DIGITALIZING THE GLOBAL TEXT

East-West Encounters in Literature and Cultural Studies

SERIES EDITORS
Bennett Yu-Hsiang Fu, Paul Allen Miller, Chi-she Li

This series is jointly published by National Taiwan University Press and the University of South Carolina Press.

DIGITALIZING THE GLOBAL TEXT

Philosophy, Literature, and Culture

EDITED BY

Paul Allen Miller

THE UNIVERSITY OF SOUTH CAROLINA PRESS

臺大出版中心
NATIONAL TAIWAN UNIVERSITY PRESS

Published by the University of South Carolina Press
Columbia, South Carolina 29208
Published by National Taiwan University Press
Taipei City, Taiwan 10087

www.sc.edu/uscpress
eng.press.ntu.edu.tw

Manufactured in Taiwan

28 27 26 25 24 23 22 21 20 19
10 9 8 7 6 5 4 3 2 1

Library of Congress Cataloging-in-Publication Data
can be found at http://catalog.loc.gov/.

ISBN 978-1-64336-058-4 (hardback)
ISBN 978-1-64336-059-1 (ebook)
GPN 1010801531

Contents

Introduction

The present book in both its topic and its transnational makeup has come at a very particular moment. A few short years ago, globalism seemed to be both a known and an inexorable phenomenon. With the end of the Cold War, the opening of the Chinese economy, and the ascendancy of digital technology, the prospect of a unified flow of goods and services, of people and ideas seemed unstoppable (Moraru). Political theorists such as Francis Fukuyama proclaimed "the end of history." Yes, there were pockets of resistance and reaction, but these, we were told, would be swept away in a relentless tide of free markets and global integration that would bring Hollywood, digital finance, and fast food to all. Religious fundamentalism, revanchist forms of nationalism, attachments to traditional sexual identities would melt away before the forces of what were variously termed "modernity," "postmodernity," and Empire. A kind of relentless, technocratic rationality would sweep all in its wake, bringing a neoliberal utopia of free markets, free speech, and ever-increasing productivity. Were there, in the words of a seventies classic, "limits to growth" (Meadows et al.)? If so, they would be either transcended or accommodated by the same forces that threatened their breach. Climate change would be managed through a combination of technological innovation and agreed-upon regulation. Population control would be achieved by education, prosperity, and women entering the workforce.

There would, of course, be differences of opinion about the proper mix of markets and regulatory regimes, of individual versus collective decision-making, but not about the road where reason led. There were no irremediable opacities, no values that were not calculable, no passions that would not, in the end, yield to a calculus of maximizing utility. It would be possible for us all to exercise our capacities for rational choice and the pursuit of personal happiness within a bounded sphere of agreed-upon rights and interests. Those who said otherwise were either deliberate obscurantists or criminals or were mad. The role of culture in such a world was in the first instance to be determined by the market—what would people pay for—and in the last by the needs of collective mental and social hygiene: the promotion of "healthy" lifestyles and forms of enjoyment.

Of course there would remain stubborn inequalities. Many of these were necessary. Within our communities there would need to be a technocratic elite of financial regulators, investment bankers, CEOs, public health officials, scientists, and assorted members of the creative classes. These people would need to be rewarded for their efforts and expertise, whether they worked for Google, the World Bank, the Chinese Communist Party, or Pixar. A rising tide lifts all boats: but amid the kayaks and canoes, there would have to be supertankers and luxury liners. Likewise, between our communities there would remain certain historical inequities, the results of poor decisions, limited resources, deliberate exploitation, racism, and colonialism. Certain interventions might need to be made, persistent pathologies addressed, to ensure that the global order remained intact, that unrest did not produce disruption, that the flow of goods and services should proceed with minimal interruption.

Necessarily there would be disputes. In the "rules-based" international order (Peel), outliers would need to be punished and sanctions would need to be applied; and while there would be disagreements about proportionality of response and even about who was deserving of that response, what made this a global system was the recognition of that order, the establishment of certain widely accepted benchmarks, and, implicit in that establishment, the acceptance of modernity's relentless march. The technocratic elite of the French Socialist Party, the German Christian Democratic Union, Mitt Romney's Republican Party, and Mexico's Partido Revolucionario Institucional all shared these same basic assumptions, even as they differed on precise policy prescriptions. Indeed, but a few short years ago, if one listened to the discourse of the American media, of the European Union, of Hillary Clinton and Goldman Sachs, of Barack Obama and Hu Jintao, one heard a series of remarkably similar statements that all followed in this general line.

Major institutions of higher learning around the world followed suit, producing students with defined skills for a global market. Educational outcomes were assessed along a universal quantitative grid that sought to iron out cultural differences, eliminate the idiosyncratic or recalcitrant, and measure all things by agreed-upon benchmarks and norms. Diversity and inclusion were celebrated as long as no one was too diverse, too difficult to include. Clean-cut African Americans in blue blazers were welcome, as were Muslim women who did not wear the hijab. Gays could marry and have families just like "the rest of us." The hegemony of global capital possessed an ethos, a style of dress, and norms of politesse that were in a sense open to all as long as no one insisted on being *too* different, and it was the job of universities to produce more of these model citizens across the globe, so that a rational and domesticated capitalism could cater to their tastes.

Digital reproducibility, moreover, as I argue in the first essay, is the predicate for one common form of globalization: the dream of a universal culture in which films, food, and fashion flow effortlessly across a digital pipeline. Adorno's nightmare of the "culture industry" may finally find its realization in the fusion of Disney, Amazon, and Whole Foods with the Spelling report's vision of higher education as a "mature industry" (U.S. Department of Education). Such a world—to paraphrase Benjamin, the work of life in the age of digital reproduction!—is also necessarily that of perfect commodification, one in which use value has been all but completely reduced to the liquidity of surplus value, in which ones and zeros have become synonymous with the flow of global capital.

I do not mean to sound too critical of all this technocratic and commodified global optimism. The reduction of difference and opacity to the calculable, of the insistent noise of the analog to the crisp increments of the digital, makes possible a form of global rationality that we may soon regard with a form of nostalgia. The global and the digital go hand in hand, with the rational reduction of the phenomenal world to a set of interchangeable units of ones and zeros, which is both the predicate of global capitalism and sorts ill with a revanchist dedication to the local and particular. The neoliberal university, also, has as its ideal the perfect fungibility of knowledge and experience. From teaching evaluations, to assessment, to value added, the outcomes produced by courses as diverse as Biology, Accounting, and Modern French Literature should be quantifiable in comparable if not identical ways and a rubric produced in which each could be evaluated along a range of identical terms.[1]

Nonetheless, as we have begun to experience in earnest the backlash against a global world founded on digital fungibility, the perils of appeals to nationalism, identity, and authenticity have become only too apparent. The collapse of Soviet Communism left an ideological vacuum that offered no recognized place from which to oppose global capitalism. What was the alternative? The anxieties, fears, and resentments produced by this global order among those who were left behind, who were alienated, exploited, or unrecognized by its ascendance, were often manifested in a variety of assertions of particularity. This is what it means to be a real American, a true Muslim, *un français de vieille souche,* a proper Chinese. The Other is coming to take what is ours, and we must defend ourselves! The Other is within and must be driven out.

The results have been frightening on any number of levels: the rise of nationalist and anti-immigrant sentiment in Europe; the Rohingya crisis in Myanmar; the U.S. government taking immigrant children from their parents. Of course all of these crises have their origins in prior movements. The collapse of the former Yugoslavia revealed the presence of nationalist and genocidal sentiments many thought long vanquished in Europe. Al-Qaeda and ISIS trace their roots to the Soviet invasion of Afghanistan. The worst excesses of the Israeli Right find their origin and justification in the horrors of the Holocaust. We are accustomed to speaking of the ancient roots of many of these conflicts, and while in once sense such deeply rooted hatreds can seem all the more intractable, it is also what makes them particularly susceptible to being subsumed into a global narrative of rational progress. These enmities are portrayed as relics, as atavisms, as the ghosts of a now-dead past whose transcendence by reason and utility is both inevitable and urgent.

And yet, in producing this narrative of improvement, we may well be fooling ourselves. While hatred and persecutions of those who are different have always existed, the nation-state, nationalism, and deliberate genocidal policies are peculiarly modern phenomena. The roots of slavery may run historically deep, but racialized slavery, buttressed with "biological" theories of ethnic superiority, was unknown. In the ancient world, you were enslaved not because of your phenotype but because you or your forebears were captured in war or you were unable to pay your debts. The Romans sought to destroy ancient Israel as a political unit, when it destroyed the Second Temple, because portions of the population and members of the religious establishment refused to submit to the Roman imperial regime, which included recognition of the divine status of the emperor. But it would have never entered their minds to seek out people of Jewish blood, to track them down across the empire, or systematically to exterminate any ethnic group. Biological racism is a peculiarly modern category. This is in no way to diminish the brutality and often spectacular cruelty of the premodern East or West, but as Michel Foucault's *Surveiller et punir* has taught us, our sense of progress is often exaggerated.

Indeed it was in the immediate aftermath of his work on prisons that Foucault began developing his concept of biopower. Biopower is a form of political power that is proper to the nation-state and to the emerging order of capitalism. It is a form of governing or "governmentality" that takes as its object a "population," a people. If government's role is to foster the people, to look after their health and welfare, to protect them from harm, then that people must be defined as a unity. They are not the subjects of a sovereign but an organic unit. They have a kinship to one another, an identity that must be defended. They are French, they are German, they are Dutch. These identities are assumed to have an ontological status. They are real, not merely conventional. In the wake of this conception of a population as a unity that finds its fullest representation in the nation-state come disciplines such as public health, population genetics, and scientific and philosophical investigations into the moral, corporeal, and sexual hygiene of a given people, *Volk,* or nation. In volume 1 of *Histoire de la sexualité,* Foucault outlines the emergence of biopower as follows:

> We know how many times has been posed the question of the role that an ascetic morality was able to have in the initial formation of capitalism: what happened in the eighteenth century in certain Western countries, and which has been linked by [*par*] the development of capitalism, is another

> phenomenon and perhaps of greater scope than this new morality, which seemed to disqualify the body; it was nothing less than the entry of life into history—I mean to say the entry of the phenomena proper to the life of the human species into the order of knowledge and power—into the field of political techniques. It is not a question of claiming that at this moment was produced the first contact between life and history. On the contrary, the biological pressure on history had remained for millennia extremely strong; epidemics and famines constituted the two great dramatic forms of this relation that stood placed beneath the sign of death; through a circular process, the economic and principally agricultural development of the eighteenth century, the more rapid increase in productivity and resources than in the demographic growth that it favored, permitted these profound menaces to loosen their grip a bit: the era of the great ravages of hunger and the plague—except for certain resurgences—is closed before the French Revolution; death began no longer to threaten life directly. But, at the same time, the development of knowledges concerning life in general, the improvement of agricultural techniques, observations and measures aiming at life and the survival of men, contributed to this loosening: a relative mastery of life removed some of the threats of death. (187)

It is in the context of this discussion of power's newfound abilities not just to ward off death but also to foster and form life, to manage the biological growth of the species, to control populations, indeed to take populations per se as objects of knowledge and hence manipulation, that Foucault sums up the revolutionary nature of this change by stating, "Man, for millennia, remained what he was for Aristotle: a living animal and also capable of a political existence; modern man is an animal in whose politics his life as a living being is in question" (188). Foucault's point is that for modern humans, faced with a radically different technical and scientific reality than was found in Aristotle's classical *polis,* the fact of living has itself become the object of politics in a way that it was not or could not be for the ancient or even the early modern world.

Thus we come to the belated realization that the same forces that created the movement toward a global technocratic order are those that threaten most to tear it asunder. In many ways this is a classical Hegelian reversal first articulated by Adorno and Horkheimer's *Dialectic of Enlightenment,* in which the forces of instrumental reason that produced the Enlightenment are shown to be the same forces that make possible National Socialism and the final solution. And on several occasions Foucault himself, while always having at best an ambivalent relationship to Hegel, late in life spoke of the kinship he felt to the work of the Frankfurt School. Nonetheless what Foucault offers in volume 1 of *Histoire de la sexualité* and in such lecture courses as *Il faut defendre la société* and *La naissance de la biopolitique* is in some ways a more rigorous account. For the essence of his argument, and I am now ruthlessly schematizing a much more nuanced set of positions, is that as new strategies of governance evolved at the nexus of economic and political change at the end of the eighteenth century, there grew alongside them (both fostering and fostered by them) a series of new sciences and technologies that in turn defined and, in a real sense, created new objects. The classic example of this for Foucault is the discourse of sexuality. Sex as a thing, as a unified phenomenon—as opposed to a series of actions, organs, sensations, and norms that could at times be related to one another and at others totally separate—is the creation of the discourse of sexuality, he argues at the end of volume 1 of the *Histoire.* Once people possess a "sex," they can then have an orientation to it or a "sexuality"—most prominently they can be homo- or heterosexual. But as the discourse of the great nineteenth century sexologists demonstrates, these broad categories can be subdivided into an evermore discrete series of categories, ever smaller numbers of boxes into which norms and their deviations can be placed. And so people become things, and those things define their identities. They are male or female, heterosexuals or homosexuals, sadists or masochists, oversexed, undersexed, masturbators, fantasists, or frigid women, and these qualities define their being.

In a similar way, other social types are created by these same typologizing, social scientific discourses. Indeed there develops a vast array of criminals and deviants, of personality types, ethnic types, and their associated pathologies. The sciences that are formed to address the perceived problems associated with these types, at the same time, both create and homogenize their objects of knowledge. They give those objects definition, create repositories of statistical knowledge about them, and begin to pose the question of what is to be done to or with them.

If a given group can be defined as harmful to the social whole, a kind of pathogen to the organic and biological unity that should genetically constitute our society as a "people" and politically as a nation-state, if we are to defend our society, must not that group be controlled, modified, at the limit, eliminated? This is how programs of forced sterilization were established not only in Nazi Germany but also in the American South. There is a kind of infernal logic here that the attempt to address actual problems (public health is a good thing) creates objects where they did not exist before and then subjects those objects to the possibility of technological manipulation. New ontologies and identities are created.

At the same time, as Foucault also points out, these new objects and identities create new possibilities of resistance. There can be no gay liberation movement until homosexuality is recognized as an identity (as there can be no attempt to control or eliminate homosexuals as a group without the same). There can be no movement for a Jewish state without Jews' being recognized as a people, as possessing an identity that transcends religious preference and becomes an inherited nature, something that one either is or is not, just as there can be no final solution without the same. None of this is to say, as Foucault makes clear, that people were not persecuted for their religious practices or their sexual acts throughout the Middle Ages and into the early modern period, but these preferences and practices were not considered immutable parts of the person's identity rooted in their biological makeup. By the same token, our ability today to bisect and dissect our digital information into ever smaller discrete units not only allows the creation of ever smaller and more defined demographic groups to be studied—white working-class rural voters, female preteen consumers of K-pop, male Muslim urban immigrants between ages fifteen and twenty-five—but it also creates identities that are subject to manipulation by a wide variety of actors, from Russian troll farms, to Disney, to Al-Qaeda. The very forces that have created the global order are the same as those that are splitting it apart, and these contradictory actions are not so much the unintended consequences of the actions of a well-intentioned elite as they are built into the very fabric of late capitalist modernity. To sum up, the world that gave us Donald Trump and Brexit is the same as that which produced the European Union and the Asian Miracle.

The present set of essays situates itself squarely at this nexus of forces. Together they examine how literature, culture, and theory in the global and digital age both enable the creation of these simultaneously utopian and dystopian worlds and offer a tactical resistance to them. The papers in this volume originated in the first of three joint conferences held between the literature faculties of National Taiwan University, Ewha University, and the University of South Carolina. "Literature and the Global Public: A Transnational Symposium" was held on the NTU campus in Taipei on October 28, 2016, and it was made possible by NTU's generous sponsorship.

The essays are divided into three categories. The first group, "The Local and the Global in the Digital Age," is the most general. It looks at the intersection between the possibilities opened by digital technologies for a wide dissemination of cultural artifacts and the ways in which those very technologies undermine the local characteristics that give those artifacts the power to resist a relentlessly homogenizing capitalist order. The second group, "Going Global: Digital Popular Culture," offers a more in-depth look at two digital pop culture phenomena, K-pop and interactive narrative structures in video games and beyond. Thus where the first section offers an overview of global culture in the digital age, examining the concepts of the digital and its resistance, international literary trends, the global phenomenon that was the two-hundredth anniversary of Richard Wagner's birth, and the international epistolary novel in the age of email, the second focuses much more on two specific digital phenomena of global significance: music videos and gaming systems. The final section, "The Global Object World: Literature and Ontology in Late Capitalism," looks from three separate perspectives at what Foucault would label the ontology of the present. It asks how we got here and what is the nature of our being in the commodified world of global capital.

I lead off the collection with an essay on strategies of resistance. My essay, "On Being Old and Queer: Plato's *Seventh Letter* in the Digital Age, or Resisting Neoliberalism," argues that the forces that push toward digitalization are the same as those that push for global commodification. After a more general introduction to the topic, the essay begins with a brief reading of chapter 1 of volume 1 of Marx's *Capital* on the origins of the commodity and the money form and then moves on to the work of Foucault and Plato's *Seventh Letter.* The essay's title alludes to Foucault's late lectures and to the status of the ancient world and its artifacts as objects whose value stubbornly resists being consumed by the reigning neoliberal calculus. In the last years of his life, Foucault focused intensely on Plato's *Seventh Letter.* There, Plato argues that no serious philosopher commits his thoughts to writing but rather relies on direct interpersonal dialogue and the insight those intense, emotionally charged conversations produce. Many today view Plato's argument as ironic or reactionary. How could writing's power to reproduce itself identically, regardless of context, be opposed by the advocate of universal ideality? Foucault contends that Plato's point is not to oppose writing per se—the ancient world's incipient digitality—so much as it is to favor *tribe,* the labor of the self on the self, literally the "rubbing" or "friction" between teacher and student that produces the spark of enlightenment, a moment of unrepeatable intelligibility. In the end what is most authentic is not the normative and the infinitely reproducible, which functions like the money form of exchange value, but the moment of irreducible insight, of queer intelligibility, which makes possible a form of self-relation and of relation to others that is based on curiosity and care. This insight must be informed by data and may be cosmopolitan in its scope but is never reducible to information or mere exchange, nor is it able to be globalized in its imperial reach.

This dialectic of the irreducibly local and the truly global in turn features centrally in Alexander Beecroft's "Local Cultures, Global Audiences: The Dream (and Nightmare) of the World Novel." Beecroft argues that global literary culture in the early twenty-first century seems caught in a dilemma analogous to that of early twenty-first-century politics. We are poised between two understandings of globalization. While vast impersonal forces propel us toward a globalized economy and culture, in culture as well as in politics, he notes, we argue bitterly over the desirability of a planetary culture. Global trade and social media can knit together widely scattered groups, expanding the reach of even the most restricted literary languages. Nonetheless, there seems to be a real danger that the power of a globalized market, will transform the cultural world from a series of interconnected national and regional cultural dialects and idiolects into a vast planetary lingua franca, in which active readers morph into cultural consumers, passively absorbing nearly-identical products, produced wherever costs are lowest. Books and blue jeans a like flow from producer to consumer through the global supply chain. In recent years, we have seen the rise of both a right and left populist resistance to globalization: a movement to fight back against the homogenization of global culture.

Nonetheless, Beecroft contends, the globalization of literary culture need not produce blandness and uniformity. New technology in principle makes publication easier and cheaper, making it possible for less commonly spoken languages to acquire written literatures and for nascent and threatened literary languages to thrive. The lower costs of digital publication make literatures in languages such as Slovak, Albanian, and Kurdish, financially viable. As it becomes possible to package texts as commodities for global consumers, it should also become easier to find and reach niche markets, whether linguistic minorities or countercultural and counterhegemonic groups, and this very market segmentation could present fresh opportunities for more sophisticated cultural engagements with globalization.

Beecroft's essay begins by examining recent arguments about a possible global literary culture. Reading the works of two recent writers, both Italian, he suggests that there is reason for optimism: while the pressures toward uniformity are real, globalization may yet leave room for a complex, multivoiced cultural dialogue. In fact the authors discussed offer signs of the emergence of a new grammar of the global novel, of the gradual emergence of a series of tropes that are adapted to the needs of global narration in our era, and play much the same role as epistolary fiction did in the eighteenth century with the emergence of the nation-state.

It is precisely the emergence of a new global and electronic epistolary fiction that forms the basis for our third essay, Bennett Fu's "Global Public, Digital Public: Neo-epistolarity and Tactical Consumption in *À toi*." Picking up where Beecroft leaves off, Fu's essay analyzes Vietnamese Franco-Canadian writer Kim Thúy and Slovak Swiss novelist Pascal Janovjak's coauthored epistolary text *À toi* (To You, 2011), which is structured as a series of emails written between October and December 2010. These often-short messages exchanged between a wide range of geographical locations—Montreal, Hanoi, Ramallah, and Dhaka—discuss their multilingual, multicultural writers' often ambivalent relationships with language, identity, and writing. Through a series of emails exchanged about quotidian trivia, the writers share the story of their various cultural exclusions and their experiences of displacement. She is a French-speaking Canadian novelist of Vietnamese heritage, and he is a son of mixed French and Slovak parentage who, though born in Switzerland, grew up and worked in Lebanon, Jordan, and Bangladesh. The resulting work can only be termed global literature, but it is also irreducibly local in its evocation of a series of discrete cultural and geographical locations.

À toi exemplifies what Fu terms "neo-epistolarity." In the world of letters, as in the world of goods, neo-epistolarity creates a virtual space of community and solidarity across boundaries. Fu argues that these "virtual" epistles serve to create a new digital instantiation of the Habermassian public sphere, a space where individuals can come together freely and discuss individual and social problems. These writers' collaborative work, Fu contends, also cements certain correlations between epistolarity and Certeauean consumption/production as a tactic of resistance. Writing becomes a form of agency that liberates Thúy from the constraints of life as an Asian woman and as a foreigner, while the shifting global perspective allows her and her coauthor to create new cultural vistas that become public through this virtual epistolary form.

We end this first section on a relatively more hopeful note with Nicholas Vazsonyi's examination of the worldwide celebration of the two-hundredth anniversary of Richard Wagner's birth. In "Wagner in China: Negotiating the National, the Universal and the Global," Vazsonyi investigates what the relationship is between music and our concept of home, particularly our spiritual home. He asks, if our home is displaced or lost or we are exiled from it, can music return it to us, bring it back through powers of recollection, or at least provoke in us that most Odyssean of emotions, nostalgia, the pain that comes from longing for *nostos* (return)? It is the case that music is often the most evocative of the arts in terms of memories. Certain songs are associated with certain experiences; a given melody or even but a few notes can conjure up an entire emotional world. But Vazsonyi demonstrates that this return can take many forms and can happen in many different places. There is something *unheimlich* about our musical home, which allows us to experience it even when we are far away—listening to Wagner in Shanghai, Peking opera in Berlin, or Beethoven's "Ode to Joy" in Taipei, New York, or Johannesburg.

In many ways music is also the most global of the arts. It is not limited by language, and whether we are discussing popular or classical music, it often spreads around the globe literally at the speed of light. But is the global appeal of the music of a composer such as Wagner, whose birth was celebrated around the world, the same as a universal appeal? That is to say, even as people from widely different backgrounds and widely different cultures may thrill to the opening bars of "Ride of the Valkyries," do they have the same experience, and if not, then in what sense can they be said to be experiencing the same object? Moreover if different people are having different experiences and, in not insignificant ways, perceiving fundamentally different objects, then in what meaningful way can that object be spoken of as a universal, even if it is indisputably a global, phenomenon? The paradox becomes all the sharper when we are dealing with a composer such as Wagner, who is so deeply and problematically associated with German nationalism and with the harsh peculiarities of German history and culture.

As we noted above, the paradoxes of the local, the global, and the universal are not simply limited to the artifacts of high culture: novels, philosophy, opera, and the like. Popular music and culture participate in this same overdetermined dialectic. If opera is the *Gesamtkunstwerk* of high culture, the music video is arguably the "complete art work" of the popular realm, combining music, poetry, visual art, and dance. Julie Choi in "Right to the City: The Metropolis and 'Gangnam Style'" offers a close reading of this international pop sensation to open the second section of the book. First uploaded on July 15, 2012, "Gangnam Style" was the first video ever to reach one billion views. The content, style, and history of the video, Choi argues, speak both to its utopian credentials as well as to its cynicism. It is a call to arms for the urban dispossessed to take back the topography of Gangnam and at the same time a celebration of the excesses of glamorous consumption.

The psychedelic spectacle that calls itself "Gangnam Style" presents a rich and colorful array of metropolitan experience that is starkly distinguished from the monotony of the rational workday. Daily life is transposed into leisure, and festivity becomes possible in city spaces planned and developed for capitalist production. In the tradition of the modernist flaneur, Psy narrates the city from the perspective of the scavenger making his way through the glorious detritus of contemporary commodity culture. What "Gangnam Style" manages to do, Choi argues, despite all the odds and perhaps despite the intention of the artist himself, is to upend the inhumane coordinates of the postmodern city.

We continue our examination of global popular-culture forms with Mou-Lan Wong's "The Garden of Living Paths: Interactive Narratives in Global Geek Culture." Wong begins with a reading of Jorge Luis Borges's famous story "The Garden of Forking Paths," in which we learn of Ts'ui Pên's novel of the same name. This Chinese narrative, we are told, has baffled readers for many generations with its multiple, chaotic, and often contradictory plot lines. In the course of a seemingly unrelated series of events taking place in Britain during the First World War, Borges tells us how a descendant of Ts'ui Pên comes to understand that *The Garden of Forking Paths* is not what it has long seemed, an inchoate mess, but actually a book that attempts to narrate all the possible outcomes of the protagonist's decisions in life without at the same time including a specific registry or index in the manner of, for example, Julio Cortázar's *Hopscotch.* Thus every seemingly contradictory plot twist is in fact simply another branch in this refractory narrative as all possible options are continuously charted, creating both new narrative trajectories and at the same time looping back and intersecting with previously articulated parallel plot developments. Upon coming to this realization, Yu Tsun, Ts'ui Pên's descendant, comprehends that *The Garden* is neither unintelligible nor a monumental failure but is an innovative experimental model for nonlinear temporality. In *The Garden* time seems forever to branch outward to create new possible futures.

Wong observes that in many ways what Borges's story imagines in 1941, in its own admittedly limited and linear way, is what digital technology would later make possible as hypertext. Although scholars such as Noah Wardrip-Fruin and Lev Manovich, in their *New Media Reader,* and Perla Sassón-Henry, in her *Borges 2.0,* have used Borges as a starting place for their examinations of the various points of contact and intersection between literature, science, and a variety of digital narratives, hyperfictions such as Michael Joyce's *Afternoon: A Story* have not generally been the object of serious academic examination. Moreover, even as hypertext has now been combined and incorporated into multimedia experiences, particularly in video games and other formats, little research has been done on the relation between Borges and these new media. Wong's essay surveys printed and digital interactive narratives from choose-your-own-adventure books to video games. It explores the idea of experiencing multiple timelines through the looping effect of rereading branching narratives and charts how Borges's original concept has become a conceit of global digital culture.

In our final section, we shift from the dialectics of the local and the global, the popular and the high, in contemporary digital culture to questions of ontology in the world of globalism and late capital. While a "return" to ontology has recently come to the fore in the work of thinkers such as Quentin Meillassoux, with his argument for a post-Kantian materialism, and in that of the advocates of object-oriented ontology, in fact the ontological has never really left us. Despite Meillassoux's attacks on the "correlationism" of philosophers such as Derrida and Foucault (Zalloua chap. 5), few thinkers operating in the wake of Heidegger have truly left the ontological question behind. Sartre sought a phenomenological ontology of freedom. Foucault argued for an ontology of the present, and Derrida sought to deconstruct the closure of Western metaphysics, an occlusion that necessarily opened onto a new way of being.

Meili Steele opens his essay, "The Ontological Turn: A New Problematic for Literature and Globalization," by invoking not the object-oriented ontology of Graham Harman but that of older traditions: the Heideggerian work of Charles Taylor and the post-Foucauldian work of Talal Asad. Taylor, as Steele observes, makes a strong argument for the ontological priority of the social as the enveloping context that makes possible both subjective judgment and the objects that subjects seek to define. He argues for an articulation of our social embedding that is deeper and more determining than the concept of ideology found in thinkers such as Said, and this is something, Steele contends, that Taylor shares with those like Asad who work in a more Foucauldian line. But where Taylor often looks at the social whole as determining our possibilities of meaning, Asad, following more closely Foucault, examines specific structures of power and domination. He focuses particularly on the ways in which Western notions of secularism maintain Christian structures of thought, which become increasingly oppressive in a global context, especially when portrayed not as a set of culturally specific norms but as a form of pure, objective neutrality. Moreover, as Steele observes, when non-westerners examine French or American secularity (or feel themselves examined by it), they often do not see what from an internal perspective is understood as the slow historical development of fair solutions to conflicts about morality, politics, and religion. Rather they perceive a kind of externally imposed, abstract morality that both defines a space of judgement and within that space sets itself up as the arbitrator of all forms of both religion and irreligiosity, treating them as sets of objects to be measured, judged, and corrected by a disembodied and omniscient reason. Secularism, in such cases, may be less the antidote to fundamentalism than a contributing cause.

The ontological approach, Steele thus argues, offers us a variety of possibilities for understanding the nature of conflicts. It can open up temporality so that we can see how conflicts emerge historically over long periods. It can also give us access to the wide range of structures that make up the collective mind that we study. We are not limited to the study of ideas and beliefs present to the minds of historical actors, for those ideas and beliefs can be formed only against the background imaginaries that constitute their horizon of understanding. Steele closes by arguing that literary discourse is particularly adept at exploring different dimensions of these background imaginaries—the way they set up worlds, languages, characters, views of causality and consciousness, and the like. The ontological approach, as he argues, is less a return to a precritical encounter with things in their ontological purity than an understanding of how we constitute and are constituted by an object world that both exceeds our grasp and determines our being.

Steele's emphasis on the ways in which literature both gives access to the ontological realm and helps us imagine being otherwise offers a peculiarly apt introduction to Chi-she Li's "Altered Realism in Ontological Fiction: *Never Let Me Go* and *Point Omega*." Li's argument in this essay is twofold: that we are currently living through a fundamental shift in our understanding of ontology and that we can trace that shift in the evolution of the realist novel. Starting from the grounding assumptions of object-oriented ontology that humans' experience of the world cannot be privileged, Li returns to the Bakhtinian notion of dialogue as the privileged moment in the constitution of the realist novel. This move may seem paradoxical at first, since we are so accustomed to an anthropocentric privileging of human consciousness in our understanding of voice and dialogue. But in the digital world of robotics and of the Internet of things, this may no longer be the case. Artificial intelligence has made the line between human and nonhuman increasingly hard to defend, as have various advances in medicine and biomechanical engineering. When does an artificially created being cross the threshold to humanity? When can we engage it genuine dialogue? If we can have meaningful, even if nonverbal, exchange with nonhuman actors, how does that fundamentally reconfigure our understanding of the origins, nature, and limitations of human consciousness?

These are the questions, Li argues, posed by Kazuo Ishiguro's *Never Let Me Go* (2005), which portrays a British boarding school that we slowly learn is populated with clones produced for organ harvesting, and Don DeLillo's *Point Omega* (2010), which centers on documentary filmmaker Jim Finley's journey to the desert. In each case objects that are in no sense considered conventionally human become actors and agents within the narrative, dialogically interacting with the other characters. The enveloping context that makes possible both the subjective judgments of the human actors and the objects those subjects seek to define is shown to be radically undifferentiated or at least not defined by the difference between the human and the nonhuman, between subjects and objects. Thus the ontological assumptions of the great conventions of nineteenth-century realism, which are humanist to their core, are upended by these novels and used to portray a brave new world in which humans not only manufacture their environment but also are equally manufactured by it.

The world of commodity capitalism is that from which both globalism and the digital sprang. As I argue in the first essay, the notion of global culture and the possibility of its reduction to a digital flow of ones and zeros is predicated on a dominance of exchange value over use value that defines the birth of the commodity. By recovering forms of thought and experience in the work of writers as various as Plato and Foucault, I contend, we gain access to a lifeworld that resists commodification, in much the same manner that the works examined by Beecroft remain stubbornly tied to the particularities of local experience, even as they appeal to a transnational literary market. Throughout this volume we examine extensions and variations on these basic insights and look at the ways in which culture and the imaginary posit forms of resistance to the homogenizing forces of global capital: from Fu's reinvention of the public sphere in a neo-epistolary novel that gives voice to the diasporic and the marginalized; to Vazsonyi's reconceptualizing of what it means to be "at home" through the power of music; to Psy's carnivalization of the serious world of economic production by means of parody and dance in "Gangnam Style"; and to the liberating displacement of human consciousness via the representation of complex and multilinear temporalities inspired by Borges. We arrive finally at Steele's and Li's undermining of the ontological privilege of the individual human consciousness posited by rationalist philosophy and classical as well as neoliberal economics.

With our final essay, we go back to the point or origin of both classic realism and the ontological dominance of the commodity form in modern thought. Hisup Shin's "Ghost in the Machine: Fetishism and the Laboring Body in Marx, Dickens, and Mayhew" returns us to the scene of the crime. Shin's aim in the essay is to explore the theory of fetishism as a site of conflicting discourses traversing a variety of intellectual and social fields from anthropology to the economy at a time when England was becoming increasingly materialist in its modern outlook. Originally coined to designate a specific type of material experience that is deemed unscientific and primitive, the term *fetishism* gained further significance when Marx adopted it in order to capture dehumanizing patterns of materialistic life under capitalism. Commodity fetishism more precisely refers to the process whereby commodities seem to take on a life of their own, in which produced objects become agents by concealing the labor that produced them, the history that made them possible. Shin argues that while Marx's use of the term is primarily critical in diagnosing the way in which individuals (laborers) are compelled to adopt thing-like attributes in their participation in the commodity market, it also offers an alternative insight into the very same features of dehumanization, a fetishist insight extending beyond the Marxist frame of critical thinking. In particular this essay argues that this insight organizes a unique bodily figuration assigned to physical labor—a bodily type whose theoretical and historical significance becomes discernible in its intervention in the way in which the nineteenth-century discourse of political economy reproduces "a recognizably Victorian disgust for the body." Thus the object-oriented ontologies of the twenty-first century are revealed to be dependent on the commodity form as the fundamental definition of being in our late capitalist world, and it is precisely the abstraction that commodity production designates in its privileging of exchange over use value that makes possible a world market in which Dickens is as much a commodity in Korea as K-pop is in California, in which goods and services float free from their specific cultural contexts and all that is solid melts into air.

Note

1. Compare Govers's account of globalization and the neoliberal economy (12–15).

Works Cited

Adorno, Theodor. *The Culture Industry*. Ed. J. M. Bernstein. London: Routledge, 2001.

Adorno, Theodor, and Max Horkheimer. *Dialectic of Enlightenment.* Trans. John Cumming. Allen Lane, 1973.

Benjamin, Walter. "The Work of Art in the Age of Mechanical Reproduction." *Illuminations.* Ed. Hannah Arendt. Trans. Harry Zohn. Schocken Books, 1969. 217–51.

Foucault, Michel. *Surveiller et punir: Naissance de la prison.* Gallimard, 1975. Translated by Alan Sheridan as *Discipline and Punish: The Birth of the Prison* (Pantheon, 1978).

Foucault, Michel. *Histoire de la sexualité.* Vol. 1, *La volonté de savoir.* Gallimard, 1976. Translated by Robert Hurley as *The History of Sexuality.* Vol. 1, *An Introduction* (Random House, 1978).

Foucault, Michel. *Il faut defendre la société: Cours au Collège de France 1976.* Eds. Mauro Bertani and Alessendro Fontana. Ecole des Hautes Etudes/Gallimard/Seuil, 1997. Translated by Robert Hurley as *Society Must Be Defended* (Picador, 1997).

Foucault, Michel. *La naissance de la biopolitique: Cours au Collège de France 1978–79.* Eds. Michel Senellart. Ecole des Hautes Etudes/Gallimard/Seuil, 2004. Translated by Graham Burchell as *The Birth of Biopolitics* (Picador, 2009).

Fukuyama, Francis. *The End of History and the Last Man.* Freedom Press, 1992.

Govers, Robert. *Imaginative Communities: Admired Cities, Regions, and Countries.* Reputo, 2018.

Meadows, Donella H., Dennis L. Meadows, Jørgen Randers, and William W. Behrens III. *The Limits to Growth: A Report for the Club of Rome on the Predicament of Mankind.* Potomac Associates, 1972.

Moraru, Christian. *Reading for the Planet: Toward a Geomethodology.* University of Michigan Press, 2015.

Peel, Quentin. "Threats to a Rules-Based International Order." *Australian Outlook.* May 25, 2018. https://www.internationalaffairs.org.au/australianoutlook/threats-to-rules-based-international-order/.

Sassón-Henry, Perla. *Borges 2.0: From Text to Virtual Worlds.* Peter Lang, 2007.

U.S. Department of Education. *A Test of Leadership: Charting the Future of U.S. Higher Education, A Report of the Commission Appointed by Secretary of Education Margaret Spellings.* 2006. http://www.ed.gov/about/bdscomm/list/hiedfuture/reports/final-report.pdf.

Walrdrip-Fruin, Noah, and Nick Montfort, eds. *The New Media Reader.* MIT, 2003.

Zalloua, Zahi. *Theory's Autoimmunity: Skepticism, Literature, and Philosophy.* Northwestern University Press, 2018.

Part One

The Local and the Global in the Digital Age

On Being Old and Queer

Plato's *Seventh Letter* in the Digital Age, or Resisting Neoliberalism

Paul Allen Miller

The first premise of digitality is infinite reproducibility. The analog world of mechanical clocks and vinyl sound, of the individual typescript or hand-produced painting, is haunted by an irreducible particularity, a residual materiality, that on however infinitesimal a level precludes the perfect repeatability of a string of ones and zeros. Digital reproducibility is also the predicate for one common form of globalization: the dream of a universal culture in which films, food, and fashion flow effortlessly across a digital pipeline from Seoul to Shanghai to SoHo, a dream of K-pop, Disney, and KFC. Such a world is that of perfect commodification, one in which use value has been reduced to the liquidity of exchange value, in which ones and zeros have become synonymous with the flow of global capital. The malls and movies of Taipei, Muscat, and Atlanta are all but indistinguishable. Adorno and Horkheimer's nightmare of the culture industry may finally have found its full realization in a fusion of Netflix, Amazon, and Whole Foods with the Spelling report's vision of higher education as a "mature industry" (U.S. Department of Education).

This dream is resisted on multiple fronts today. On the one hand, there are the reactionary forces of nationalism and parochialism embodied in the pronouncements of Donald Trump on the international conspiracy of global financial and media elites, the unsubtle xenophobia marshaled by the supporters of Brexit, the rise of the Rassemblement National in France, and Russia's aggressive stoking of nationalist resentments from the Ukraine to Western Europe to Facebook. All the phantasms of ethnic and religious purity that haunt the contemporary imagination, from Islamic extremism to Islamophobia, from American chauvinism to "Korean Messianic Exceptionalism" (Lim), are themselves reactions to a form of globalist hegemony that threatens to annihilate both cultural specificity and traditional patterns of life.[1] In this brave new world, presidential adviser Stephen Miller can, from the podium of the White House, attack "cosmopolitan elites," while unconsciously echoing Stalin's anti-Semitic postwar campaign against "rootless cosmopolitans" (Greenfield). Neofascist and nativist sentiments are on the rise around the world as increasing numbers of people feel their traditional ways of life threatened by faceless "elites" they neither see nor understand.

On the other hand, there remains a progressive, principled resistance to the reducibility of experience to a fungible, commodified standard. That resistance is embodied in everything from the increased valuation of local food traditions to an embrace of multiculturalism that is actually multiple and not simply the lowest common denominator of global marketing. People support local farmers, refuse to shop at big box stores, champion indigenous rights. We hunger for the authentic, the peculiar, the queer amid an increasing global uniformity. High-end cultural tourism caters to this market, even as it ironically commodifies its resistance to commodification. The nostalgia for an authentic, preindustrial past becomes itself a major marketing strategy for everything from artisanal cheese to craft beer to the Cracker Barrel chain of "country store" restaurants, complete with rocking chairs and prefabricated weathered wood. We want our authenticity delivered on a plate.

In this essay I want to argue that one of the most powerful loci of resistance to the forces of global commodification, at least within higher education, is the traditional humanities. The contemporary, neoliberal university assumes digitality and reproducibility (Di Leo). We need to be able to show the added value of every class and to quantify that addition in uniform terms. The neoliberal university has as its ideal the perfect fungibility of knowledge and experience. From teaching evaluations, to assessment, to value added, biochemistry and romantic poetry should be quantifiable in comparable if not identical ways and a rubric produced in which each could be evaluated along a range of possible axes using identical terms.

Knowledge in the humanities, however, is never fully universalizable, because it is always tied to the particular experience of reading a text, viewing a painting, listening to or playing a piece of music, or personally engaging in philosophical dialogue and reflection. That experience is not reducible to the information contained within a given text, work of art, or score. It is not that these works do not contain information and that this information cannot be extracted, used, stored, and even sold. It is not that a value cannot be placed on that information or even that the work itself cannot become a commodity—books are sold, paintings become prints, musical performances CDs. In the process, as Benjamin noted, they lose the aura of the hand-produced original, their artisanal particularity. But even so the experience of the work remains strictly unrepeatable and as such irreducible to the information contained therein (Miller, "The Repeatable and the Unrepeatable"). This is as true of the new global fiction described by Alexander Beecroft in the present volume as it is of the irreducible particularity of Dickens's London or Balzac's Paris. The analog world of traditional liberal education resists reduction to a commodified fungibility. It aspires to universality but remains rooted not only in the particularity of its production but also, more importantly and more radically, in the particularity of its experience.

Within this context the peculiar hybrid phenomenon of digital humanities is symptomatic of our current juncture, for while new media are not inherently oppressive, they are also never simply neutral. To paraphrase Jameson, himself citing Louis Hjelmslev, there is always a content to form (Jameson 58). The shift from orality to literacy made possible not simply the preserving of information, but also new ways or organizing, presenting, and arguing about that information and hence new ways of thinking, new forms of experience. The same is true for the printing press. It is no different for the digital world.[2] Digital humanities' role in the world of neoliberal academe should not then be understood as that of an empty vessel waiting to be filled with content, old or new, as a neutral purveyor of information. Rather digital humanities must pose itself certain very explicit questions. What sort of knowledge will it produce and to what ends? For whom will it produce that knowledge? To what extent does it legitimate the continued teaching of the humanities within the neoliberal university, and to what extent does it actually threaten to undermine that teaching and to substitute information for experience?

There is no doubt that digital humanities as currently constituted can produce vast amounts of useful, reproducible data, which the individual reader could not. Data mining makes it possible to trace words, themes, motifs, and devices across vast corpora. If you want to map the themes of global chick lit (Folie), catalog every use of the word *novel* or of its translational equivalents across the globe, or simply create a searchable database of classical Chinese poetry, digital humanities can do that far more effectively and efficiently than individual readers can. This is actual data, knowledge that is recognizable as knowledge to scientists, grant funders, and university administrators. It is infinitely reproducible and always self-identical. It makes it possible to put forth claims and defend theses that would otherwise be based on conjecture and anecdote. This is all to the good.

What digital humanities does not do, and what it cannot do, is explain why you should read a novel or a poem and how that experience differs from uploading information about that novel or poem, or the phone book, or global sea levels, or anything else that is able to be reduced to a flow of data. There are certain contexts where we absolutely want our information to be as uniform and measurable as possible: the tensile strength of steel, the amount of carbon in the atmosphere, the effects of a new cancer treatment. Likewise, for sociological and historical studies, the information cataloged in vast databases in which Poe would sit cheek by jowl with Pindar and Pirandello could be immeasurably valuable, but nothing in those databases can tell you why we should read, let alone expend public resources to teach, those texts per se. Digital humanities is, on a certain level, not humanistic at its core, because it separates the accumulation and exchange of information from the experience of producing it. In this respect it treats that information more like a commodity in the global marketplace than the artisanal product of a unique and unrepeatable experience. And this is precisely what Plato in his *Seventh Letter* stands against.

Of course digital humanities is not unique in this regard, merely a particularly symptomatic phenomenon. In our world of constant accountability and quantitative assessment, the central question all humanities scholars must face is: Do we consider liberal education a commodity? Is it just another product on offer from the culture industry, no different in principle from various other forms of *Bildung* and entertainment, whether vocational training, self-help books, or reruns of *The Apprentice?* And if so, what does that mean for forms of learning and forms of life that do not conform to this hegemonic model, that are nonnormative, that do not reaffirm or derive from the dominant lifeworld, forms that may be old or queer, like Plato and the long history of commentary on his work? Are they not to be shunted aside? Where is the market for them? How do they increase our graduates' earning potential? Are they not expensive luxury goods, which are fine for those who enjoy them and have the ability to pay but are possessed of no intrinsic value beyond that set by the market of exchange? In many ways Marx's understanding of the commodity must remain central to the comprehension of our present situation: for the commodity is the ideal object of the digital universe. It is the world of experience reducible to its most basic quantitative (and hence infinitely iterative) expression. The commodity in capitalist production and exchange functions as the fundamental definition of the object qua object, as what literally counts as real, precisely because the commodity is completely reducible to a universal quantitative expression.

Marx's origin story goes something like the following: In the beginning two producers stood before each other, each holding an object that possessed utility for the other. One had a pound of flax, the other a pound of coal. These objects in their sensuous qualities and their potential uses could not be more different. There is no practical situation in which the one can be substituted for the other. But through the magic of commodity exchange, they become part of an endless chain of substitutions, in which each can become the equivalent of every other object in this universe, be it boots, books, or bourbon. What these objects have in common is not a material property shared by the things themselves. It is the fact that they were produced, that they are the products of human labor, and the same is true for all the other objects that circulate in the magical ether of exchange. What they have in common is their labor value. That value may have only a tangential relationship to the actual use value of the object for a given producer or user, but it has a direct relationship to the effort expended. Likewise, though we may think of certain objects as inherently valuable—diamonds, gold, and other precious objects—none of those have any exchange value until they are mined, refined, or otherwise produced, until they enter the marketplace and assume their positions vis-à-vis one another: a pound of flax, a pound of coal, an ounce of gold, a book, a poem, or a painting. As exchanges become more routine, there arises a need to find a stable universal equivalent for the expression of the exchange values of this wide variety of objects and hence to make all objects comparable and expressible in terms of this universal equivalent. This equivalent becomes what we know as money.

The universal equivalent or money form in turn makes possible large-scale production and exchange. I can hire a group of producers, pay them for their labor, and realize in the process of exchange a surplus beyond what I have paid them. This produces not only my profit but also, and perhaps more important, an accumulation of capital, which can be used to build factories, digital platforms, and other assemblages that magnify the power of individual labor. It can also produce investments in human capital that increase efficiency and reliability through institutions of education and training such as technical colleges and the modern research university. This investment in turn makes possible the accumulation and reinvestment of potentially ever greater amounts of surplus. This accumulating surplus, then, can be used to generate new forms of monetary accumulation through finance capital and other means of speculation that are ultimately disconnected from either the original use value of the object or the experience of labor that brought it into the world. The measure of value that allowed one incommensurable object to be compared with another incommensurable object ultimately comes to replace the objects themselves, producing a flat plane of value in which widely disparate objects and activities are all rendered equivalent to one another (Marx 197). Money becomes the measure of all things, because money literally represents the digitalization of the lifeworld. Things only exist in objective reality—that is to say, they are only abstracted from subjective experience and hence the world of opinion—to the extent that they can be expressed in quantitative and repeatable forms, which in turn renders only the commodity, or at least the commodifiable, the object qua object of experience. Hence when we are asked to express the value added to a student's education of the reading of a given poem, the experience of another culture, or the development of creativity or critical thinking, this must be expressed in terms of a quantitative reduction, that is, a "scientific," "evidence-based" approach, which can be translated into some form of universal equivalent allowing the comparison of incommensurable objects, which means ultimately it must be expressed in terms congruent with the monetary form.

Within this lifeworld the humanities per se can never have value. On one level this is not unique to the humanities, since within this particular universe no thing has value in itself, but only to the extent that it is expressible quantitatively in terms of the universal equivalent. This is as true of the basic sciences, the social sciences, and the applied professions as it is of the humanities. But on another level, what separates the humanities from their confrères in colleges of engineering and business is that the point of education in the humanities is precisely to stand against the fungibility of our experiences, against their reduction to a universal equivalent, because the basic premise of that equivalent and the reason why it is so incredibly powerful lie precisely in the fact of its reduction. Within this universe, if we cannot measure the utility of reading a poem by John Donne, a novel by Toni Morrison, the *Analects* of Confucius, or a play by Bertolt Brecht, then we cannot say the value added. That value literally does not exist. At the same time, to the extent we can express this value in terms of a universal equivalent, then the particularity of the experience of necessity becomes occluded. There is no material difference between the experience of reading the text and receiving the information communicated by the text, which logically means there is no difference between reading the text and receiving it in a predigested or summary form. Hence the text itself becomes superfluous, as does the particularity of the culture from which it derives and in which it is experienced. Each is just another click on the Amazon marketplace, another choice on Spotify, an option on a menu.

In what remains of this chapter, I argue that the late lectures of Michel Foucault and his increasing focus on ancient philosophy offer us an alternative model for intellectual life, one that focuses on the authentic and unrepeatable in deliberate contradistinction to the world of normative information and the universal equivalent, a world that is instead very deliberately "old" and "queer." In the last years of his life, Foucault paid special attention to Plato's *Seventh Letter.* In that letter Plato polemicizes against writing in favor of direct one-on-one dialogue. His argument has often been seen as an ironic and reactionary position adopted by one of the greatest advocates of the power of the universal. How could writing's power infinitely to reproduce itself be opposed by the advocate of universal ideality? Foucault's argument is that the *Seventh Letter* is not so much against writing—the ancient world's incipient digitality—as in favor of *tribe,* the labor of the self on the self, which through a kind of friction produces the spark of insight, a moment of unrepeatable intelligibility (Miller, "Art of Self-Fashioning"). It is this moment of queer intelligibility that we must retain.

Edward Said and others would fault Foucault for this turn to antiquity, claiming it was a withdrawal from the political arena, a renunciation of commitment if not a direct form of reaction (Said; Macey 475). Moreover, in the history of the West and particularly the history of metaphysics as understood since Heidegger and Derrida, but even for thinkers such as Popper, Plato has been seen as the great normalizer.[3] Platonic metaphysics as generally understood, though I would argue as commonly misread, establishes certain transcendental essences that both constitute and regulate the order of things in the phenomenal world. The properly trained individual is the one who can bring the world of appearances into line with those essences, whether this be on the political, the ethical, or the epistemic levels. A place for everything and everything in its place. Such a universe functions as a locus of reproducible normativity in spades. Men and women, fathers and mothers, families and the state, each have their specific functions within the world that are ideally in accord with their essence, and when they deviate from those functions, they are to be led back into conformity with their natures.[4] The phenomenal world, however, can prove remarkably recalcitrant. For insofar as the world of appearances must always in some sense be deviant, if it is to appear at all, since by nature the world of appearances must always be different from the ideal essences to which they are to conform, then there must be a constant and contradictory effort both to hold that difference at bay and to reassert it.

The political task of displacing normalized reproducibility, then, would appear to be the opposite of what classical Platonism calls for. Rather than a reduction of the phenomenal to its ideal essence, rather than the subjection of the wandering and the deviant to the transcendental norm, it would be the celebration of the material itself, of the fact of inscription, of an unruly and queer sexuality, of bodies and pleasures, to paraphrase the conclusion of volume 1 of *The History of Sexuality.* And so maybe Said and, more recently, James Porter are right: the late Foucault represents not just an ethical turn, as is commonly observed, but an inward turn, a withdrawal from the political arena of *Surveiller et punir* and *La volonté de savoir,* a fundamentally conservative return to the self, to aesthetics, and to Plato, one that seems increasingly inviting in the age of global climactic catastrophe and Donald Trump (Porter, "Foucault's Ascetic Ancients"; Porter, "Discipline and Punish"; and Boyle, "Foucault among the Classicists, Again").

But I want to argue that such a reading is vastly oversimplified—that in Foucault's turn to Plato and ancient philosophy more generally what we see is not a capitulation to conservative nostalgia but a radical reenvisioning of what it means to be an intellectual, of what it means to speak truth to power, of what

Plato saw as the essence of philosophy. Indeed of what truth is. And in this turn to antiquity, we find a resource for resistance to a form of globalization that would seek to prioritize information over insight and see the accumulation of data and capital as ends in themselves.

The *Seventh Letter* is precisely Plato's attempt to justify his one attempt to intervene directly in politics in the course of his three voyages to Sicily and his interventions in the court of Dionysius the Younger and his young cousin Dion. It is also the locus of one of the philosopher's more famous diatribes against writing. I want to focus on one particular passage that describes Plato's relationship with Dionysius the Younger, when he returned to the island a third and final time. It is here in particular that Plato refers to what I would term the irreducible quality of the philosophical experience, and to his position that it is the irreducible quality of that experience that constitutes both the truth of philosophy and its primary contribution to the practice of governance or what Foucault would term governmentality. Such a position would seem at variance with the common reading of the *Republic* and the *Laws,* as well as the common understanding of Platonism writ large, but it is just that position that Foucault seeks to defend in his late lectures and that Plato argues for in the *Seventh Letter.* Elsewhere I have already argued, and I am certainly not alone,[5] that the orthodox reading of the *Republic* is itself an abstraction from the text and that Platonism is itself a bad or limited essentialization of the Socratic and Platonic project (Miller, *Postmodern Spiritual Practices* 108–21, 178–235; Miller, "Dreams and Other Fictions"). Foucault too is making the argument that the purpose of philosophy—both in the ancient and the contemporary world—is not to provide formulaic prescriptions concerning how our polities should be ordered or on how we should live our lives. Speaking truth to power is not a matter of voicing an opinion, of going viral on Twitter, but rather it is about a certain set of practices and experiences that are irreducible to a given opinion, to a specific set of policy recommendations or data.

It is in fact very close to what Foucault outlines as the goal of his own theoretical labor in 1980 in his course at the Collège de France, the first course that features what has been termed his turn to antiquity, *Du gouvernement des vivants.* This course opens with a description of the throne room of the Roman emperor Septimius Severus, then moves through a detailed reading of *Oedipus Tyrannus,* before finally concentrating on the function of the confession in early Christianity. In each case the question is what is the function of truth in the constitution of power, and how do different forms of truth making in relation to different regimes of power, what Foucault labels with a neologism different forms of *aléthurgie,* presume different forms of subjectivity and different relations between truth, the subject, and power. Foucault makes it clear that the vision he has of his work is not the return to some kind of "source" or "golden age," it is not the correction of the phenomenal and the particular in terms of the transcendental and the universal, but rather a persistent and consistent displacement of the relations binding the forms of subjectivity and forms of knowledge to specific regimes of truth and power. It is then precisely the opposite of what is traditionally claimed for Platonism. The Foucauldian labor is to open a queer space not only for relations of gender and sexuality but also for knowledge truth and subjectivity per se.

> For me, theoretical work does not really consist . . . in establishing and maintaining the totality of the positions that I would sustain and the fact that the presumed linkage between these different positions would form a coherent system. My problem, or the only possibility of theoretical work that I perceive, is to leave, according to the most intelligible design possible, the trace of the movements through which I am no longer at the place where I was just now. Hence, if you will, this perpetual need, or necessity, or desire, this perpetual need to bring up in some fashion the junctions at which each displacement runs the risk of modifying, if not the entire arc [of my theoretical work], at least the manner in which one can read its arc and in which one can grasp it, insofar as that arc is able to have a share in the intelligible. (*Du gouvernement des vivants* 74–75)

The purpose of philosophy is less to create a system of propositions that correspond to an unchanging or universal reality beyond themselves than to modify the relation of the self to the self through a continuous labor of seeking the truth and documenting the displacements that labor creates. But that labor can only take place in terms of the subject's relationship to truth, and the truth to which it points must always lie beyond the empirical given. The role of philosophy is not to ratify the present but to displace it, to create a brief opening, the possibility of change, of movement, of going beyond.

I will spend my few remaining pages looking directly at the passages from the *Seventh Letter* to which Foucault sought to draw our attention. Plato tells us that when he left Dionysius the first time, the latter was surrounded by people who had listened to Plato's conversations with Dion and to those who had heard them. Their heads were filled with these bits of philosophical hearsay (*parakousmatōn*) (338d3). These people gathered around Dionysius and tried to engage him in dialogue as if he had heard everything that Plato had intended, which Dionysius allowed owing to his vanity as well as to a "nature that was not completely alien to learning" (338d6–8). The critique here is clear. These are people who lack understanding. They may have heard, and they may repeat back, but they pass philosophical "formulae" back and forth to one another like tokens or badges of belonging. These are formulaic responses, which in their unchanging repetition do not gain in truth but rather lose the specific value they possessed in their initial articulation. Dionysius would then go on to take these bits and pieces of philosophical language and record them in a book, which he attempted to pass off as representing his own original philosophy (341b1–6). Such an undertaking is by nature, Plato claims, wrongheaded; for it assumes that philosophical knowledge is information, like mathematical formulae, or names and dates, or observational data, which can be written down and repeated, and in that repetition there is a confirmation of its truth value. No matter how many times you count the number of stones, two plus two is four. Astronomy as an empirical science depends on the same observations being able to be made again and again. The more times these statements can be said and received as true, the stronger their correspondence value. Statement and meaning coincide and are confirmed in the world. Laws are propounded, things defined, types delimited, genders and genres established. You can write these things in a book and pick that book up in a different time and place and they will be, or at least they will purport to be, the very same things.

But philosophy, at least as Plato understands it, is not like that. Rather he says those producing such books "do not understand anything about the matter":

> And that is why there are not any writings from me, nor will there ever be, about these things: for what is spoken here is not the same as in other sciences, but as a result of a great amount of time being spent together (*sunousia*) concerning this very matter and of living together, suddenly just as a light is kindled from a fire that has blazed up, that very thing having been born in the soul then nourishes itself. (341c–d)

This is what I have termed in another context unrepeatable knowledge, a form of knowledge that is deeply contextual and experiential ("Repeatable and the Unrepeatable"). It is closer to the truth of psychoanalysis or of reading a poem than physics: a moment of interpretive insight contingent upon a particular set of events and associations. It is not the case, of course, that these flashes of light do not transcend their immediate context, that they do not illuminate what surrounds them, but they are never universalizable as such, and when they are decontextualized, reduced to formulas in the here and now, they become oppressive, they become the Law, and their very transcendental quality becomes a finite and enforceable typology. For Plato, at least in the *Seventh Letter,* and at least as read by Foucault, this is not philosophy. Philosophy is something far more powerful, far more destabilizing, and far more queer.

"Knowledge" as normally understood for Plato, then, is a repeatable structure. It is information that is dependent upon a framework that seeks to align language (*onoma*), argument (*logos*), and image and perception (*eidōlon*), the totality of which is called *epistēmē,* often translated "knowledge."[6] But for Plato philosophy's concern is not so much with these three elements and their correct alignment to produce repeatable knowledge as with the contingency of those structures in relation to what makes them possible, which he calls being (*on*) and the known (*gnōston*) (342 a–b). Any identifiable phenomenon has a name—let us say "woman," though Plato uses the example of a circle. We can then make propositions about that phenomenon. For example women are mothers. We can then check that proposition against the image we receive of women, whether through culture or personal experience—yes, my mother is a woman—and when we perceive an alignment between these three, we then have *epistēmē*. But while certain forms of empirical research would stop there and might even deduce certain consequences from that (i.e., women have certain anatomical characteristics, women have certain emotional characteristics, women have certain roles in societies and families), philosophy on Plato's understanding, and I would argue on Foucault's, does not stop there. It involves a continuous running up and down of these categories, rubbing them against one another and finding the friction points between them (343e). In the same manner, Socrates in the elenchus continuously seeks agreement with his interlocutor about a given proposition and then tests that proposition against a variety of cases, generalizations, and counterexamples, leaving the interlocutor not in the possession of firm knowledge, from which they can deduce positive prescriptions concerning the nature of things or the organization of social life, but in a state of perplexity or *aporia,* as the solid links between names, arguments, and perception become frayed and a moment of what belies any contingent epistemic reality becomes visible (compare *Sophist* 230a–d; Hadot 55–57, 103; Nehamas 82–85; and Blondell 100, 124). To return to our example, then, the reality of "woman," which seemed to inhere in both the name itself and the propositions in which it appeared and to be confirmed by personal perception and the social imaginary, suddenly seems to float free of those constraints. What seemed rock-solid reality is now shown to lack being, and attempts to enforce that reality through, for example, laws that seek to control the toilets people are allowed to use or the sexual habits they practice are revealed to be arbitrary exercises of power and control. Hence Plato concludes in the *Seventh Letter,* in a passage to which Foucault explicitly draws our attention (*Gouvernement de soi et des autres* 232):

> It is necessary to learn these things, the true and the false, at the same time from the whole of being, with all the work [*tribēs,* literally "rubbing, friction"] and much time I spoke of at the beginning. But rubbing [*tribomena*] each of these things together against one another with exertion, names and arguments, observations and perceptions, testing them in good faith and using questions and answers without rancor or envy, reflection and intellect shine forth, extending to the limits of human potential. (344b)

The recollection here of the earlier image of the light of understanding blazing forth is clearly deliberate. The vision of philosophical activity here is precisely the opposite of Dionysius's compiling a set of propositions heard here and there and presenting them as though they were the object of philosophy or of producing data sets that purport to show the achievement of learning outcomes, the development of critical thinking, or the "value" of an education.

Rather the mission of philosophy is precisely to disrupt such paradigms and the object world they must presume to exist. To return to the passage from Foucault cited earlier, "My problem . . . is to leave, according to the most intelligible design possible, the trace of the movements through which I am no longer at the place where I was just now," or to recall another justly famous formulation, from volume 2 of *The History of Sexuality:*

> But, then, what is philosophy today—philosophical activity, I mean—if it is not the critical work that thought brings to bear on itself? In what does it consist, if not in the endeavor to know how and to what extent it might be possible to think differently, instead of legitimating what is already known? (*Use of Pleasure* 9; *L'usage des plaisirs* 14–15)

The role of the philosopher in Foucault's last lectures is precisely to speak the truth to power, to have the "courage of truth" (*Courage de la vérité*). That truth is not a set of infinitely repeatable propositions, let alone a prescription telling others how they should live or where they should seek their pleasure, but rather it is the result of a continuous labor, a continuous friction, a patient work in the archive that carefully, over time, destabilizes our most fundamental epistemic realities and thereby offers the possibility to remake even our most fundamental certainties and to expand the realm of the possible.

In Foucault's last lectures, he turned to the Cynics. At a time when he was obviously ill and increasingly frail, he continued to give his weekly lectures at the Collège de France. He spoke of the ancient philosophers who, like the Platonists, traced their lineage to Socrates but who refused to accumulate a body of doctrine, lived their lives in the public square, begged, ate scraps, and masturbated in public. The Cynics were the "dogs" of philosophy. They were the street-corner preachers who confronted us with our conformity, our petty hypocrisies, our dishonesties. Their near naked bodies themselves were a locus of truth. Foucault in his penultimate lecture says:

> Cynicism was not simply a crude, insolent, and rudimentary reminder of the problem of the philosophic life. It posed a very important question, or rather, it seems to me, it gave its position on the theme of the philosophic

> life by posing the following question: life, in order truly to be the life of truth, should it not be an other life, radically and paradoxically other? (*Courage de la vérité* 226)

This call for a radical otherness, as defined by the Platonic spark or the Cynic provocation, is at the center of the final Foucault, and it is this same call that I would argue we must heed. In the end what is most authentic is not the infinitely reproducible but the moment of irreducible insight, of queer intelligibility, which makes possible a form of self-relation and of relation to others that is based on curiosity and care, one that must be informed by data and cosmopolitan in its scope but is never reducible to information nor globalized in its imperial reach. At the end of his lecture notes, though he did not have time to utter these words, Foucault writes, "But to finish what I want to insist on is this: there is no instilling of truth without an essential position of alterity: truth is never the same; there can only be truth in the form of another world, another life" (*Courage de la vérité* 311). While accountability and assessment are not evils in themselves and can be forces of rationality and the means to achieving a more just, beautiful, and better world, the reduction to the universal equivalent and the object world it defines is to be resisted at all costs.

Notes

1. See the digitalist dystopias portrayed in novels such as *The Circle* (Eggers) or movies such as *Blade Runner* (Scott).

2. There is a very large, varied bibliography on these questions; some of the more important high points can be found in Parry; Lord; Havelock; McLuhan; Ong; and Kittler. See also Miller, *Lyric Texts and Lyric Consciousness.*

3. See Heidegger ("Age of the World Picture" and "Plato's Doctrine of Truth"); Derrida ("Pharmacie de Platon" 96, 126); Popper; and Miller (*Diotima at the Barricades*).

4. The bibliography is lengthy, and other examples could be added; but see, most prominently, Irigaray ("Cosi fan tutti"; *Ethique de la différence sexuelle; Je, tu, nous*); Derrida (*Eperons*); Butler (42); Hodge (203–4); and Mortensen (11–13, 59–63, 80–81).

5. See, for example, Derrida (*Khôra* 81–83), but also a wide range of works that indicate that the Socratic and Platonic project is not a dogmatic knowledge of unchanging essences but an unending pursuit of wisdom in the midst of aporia and perplexity. Notable examples are Festugière (42–43, 191); Saxonhouse (82); Brown (164–65); Hadot (104–6); and Hunter (86–87).

6. Plato is not always consistent in his use of these terms. As Brisson and Pradeau observe in *Dictionnaire de Platon,* elsewhere *epistēmē* has a meaning much closer to what Plato here terms *gnōsis.*

Works Cited

Adorno, Theodor, and Max Horkheimer. *Dialectic of Enlightenment.* Trans. John Cumming . London: Allen Lane, 1973.

Benjamin, Walter. "The Work of Art in the Age of Mechanical Reproduction." *Illuminations.* Ed. Hannah Arendt. Trans. Harry Zohn. New York: Schocken Books, 1969. 217–51.

Blondell, Ruby. *The Play of Character in Plato's Dialogues.* Cambridge: Cambridge University Press, 2002.

Boyle, Brendan. "Foucault among the Classicists, Again." *Foucault Studies* 13 (2012): 138–56.

Brisson, Luc, and Jean-François Pradeau. *Dictionnaire de Platon.* Paris: Ellipses, 2007.

Brown, Wendy. "'Supposing truth were a woman . . .': Plato's Subversion of Masculine Discourse." *Feminist Interpretations of Plato.* Ed. Nancy Tuana. University Park: Penn State University Press, 1994. 157–80.

Butler, Judith. *Bodies That Matter: On the Discursive Limits of "Sex."* New York: Routledge, 1993.

Derrida, Jacques. *Eperons: Les styles de Nietzsche.* Paris: Flammarion, 1978.

——. *Khôra.* Paris: Galilée, 1993.

——. "La pharmacie de Platon." *La dissémination.* Paris: Seuil, 1972. 74–196.

Di Leo, Jeffrey R. *Corporate Humanities in Higher Education: Moving beyond the Neoliberal Academy.* New York: Palgrave Macmillan, 2015.

Eggers, Dave. *The Circle.* New York: Knopf, 2013.

Festugière, A. J. *Contemplation et vie contemplative selon Platon.* 2nd ed. Paris: Vrin, 1950. Original, 1935.

Folie, Sandra. "Beyond Ethnic Chick Lit—Queering the Field of 'World Women's Literature.'" Delivered at Littérature comparée et Gender—Queer vers un dépassement des identités, Journée d'études, September 16, 2016. Université Sorbonne Nouvelle—Paris 3.

Foucault, Michel. *Le courage de la vérité: Le gouvernement de soi et des autres II. Cours au Collège de France.* 1984. Ed. Frédéric Gros. Paris: EHESS/Gallimard/Seuil, 2009.

——. *Du gouvernement des vivants. Cours au Collège de France.* 1979–80. Ed. Michel Senellart. Paris: EHESS/Gallimard/Seuil, 2012.

——. *Le gouvernement de soi et des autres. Cours au Collège de France.* 1982–83. Ed. Frédéric Gros. Paris: Gallimard/Seuil, 2008.

——. *Surveiller et punir: Naissance de la Prison.* Paris: Gallimard, 1975.

——. *L'usage des plaisirs. Histoire de la sexualité,* vol. 2. Paris: Gallimard, 1984.

——. *The Use of Pleasure. The History of Sexuality,* vol. 2. Trans. Robert Hurley. New York: Random House, 1986.

——. *La volonté de savoir. Histoire de la sexualité,* vol. 1. Paris: Gallimard, 1976.

Greenfield, Jeff. "The Ugly History of Stephen Miller's 'Cosmopolitan' Epithet: Surprise, Surprise—The Insult Has Its Roots in Soviet Anti-Semitism," *Politico* August

3, 2017, http://www.politico.com/magazine/story/2017/08/03/the-ugly-history-of-stephen-millers-cosmopolitan-epithet-215454.

Hadot, Pierre. *Qu'est-ce que la philosophie antique?* Paris: Gallimard, 1995.

Havelock, Eric A. *Preface to Plato.* Cambridge, Mass.: Harvard University Press, 1963.

Heidegger, Martin. "Plato's Doctrine of Truth." Trans. Thomas Sheehan. *Pathmarks.* Ed. William McNeill. Cambridge: Cambridge University Press, 1998. 155–82.

——. *The Question Concerning Technology and Other Essays.* Trans. William Lovitt. New York: Harper Torchbooks, 1982.

Hodge, Joanne. "Irigaray Reading Heidegger." *Engaging with Irigaray: Feminist Philosophy and Modern European Thought.* Eds. Carolyn Burke, Naomi Schor, and Margaret Whitford. New York: Columbia University Press, 1994. 191–209.

Hunter, Richard. *Plato's Symposium.* Oxford: Oxford University Press, 2004.

Irigaray, Luce. "Cosi fan tutti." *Ce sexe qui n'en est pas un.* Paris: Minuit, 1977. 83–102.

——. *Ethique de la différence sexuelle.* Paris: Minuit, 1984.

——. *Je, tu, nous: Pour une culture de la différence.* Paris: Grasset, 1990.

Jameson, Fredric. *The Political Unconscious: Narrative as a Socially Symbolic Act.* Ithaca: Cornell University Press, 1981.

Kittler, Friedrich A. *Gramophone, Film, Typewriter.* Trans. Geoffrey Winthrop-Young and Michael Wutz. Stanford: Stanford University Press, 1999.

Lim, Jason. "Korea's CULTural Exceptionalism," *Korea Times,* June 27, 2014, http://www.koreatimes.co.kr/www/news/opinon/2016/02/352_159946.html.

Lord, Alfred B. *The Singer of Tales.* Cambridge, Mass.: Harvard University Press, 1960.

Macey, David. *The Lives of Michel Foucault.* New York: Pantheon Books, 1993.

Marx, Karl. *Capital.* Vol. 1. Trans. Ben Fowkes. New York: Vintage, 1977.

McLuhan, Marshall. *The Gutenberg Galaxy.* Toronto: University of Toronto Press, 1962.

Miller, Paul Allen. "The Art of Self-Fashioning, or Foucault on Plato and Derrida." *Foucault Studies* 2 (2005): 54–74.

——. *Diotima at the Barricades: French Feminists Read Plato.* Oxford: Oxford University Press, 2016.

——. "Dreams and Other Fictions: The Representation of Representation in *Republic* 5 and 6." *American Journal of Philology* 136 (2015): 37–62.

——. *Lyric Texts and Lyric Consciousness: The Birth of a Genre from Archaic Greece to Augustan Rome.* London: Routledge, 1994.

——. *Postmodern Spiritual Practices: The Construction of the Subject and the Reception of Plato in Lacan, Derrida, and Foucault.* Columbus: Ohio State University Press, 2007.

——. "The Repeatable and the Unrepeatable: Žižek and the Future of the Humanities, or Assessing Socrates." *symplokē* 17 (2010): 7–25.

Mortensen, Ellen. *The Feminine and Nihilism: Luce Irigaray with Nietzsche and Heidegger.* Oslo: Scandinavian University Press, 1994.

Nehamas, Alexander. *The Art of Living: Socratic Reflections from Plato to Foucault.* Berkeley: University of California Press, 1998.

Ong, Walter. *Orality and Literacy: The Technologizing of the Word.* London: Methuen, 1982.

Parry, Milman. *The Making of Homeric Verse.* Ed. Adam Parry. New York: Oxford University Press, 1987.

Popper, Karl R. *The Open Society and Its Enemies.* Vol. 1. London: Routledge, 1945.

Porter, James I. "Discipline and Punish: Some Corrections to Boyle." *Foucault Studies* 14 (2012): 179–95.

——. "Foucault's Antiquity." *Classics and the Uses of Reception.* Ed. Charles Martindale and Richard Thomas. London: Wiley Blackwell, 2006. 168–79.

——. "Foucault's Ascetic Ancients." *Phoenix* 59 (2005): 121–32.

Said, Edward. "Michel Foucault, 1926–84." *Raritan* 4 (1984): 1–11.

Saxonhouse, Arlene W. "The Philosopher and the Female in the Political Thought of Plato." *Feminist Interpretations of Plato.* Ed. Nancy Tuana. University Park: Penn State University Press, 1994. 67–85.

Scott, Ridley, dir. *Blade Runner.* Film. 1982. Hollywood: Warner Brothers. 2007 DVD.

U.S. Department of Education. *A Test of Leadership: Charting the Future of U.S. Higher Education, A Report of the Commission Appointed by Secretary of Education Margaret Spellings.* 2006. http://www.ed.gov/about/bdscomm/list/hiedfuture/reports/final-report.pdf.

Local Cultures, Global Audiences

The Dream (and Nightmare) of the World Novel

Alexander Beecroft

Global literary culture in the early twenty-first century seems poised in a dilemma resembling that of early twenty-first-century politics, caught between two constructs of globalization. Seemingly unstoppable economic forces relentlessly propel us towards a planetary economy and culture, steamrolling any resistance in their way. With culture as in politics we are, necessarily, divided on the desirability of this outcome. In the cultural case, for example, as a scholar of ancient Greek and classical Chinese literature, both truly transnational academic disciplines, I cannot be entirely hostile to the idea of closer cultural integration at the global level, which can only provide an impetus to further research, as well as opportunities to defamiliarize old narratives about these fields and to explore new paradigms. Global trade and new media can knit together diasporic audiences globally, enhancing the reach of literary languages large and small and building new and stronger ties between regions of the world. Yet at the same time, there seems a very real danger that increased global contact, and the increased power of the market that implies, might transform the cultural world from a series of loosely connected worlds of difference into a homogenous planet of indifferent cultural consumers, passively absorbing nearly identical cultural products (film, television, fiction) produced wherever costs are lowest. Just as recent years have seen the rise of a political resistance to economic globalization, on the right as well as the left, so, too, have we seen the emergence of a resistance to cultural globalization: a movement decrying the perceived uniformity of global culture in the present and concerned that even greater homogeneity is on its way.

At the same time, there may be a more hopeful path. New technology in principle decreases the barriers to entry into publication and could make it easier for new languages to acquire written literatures and for existing but small-scale literary languages to thrive, especially in diasporic contexts. We see some version of this happening with the almost universal phenomenon, since 1990, of the further embrace of regional and minority languages everywhere from Nepal to Iraq, France to Argentina (Beecroft, *Ecology of World Literature* 273–76). Even as it becomes possible to package texts as commodities for a truly global audience, it should also become easier to find and reach niche audiences, whether linguistic minority or countercultural and/or counterhegemonic in other ways, and this might present fresh opportunities for more sophisticated cultural engagements with globalization. In what follows I examine recent arguments about a possible global literary culture. Through a quick examination of the works of two recent writers, both working in Italian, I suggest that there is reason for cautious optimism: that while the pressures toward uniformity may be real, increased globalization may yet leave room for a diverse and distinctive planetary literary culture. I suggest, in fact, that the authors I discuss offer signs of the emergence of a new grammar of the global novel, of the gradual emergence of a series of tropes adapted to the needs of global narration in our era in much the way that epistolary fiction was to the emergent nation-state world of the eighteenth-century novel.

The fear that a globalized cultural economy will lead to a homogenization of cultural products finds potent, if elementary, expression in the ways in which novels are packaged for a global readership. The cover designs for novels, for example, frequently resort to crass and simplistic imagery to reassure potential readers that the work they may be about to purchase will confirm their existing understanding of the world rather than seeking to challenge it. Novels set in Africa, or even set elsewhere but written by African writers, are usually given covers involving acacia trees at sunset, whether or not the acacia is native to their countries of origin, let alone whether the novel's setting includes the tree (Stevens). Likewise the covers of novels by women writers from Muslim nations, or concerning Muslim women in any way, almost invariably feature veiled women, whether or not the female characters in the work themselves wear the veil or whether the question is even discussed in the text (Talib). This is a superficial example of the kinds of conformity a global literary economy already demands and might demand more of in the future, but it has a real impact: more challenging works that disrupt clichés about their regions are marketed as if they confirm those clichés, possibly discouraging readers who are more open to the unexpected and encouraging more complacent readers to find their expectations confirmed by whatever they read.

But critics identify more profound ways in which the global marketplace may be shaping literary fiction in our time. Tim Parks, for example, has traced the influence of English on the syntax of Italian prose, showing an increasing tendency toward the use of subject pronouns, of the placement of adjectives before nouns, and of the use of possessives rather than reflexives to indicate body parts

("Your English Is Showing"). If the fabric of the language is changing, so is how it is being used: Parks also suggests the gradual erosion of modernist linguistic experimentation in contemporary European fiction in favor of a sparer, more easily translated style, and the avoidance of too-specific cultural or political references to the nation of origin—except in contemporary U.S. fiction, which, Parks argues, features ever-more extensive use of contemporary slang and arcane pop-culture references. American writers, he argues, can get away with these things because they are less dependent on income from translation in the first place and can rely on a greater interest in translation with English as the source, rather than the target, language ("Franzen's Ugly Americans Abroad").

Going further, the Italian critic Vittorio Coletti explores the representation of place in the *romanzo mondo* (world novel). According to Coletti the contemporary world novel uses its location, typically in a large cosmopolitan global city, as little more than a backdrop, familiar to its readers whatever their national origin because they, too, live in such cities. Local political and cultural texture is omitted, especially anything that would offer a barrier to quick translation, with perhaps the occasional gesture toward familiar and accessible aspects of foreign cultures, such as food or popular music. Coletti contrasts our contemporary moment (represented for him by what he sees as the completely generic urban settings of Scandinavian *noir* detective fiction) with the great nineteenth-century novels, narrating their nations through the careful evocation of a particular place and time: the provincial Great Reform–era England of *Middlemarch,* say, or the life of an 1840s village in Normandy in *Madame Bovary.* Indeed, as Coletti puts it, the latter novel is so deeply rooted in its particular location that it would become unimaginable uprooted and transferred to, say, the urban petit-bourgeoisie of Rome after Italian unification. Global novels, Coletti seems to suggest, are located in particular cities because they have to be, but those cities are carefully stripped of any distinguishing marks that would intrude on the global reading experience, just as the novel as a whole is voided of any individual or national characteristics.

Stephen Owen once famously and controversially compared so-called world poetry designed for translation to a food court, offering a readily accessible and nonthreatening version of local culture for global consumers ("What Is World Poetry?"; "Stepping Forward and Back"). The world novel as understood by Parks and Coletti seems like something rather more dispiriting even than that: a mid-range chain hotel, perhaps, whose coffeemaker, skin-care products, and bedding are almost identical everywhere in the world, each room ornamented with an artful black-and-white photograph of an architectural detail from some local landmark as the only reminder that this particular hotel is in Chicago rather than Cologne, Taipei rather than Tampa. But is the situation as dire as that? Must global fiction necessarily be so flat and uniform? It is instructive here to reflect on Pascale Casanova's claim that, in minor literatures, the innovative writers are those who aim at a global market, while those who write for local audiences are comparatively reactionary, preferring realism to formal experimentation:

> It thus becomes possible to understand how the very content of literary texts is linked to the place in the worldwide structure of national space from which they emerge. The political dependence of emerging literary spaces is signaled by the recourse to a functionalist aesthetic, and, taking the criteria of literary modernity as a standard of measurement, the most conservative narrative, novelistic, and poetical forms. (199)

This claim is a contentious one, and there are, of course, many examples of formalist and experimental work written for national, even local, audiences. (See, for example, the discussions of Irish language and Italian dialect poetry in McCrea, *Languages of the Night.*) Casanova's point is nonetheless an intriguing one: while writing for a local audience allows an author to engage deeply with a local culture and context in a way that a global audience will not understand and is unlikely to tolerate, that local audience may nonetheless come with constraining expectations of its own. Writers might, conceivably, seek a global audience not only for financial reasons but also because they wish to say the kind of thing, in the kind of way, that a strictly local audience might not endorse. More generally there might be other advantages of one kind or another to writing for that broader audience, and if so the global novel might represent not so much the death of local traditions as the emergence of something new and interesting.

I would argue, in fact, that the rise of the world novel is leading to the development of fresh literary tropes and devices, suitable for representing and reflecting on our changed world. Elsewhere I have discussed one such device, the "plot of globalization" (*Ecology of World Literature* 283–95; see also the longer discussion in Beecroft, "On the Tropes of Literary Ecology"). This device is a particular use of the old literary technique of *entrelacement,* or multistrand narration, weaving together distinct stories about unrelated characters that, taken together, are meant to tell us the story of globalization. This device is found in part in recent film, notably in Alejandro González Iñárritu's *Babel,* and also features prominently in much recent fiction, notably in Amitav Ghosh's Ibis trilogy and Roberto Bolaño's *2666.* Both of these works use the plot of globalization in one way or another, and both have inherently cosmopolitan casts of characters whose agency and commitments are similarly complex. Both works travel with ease through very different worlds: from the antebellum South to the subaltern world of Indian Ocean lascars to the Bengali aristocracy in one case; from European academic conferences and postwar German novelists to an African American church and to murdered women in a maquiladora-based border town on the other. The linkages made between these worlds are tenuous but rooted in the kinds of economic and power relationships we know actually exist. Both writers engage in complex and rooted ways with these characters, their worlds, and their language. This is not to say that neither is a problematic work, or that neither is thinking about the marketplace. But neither Ghosh nor Bolaño, shall we say, take the straightest shot at marketability: both create challenging, complex, and lengthy works that assume some knowledge of the worlds they describe and then provide more such knowledge.

In discussing the use of the plot of globalization in these works, I contrasted them with earlier canonical texts from similar regions: Gabriel García Márquez's *One Hundred Years of Solitude* (1967) and Salman Rushdie's *Midnight's Children* (1981). I emphasized how, for all of their vaunted magical realism, the two earlier texts focus obsessively, arguably even parodically, on the nation-state, in ways reminiscent of the great nineteenth-century works of Alessandro Manzoni or Honoré de Balzac. Marquez's village of Macondo has a life span that traces that of Colombia, from European colonization to the present, while Saleem Sinai in *Midnight's Children* is literally and precisely to the second the same age as his nation, and the events of his life (and therefore of the novel) seem obsessively to track and mimic those of Indian post-independence history. No novels could possibly be more explicitly about the nation, and yet both are read in metropolitan contexts as something other than national: as magical realism, a term that applies, in any event, very differently to each, and as works of the "Latin American Boom" and of the postcolonial Anglosphere. Both, too, use comparatively linear narrative techniques.

Alongside the plot of globalization, I'd like to suggest another literary device common to recent world novels, which is a kind of willed untranslatability, or non-translation. This, too, has cinematic parallels, being used to particular effect in another film directed by Alejandro González Iñárritu, *Biutiful* (2010). Where *Babel* revels in its global settings (Morocco, Mexico, Japan) and its interlaced narratives marked by coincidence, the characters and stories in *Biutiful* share a single city, Barcelona, though coming from many other locations. Groups of characters are native speakers of Chinese and of Wolof. Where earlier filmic traditions have tended to present dialogue by characters whose language is not that of a film's diegesis either in the original language with subtitles or (more often) spoken in the film's own language, perhaps with heavy accents suggestive of their own language, González Iñárritu chooses to present dialogue between non-Hispanophone characters in their own languages, without subtitles. At various points in the narrative, key portions of dialogue happen in Chinese or in Wolof and are not subtitled (either into the Spanish of the original film or into the English subtitles that North American viewers saw). The viewer is thus left in the position of the

Spanish characters in the film: witnesses to dialogue they cannot understand, at turns frustrated, alienated, or chastened by that experience. Rather than project the usual cinematic fantasy in which linguistic difference is erased or mitigated, González Iñárritu here gives us, in fact, Babel: a fallen world in which we need to speak to each other but can't. The refusal to translate offers a kind of rebuttal to the myth that globalization is rendering our world uniform and frictionless, reminding us that many of the barriers to understanding are as great as they ever were.

The significance of this refusal to translate is of course somewhat different on the page than it is on screen. In film, after all, some sort of sound must come out of the actors' mouths, and so the choice must be made between presenting dialogue in its original language or using the old cinematic convention of presenting that dialogue in the language of the film's narration, perhaps accented to mark the fictionality of this presentation. In prose fiction, by contrast, another possibility exists: indirect discourse, which (among other things) allows for the representation of dialogue spoken in one language in another. At the same time, there is no easy novelistic equivalent for subtitling, so that representing dialogue in another language (which happens, after all, in a novel as canonical as *War and Peace*) is generally cumbersome and unpopular. Narrative fiction tends, moreover, to use the same language and register for narration as for dialogue, with the partial exception of comic fiction (Beecroft, "Narrator and the Nation-Builder"). These metalinguistic choices, then, are at once easier and less marked in fiction than they are in film, but the decision is still a meaningful one.

Consider, for example, the following four brief passages of dialogue:

1. She said, "I love you."
2. She said in Italian, "I love you."
3. She said, "*ti amo*."
4. She said in Italian that she loved him.

Assuming that each of these four passages describe the same event, the choices between them are significant. The first, which omits any mention of language, urges the reader to consider the question of translation as unproblematic. Earlier information in the discourse may have made it clear that this speech is being translated from Italian, but we are given no reason to think that the translation is anything other than simple or immediate. The second is almost as immediate, marking the linguistic difference but implying that the phrase has been effortlessly and precisely translated. The third, by reporting the speech in Italian, does perhaps suggest that the reader needs to hear these words in their original language but offers no account of why the translation might be difficult, or how *ti amo* might possibly differ from "I love you." This third possibility, viable with a short, well-known phrase, quickly becomes unwieldy and in longer conversations is generally reserved for key words or phrases, with the remaining dialogue translated into the novel's language.

The fourth possibility, featuring indirect discourse, leaves much more room for ambiguity. We are not explicitly presented with the exact words spoken, and so implicitly we may be encouraged to wonder how exact the indirect statement is. Possibly it is a loose paraphrase of a longer or more idiosyncratic statement, though (as in this case) it would not have to be. By resorting to indirect discourse to report dialogue in another language, dialect, or register, writers are freed from finding a way to register the linguistic difference more precisely—and can also remind their audiences that translation may not be easy or straightforward. We learn roughly the import of a character's thoughts or statements but are deliberately kept aloof from the material linguistic detail. Such an approach can be particularly helpful in cases where writers have reasons to avoid conveying precise and easy access to the words of their characters, as do the two writers, Elena Ferrante and Alessandro Spina, to whom I now turn.

The recent series of four "Neapolitan" novels by the pseudonymous Italian author Elena Ferrante, published between 2011 and 2014 in Italian, with translations into English by Ann Goldman published between 2012 and 2015, offers a particularly vivid case in point. These novels became an instant sensation in the English-speaking world, selling unusually well for translated fiction and generating what was described as "Ferrante fever" (Bullaro and Love 2). While these novels also sold well in Italy, their critical reception there was more mixed and was both motivated by, and rather skeptical about, their Anglophone reception. Italian critics dismissed Ferrante's work as somewhat cynically crafted for the export market, relying on an American attachment to Naples as both a tourist center and the point of origin of many Italian American migrants; on slick, well-crafted plots; on simple, clear language; and on techniques previously honed by Italian film directors such as Paolo Sorrentino (di Paolo; de Majo).

Many of these critiques seem either unfair or slightly off-target. It's true that Naples is an Italian city with particularly strong associations for many Americans, but Ferrante's firmly unsentimental representation of the city dwells more on the chaos, poverty, squalor, and social conformity that Italians also associate with the city while studiously avoiding the picturesque qualities (of scenery and of character alike) that balance those negative characteristics in the American touristic imaginary. Food, so central both to the representation of Italian American identity and to ethnic American fiction generally, is rarely mentioned in Ferrante's account of her narrator Elena Greco's childhood in Naples, and when it is mentioned, the emphasis is on the poverty of the ingredients available and the feminine drudgery of daily food preparation, not on sunlit memories of groaning familial banquets. Moreover many of the most vivid scenes in the novels are set not in the postwar Naples of Greco's childhood but in the radical political scenes of northern cities, particularly Milan in the 1970s, a very real world but one more vivid in the Italian self-imagination than in American projections. Despite dismissive critical comparisons with Elizabeth Gilbert's 2006 *Eat Pray Love* (di Paolo), Ferrante's Naples and Italy in fact little resemble the cartoon Italy of popular Anglophone imaginings, full of genial restaurateurs and argumentative taxi drivers.

Where Italian critics of Ferrante are more accurate, I think, is in their claim that the simplicity of Ferrante's language—a spare and unfussy standard Italian—contributes to the ease and fluency of her translation and makes her works more fully accessible abroad. Yet here, too, there is something of a paradox: the very clarity and simplicity of Ferrante's Italian can generate unexpected consequences for the reader in translation. Consider, for example, the following passage from early in the first novel, *My Brilliant Friend:*[1]

> I calmed down. Lila looked around, identified the opening from which we had dropped Tina and Nu. We went along the rough bumpy wall, we looked into the shadows. The dolls weren't there. *Lila repeated in dialect,* they're not there, they're not there, they're not there, and searched along the walls with her hands, something I didn't have the courage to do. (56; emphasis added)

The two young friends, Elena and Lila, whose friendship forms the theme of all four novels, have just lost their dolls and are searching for them. A reader experiencing this passage in translation will feel, perhaps, cheated that Lila's words are reported to us in standard English and that no attempt is made to convey the vividness and particularity of the Neapolitan dialect. Surely, that reader might think, this is a case of something lost in translation, of a rich and local texture of the original text that must be flattened out in translation, due to the almost insurmountable challenges of finding a register in English that could adequately convey the emotional and cultural significance of Neapolitan dialect in Italian.

But that reader would be wrong: nothing has been lost in translation here. The Italian original reads:

> Mi calmai. Lila si guardò intorno, individuò l'apertura da dove avevamo fatto cadere Tina e Nu. Ci accostammo alla parete ruvida, grumosa, guardammo nell'ombra. Le bambole non c'erano. *Lila ripeteva in dialetto:* non ci stanno, non ci stanno, non ci stanno, e frugava per terra con le mani, cos ache io non avevo il coraggio di fare. (82; emphasis added)

Lila's dialectal reply, in other words, is not represented directly in dialect in Ferrante's original Italian either, a pattern repeated throughout the novel. Apart from a few curses strategically deployed in their original dialectal form, Ferrante consistently reports dialect in indirect discourse, marking it as dialect for emphasis or where the choice is unclear (at other times the reader will have to infer that characters are almost certainly conversing in dialect or in the standard language).[2] The effect is to remind the reader of the retrospective quality of the narration (a frame narrative at the beginning and ending of the novels is set in the present day, and there are occasional explicit reminders that the novel is being narrated from a great temporal distance). Our narrator, Elena, seems to remember every conversation of her childhood in considerable detail, but in translation, emphasizing that the gap between past life and present is for her in some degree incommensurable. The rhythms and diction of the Neapolitan dialect, the rhetoric of the working-class neighborhood, have no place, Ferrante seems to say, in the bourgeois world of social advancement and erotic independence to which the novel belongs (McCrea, "Language Change"). All of this will be meaningful, even expected, for an Italian audience, accustomed in its literary tradition both to the reporting of dialogue in dialect and to its translation into the standard language as a novelistic trope. For the reader in English translation, however, used to a language where the gaps between dialects and registers are both smoother and smaller, the productive ambiguity of dialogue in standard Italian is quite lost and suggests merely a disappointing lack of traductorial fidelity. Such strategic uses of different registers of language for different purposes are, of course, necessarily difficult to convey in translation, but the general import of Ferrante's choice here is clear even in English: there is a rich world of discourse in Neapolitan dialect, which our narrator knows very well and could choose to convey to us in some form. Instead she withholds that world from her readers, reminding us that we are tourists in the world represented by her novels, our access mediated by the forbearance of those who choose to explain it all to us.

A similar effect is used to slightly different purposes in a very different collection of works, Alessandro Spina's *I confini dell'ombra* (*The Confines of the Shadow*). Spina, né Basili Shafik Khouzam, was born in Benghazi in 1927; his father was a Maronite Christian and a wealthy textile manufacturer from Aleppo who had himself arrived (like the hero of *The Young Maronite,* the first novel in this series) in Benghazi in 1912, just after the Italians had signed the Treaty of Ouchy with the Ottomans, confirming that Cyrenaica and Tripolitania, the last remaining Ottoman provinces in Africa, had fallen to European conquerors. Spina was raised at first in Benghazi, but when war broke out in 1939, his father sent the young Alessandro and his mother to Milan. Spina remained there, pursuing his studies and thoroughly acculturating to Italy, until 1953 and Libyan independence, when he returned to Benghazi to help his father run his textile factory. Spina remained in Benghazi until 1980, running the factory and writing in his spare time, in the face of conditions that grew increasingly problematic for him as both a businessman and a writer after Muammar Gaddafi seized power in 1969. Spina began writing the novels and stories that became *The Confines of the Shadow* in the early 1960s, alongside a history of the period called *The Fall of the Monarchy,* which, at Spina's request, has not yet been published. The history had to be smuggled out of Libya when Spina left in 1980, but the novels had already been published in Italy, though with small presses, attracting little notice. Spina continued to write these books (which do not a single through-composed plot in many volumes but rather are a sequence of novels and short stories covering the history of Libya from 1911 through the discovery of oil and the rise of Gaddafi in the early 1960s) while living in retirement in a seventeenth-century villa near Bergamo, with the last in the series, *La vita della riva minore* (*The Shores of a Lesser Life*), published in 1997. In 2006 Spina assembled these works as an omnibus volume under the title *I confini dell'ombra: In terra d'oltremare* (*The Confines of the Shadow: In Lands beyond the Seas*). This won the Bagutta Prize in 2007, though still attracting relatively little attention. The whole collection is now gradually being translated into English by Darf Publishers, a company that began its history as an Arab press in Libya, then fled to London under Gaddafi, where it specializes in republishing books on the Middle East of antiquarian interest. After the Arab Spring, Darf began to take an interest in publishing contemporary Arabic fiction (especially from Libya) as well as this projected complete translation of Spina's oeuvre. Spina's translator, André Naffis-Sahely, signed on to the project just two weeks after Spina's death in 2013 (Naffis-Sahely). It's not clear who Spina was writing for. His mentor, the author Alberto Moravia, once told him there was no public for a series of books like this in an Italy that would just as soon forget its colonial past: "Per un romanzo (o ciclo) simile in Italia il pubblico non c'e" (Spina 1250). And while the translations have begun to attract some notice, that notice has been limited and slow—very much the opposite of the frenzy that greeted the Ferrante novels at approximately the same time.

Alessandro Spina's complicated identity (neither fully Libyan nor fully Italian, never a resident of his native Syria) had interesting implications for his writing of these novels, especially at first. In the 1960s, when he began to write *The Young Maronite,* he was deeply steeped in the Italian and European literary traditions. He was reasonably fluent in Arabic but had at the time neither the formal and literary sophistication that would have come with education in that language nor a sure grasp of the language of the streets of Benghazi that would have come from a life fully spent there. Spina explicitly compares himself to Joseph Conrad as a writer working in a nonnative language, but with a difference: he felt that Conrad did too little to explore the subjectivity and inner lives of his African characters, and he longed to improve on Conrad in this way. But how? To express these thoughts in Italian, a language these characters did not know, was an unimaginable project of cultural translation; but Spina himself lacked the Arabic vernacular knowledge necessary to imagine the linguistic form their thoughts would really have taken. His solution was an ingenious one, though one familiar after our reading of Ferrante: he reports the thoughts of his Bedouin characters in *The Young Maronite* only through indirect statement, signaling to the reader that we are getting an approximation only of the character's inner life, not an exact reporting of its contents. Readers are thus subtly reminded throughout the novel not only that the Bedouin characters have inner lives, but also that it is something of a privilege to gain any access to that life and that that access is neither simple nor natural. This choice could read as a kind of transcendent othering of the Bedouin, as the possessor of an inscrutably foreign mind, but Spina is careful to minimize this possibility; as his own Arabic grew more confident, and as his narration moves forward in time (so that Libyan Arabs have to some extent adapted to Italian colonialism), he drops this use of indirect discourse and grants us fuller access to the minds of his characters.

A parallel stylistic choice further clarifies Spina's intentions: the Italian colonial characters in this novel speak only in theatrical dialogue. This choice of course denies the reader access to the inner lives of the Italians in this novel but also renders them slightly absurd, as if they are characters in some opera or comic play strutting across the stage parroting a colonial superiority they seem not to believe they possess:

> OLGHINA: My first impression of this town was horrible. How the houses are painted a blinding white, how the dust lies thick on the trees like ash, the mayhem, the neglect, and the fruitless attempts to clean this up; the new military government, their hurried emergency measures. While I was riding in the carriage to the hotel, I felt a mysterious hand wrap itself around my heart. I couldn't understand the reality in front of my eyes. The further the carriage ventured down those dusty streets, the more frightened I grew.
>
> PIETRA: Are these people really such barbarians? Regardless, we clearly need to think of them as such in order to reassure ourselves. Barbarism is a crime and civilization is always right, these are what our rights amount to. In other words, we don't want victims, we want criminals. Civilization always amounts to bloody retribution. (114)
>
> OLGHINA: La prima impressione arrivando in città è stata orribili. Il bianco abbacinante delle case, la polvere posata come cenere sugli alberi, il disordine, l'abbandono, e la sterile opposizione a tutto questo: il nuovo provvisorio dei militari, come frettolose misure di emergenza. Sulla carrozza che mi portava in albergo, una mana misteriosa mi stringeva il cuore. Non mi riusciva né di capire né di accettare la realtà che avevo

sotto gli occhi. Più la carrozza si inoltrava nelle vie polverose, più la paura cresceva.

PIETRA: Questi uomini sonno davvero dei barbari? Comunque noi abbiamo bisogno di crederli tali per rassicurarci. La barbarie è colpa e la civiltà ragione, ecco i nostri diritti. In altre parole, non vogliamo vittime ma colpevoli La civiltà diventa sanguinaria giustizia. (97)

Between the Bedouins whose inner lives are paraphrased in Italian and the Italians who seem to be nothing but vainglorious performers, it is the Maronite family of the protagonist (the characters who most resemble the author, of course) whose inner and outer selves are the most fully realized. The lack of inwardness of the Italian characters underscores the hollowness of the Italian colonial project, which Spina frequently compares to a theatrical production while also asserting that Italy as a colonial power is barely more "civilized" than the country it has conquered. These stylistic choices peculiarly fit Spina's own complex situation in an independent and postcolonial Libya: as a diasporic businessman from elsewhere whose education and intellectual proclivities align him with the Italians but who is at the same time profoundly unadmiring and unsympathetic to Italy's colonial ambitions. Spina thus skillfully and subtly focalizes his narrative around the characters he knows best, providing an eccentric position from which his readers can observe the colonial situation, not as the Italians they are, nor as the colonized subjects they cannot quite imagine themselves to be, but as intermediaries, traveling in both worlds yet not quite fluent in either. For the use of these formal experiments in the service of representing empire alone, I would suggest, Spina deserves further study and attention, while the refusal to translate we have seen in both Ferrante and Spina adds to our understanding of the world novel. In so doing they remind us that global novels, and global audiences, may allow for more complexity than critics fear—and, as Spina in particular suggests, global readerships may prove even more receptive to certain sorts of complexity than the traditional national audience. There is no guarantee that the novel will thrive in its new global context, but reports of its demise may be exaggerated or premature.

Notes

1. See also the brief discussion of this passage in Cavanaugh.

2. Although interestingly here Lila's repetition is not an exact one: instead of following the narration in using the verb *essere,* Lila's indirectly reported dialogue uses *stare,* a substitution that brings her construction closer to the dialect original, which would have been something like *nun ce stanno.* Even when dialect has been banished from the novel, its specter lingers in places.

Works Cited

Beecroft, Alexander. *An Ecology of World Literature: From Antiquity to the Present Day.* Verso, 2015.

——. "The Narrator and the Nation-Builder: Dialect, Dialogue, and Narrative Voice in Minority and Working-Class Fiction." *Canadian Review of Comparative Literature/ Revue Canadienne de Littérature Comparée,* vol. 42, no. 4, 2015, pp. 410–23.

——. "On the Tropes of Literary Ecology: The Plot of Globalization." *Globalizing Literary Genres: Literature, History, Modernity,* edited by Jernej Habjan and Fabienne Imlinger, Routledge, 2016, pp. 195–212.

Bullaro, Grace Russo and Stephanie Love, editors. *The Works of Elena Ferrante: Reconfiguring the Margins.* Springer 2016.

Casanova, Pascale. *The World Republic of Letters.* Harvard University Press, 2007.

Cavanaugh, Jill R. "Indexicalities of Language in Ferrante's Neapolitan Novels: Dialect and Italian as Markers of Social Value and Difference." *The Works of Elena Ferrante: Reconfiguring the Margins,* edited by Grace Russo Bullaro and Stephanie Love, Springer, 2016, pp. 45–70.

Coletti, Vittorio. *Romanzo mondo: la letteratura nel villaggio globale.* Il Mulino, 2011.

de Majo, Cristiano. "La Narrazione Esotica Italiana All'estero." *Rivista Studio,* Jan. 2015.

di Paolo, Paolo. "Il Caso Ferrante, Il Romanzo Italiano Secondo Il New Yorker." *La Stampa,* 13 Oct. 2014.

McCrea, Barry. *Languages of the Night: Minor Languages and the Literary Imagination in Twentieth-Century Ireland and Europe.* Yale University Press, 2015.

McCrea, Barry. "On Language Change and Social Class in the Novel." *From Enlightenment to Rebellion: Essays in Honor of Christopher Fox.* Edited by James G. Buickerood. Bucknell University Press, 2018. Pages 253–266.

Naffis-Sahely, André. "Spina's Shadow." *Nation,* July 2014.

Owen, Stephen. "Stepping Forward and Back: Issues and Possibilities for 'World' Poetry." *Modern Philology,* vol. 100, no. 4, May 2003, pp. 532–48.

——. "What Is World Poetry?" *New Republic,* vol. 203, no. 21, Nov. 1990, p. 28.

Parks, Tim. "Franzen's Ugly Americans Abroad." *NYRblog,* 11 May 2011, http://www.nybooks.com/blogs/nyrblog/2011/may/11/franzens-ugly-americans-abroad/.

——. "Your English Is Showing." *NYRblog,* 15 June 2011, http://www.nybooks.com/blogs/nyrblog/2011/jun/15/english-showing/.

Spina, Alessandro. "La posterità dell'ombra: Una conversazione." *I confini dell'ombra: In terra d'oltremare,* Morcelliana, 2007, pp. 1239–66.

——. *I confini dell'ombra: In terra d'oltremare,* Morcelliana, 2007.

——. *The confines of the shadow: in lands overseas.* Volume 1. The young Maronite; The marriage of Omar; The nocturnal visitor. André Naffis-Sahely, translator. Darf Publishing, 2015.

Stevens, Simon. "Like so Many (Wildly Varying) Writers on Africa, Adichie Gets the

Acacia Tree Sunset Treatment . . . (@AfricasaCountry)Pic.Twitter.Com/ZMQtirfrQ9." @SimonMStevens, 7 May 2014.

Talib, Adam. "Translating for Bigots." *ArabLit,* 4 Nov. 2013, https://arablit.org/2013/11/04/translating-for-bigots/.

Global Public, Digital Public

Neo-epistolarity and Tactical Consumption in *À toi*

Bennett Yu-Hsiang Fu

On the last day of 1999, right before the dawn of the new millennium, Quebecois writer Nicole Brossard wrote: "En résumé: le 31 décembre, 1999, lorsqu'à minuit, j'ouvrairai une bouteille de champagne, il est certain qu'en la même seconde, ma page sera blanche comme une page de garde" (qtd. McPherson 3; In brief: on December 31, 1999, at midnight, I will open a bottle of champagne, and surely at the same second, my page will be blank like a front page).[1] Brossard's note on the "page de garde," indicative of the Francophone Canadian literary development yet to occur in the new millennium, points to changing contours in Quebecois literature. On the threshold of the new century, French Canadian literature had already reaped a harvest after its first jubilee since the "dark age" of Quebec.[2] Distinctive in its historical and literary development, Quebec underwent a decade of quiet revolution in the sixties that unshackled the province from religious dictatorship. *La Révolution tranquille* turned Quebec into a secular, Francophone center, peacefully assaulting Anglophone dominance. Literature during the long revolution and transformation became a vital shaping force as "Quebec recognized its colonized status and mentality, rejected the old thinking, and reformed the institutions that had perpetuated that status" (Brière 152). In the cultural and literary renaissance, the French language, serving as the emblem of "modernity and progress," opened up a normed center "where culture, language, and memory are constantly being constructed and kept in congruence by national mythmaking" (Brière 158).

Against the backdrop of literary development in national mythmaking, this essay, by discussing epistolarity in a digital age, strives to fill in the *page blanche* of contemporary Quebecois writing in terms of the "global" and "digital" public. These two axes, "global" and "digital," however, underline a crucial dilemma faced by modern French Canada and Quebec's claim to go global, public, and digital: "Nationalism can only be asserted successfully by an identification with technological advance; but technological advance entails the disappearance of those indigenous differences that give substance to nationalism" (Grant 76). I wish to reexamine a hidden Francophone literary tradition usually dismissed and downplayed by the unquestioned authority of the Canadian national public and to reorient Quebecois writing along global chronologies. The primary challenge to global chronologies responds to the reconceptualizations of time and history in the sending, reading, and receiving of digital forms and messages. These reconceptualizations, complicated and expedited by digitality and publicness, expose epistolarity to a potential public—not to be circumscribed by the regional or national localities—that situates the circulation of textuality in a global setting. With an analysis rethinking how writing in the global setting differs from regional or national settings, I hope to lead Franco-Canadian epistolarity to an attention to the "new and shifting notion of the Asian Canadian" (Ty and Goellnicht 7) and to address critical genre-gender and *langue-langage* reconfigurations in literary studies in a global age.

▶ Gendered Tactics, Tactical Consumption

Letter writing is an ancient and still-common cultural practice, but as a literary genre, the epistolary novel is usually dismissed from contemporary scholarly discussions and canonical formations. Here I take on two primary challenges: reconceptualizing the discursivity of epistolarity and resituating this genre in canon formation and literary scholarship. To do so I choose Vietnamese Franco-Canadian Kim Thúy's collaborative epistolary work with Slovakian Franco-Swiss Pascal Janovjak and focus on epistolarity to articulate the challenges. The complexity of the collaborative work of translational and transcultural exchange is enhanced by the nominal compound's ethnolinguistic incongruities (i.e., hyphenated Vietnamese Franco-Canadian and Slovakian Franco-Swiss) and the authors' taxonomical ambivalences either in (continental) French literature or in (predominantly English) Asian North American literature. Thúy's first novel, *Ru,* published in 2009, won a host of prizes in both Canada and France. A lyrical, highly autobiographical narrative, *Ru* has been translated into many languages and published in some twenty countries. After the success of *Ru,* Thúy experimented with a new form of publishing, compiling in the book *À toi* (2011) emails between Thúy and Janovjak about their relationships with language, identity, writing, and exile. Thúy was born in Vietnam and raised in Montreal, while Janovjak was born in Switzerland and grew up and worked in Lebanon, Jordan, and Bangladesh. Through their email exchange on everything from quotidian trivia to political polemics, both writers share their exclusion and displacement whether in the Middle East, in Asia, in Europe, or in North America. As the introductory page reads, "Ils se sont rencontrés un soir, dans un hôtel de Monaco. Au petit déjeuner, ils se sont racontés. Et puis elle est repartie à Montreal, et il a regagné Ramallah" (6; They met one night, in a hotel in Monaco. They talked over breakfast. And then she returned to Montreal, and he to Ramallah). Thúy and Janovjak's short emails pepper each other with sensory memories of their childhoods in various countries, where the customs and reflections of those places are told from the viewpoint of an integrated outsider with a limited-omniscient style.

My analysis hinges on epistolarity in a new, digital form, but to examine this vein of the Quebecois literary movement and to review the literary development of such a specific genre, it is necessary to annex Quebecois letters to continental French literary trajectories as well as to contemporary Canadian literary development. This developmental context should be first traced from two standpoints. On the one hand, observing the minority movements entering Canadian writing in the 1980s, Canadian critic Linda Hutcheon coined the term "ex-centrics, the off-center" (*Poetics of Postmodernism* 41) to characterize the nationalist politics vis-à-vis independent Canadian identity and culture in Canadian writing. In the rethinking of margins and edges, Hutcheon posits Anglophone Canadian preoccupations with feminism and postmodernism in contemporary Canadian literature before the new millennium (*Canadian Postmodernism* 108). She mentions that the paradox of both postmodernism (within and against major ideologies of modernism) and feminism (within and against long-standing male-dominated canons) in English Canadian literature resonates with the "existing Canadian emphasis on regionalism" (*Canadian Postmodernism* 9). On the other hand, in the second half of the twentieth century, Francophone writing in Canada, similar to the Anglo-Canadian writing still striving to find a voice, was still in the shadow of two French literary movements in terms of innovative form and genre: the *nouveau roman* in the 1950s (loosely defined within postmodernism) and écriture *féminine* in the 1970s (as a result of first-wave feminism). As noted, both Anglo- and Franco-Canadian literatures write paradoxically from the within and from the off-center, from the canons but against the canons. Epistolarity as a genre articulates this kind of paradoxicality. Concerning the literary genre, if traced even further back to a specific generic lineage, writers (especially unacknowledged, marginalized authors) used epistles as a form to write about overseas adventures or illicit love since the sixteenth century.[3] According to Derrida, genre plays the role "de principe d'ordre: resemblance, analogie, identité et différence, classification taxinomique, ordonnancement et arbre généalogique" (286; of the principle of order, resemblance, analogy, identity and difference, taxonomic classification, arrangement, and genealogical tree), but he also argues for the impossibility of the purity of genres, for a "loi d'impureté ou un principe de contamination" (253; law of impurity or a principle of contamination), thus producing "participation sans appartenance" (256; participation without belonging). In this precise sense, the epistolary novel, from subgenre to genre and from the literary margin to the center, can serve as a site conflated with parameters of communication theory (e.g., authentication vs. fictionalization), mediality, and discursivity. Finally new literary variations developed along these axes in Canada have been further elaborated by recent immigrant writers, many from the Maghreb and East Asia. The predominately Haitian and Maghreb Francophone writers in Canada, unlike the Anglophone "postcolonial" authors, have produced an écriture *migrante,* which is quite peculiar to Francophone literature in Canada.

This essay attempts, on the one hand, to look into how Francophone literary movements influence emerging narrative voices in Quebecois writing and, on the other, to find new poetics formed by Asian Francophone writing. I argue that Thúy uses letter writing to develop what feminist theorists call "relational autonomy" with the premise that all people are socially embedded and formed not against relationships with others but in the context of these relations (Mackenzie and Stoljar 18). Because reflection and choice as female agency through writing are crucial in "relational autonomy," for Thúy as an immigrant writer writing from the ex-centrics, like the women writers writing from the margins in the eighteenth century, these published emails define her relationships and her world. In other words engaging in correspondence helps her "to achieve moments and degrees of autonomy within the context of human relationships—from family and friendship to social and gender systems" (Goodman 3).

Epistolarity as understood in this essay is well summarized by Dena Goodman: "If the diary has been more often seen as the site of production of modern subjectivity [for women writers], correspondence is the form of writing par excellence of the socially embedded modern subject, because, for the letter writer, unlike the self-absorbed diarist, other people exist as autonomous subjects like herself" (3). In other words the gendered epistolary matrix "presuppose[s] a reader as the very pretext for writing and shape[s] the sort of subjects they would become through it" (335). However, unlike the many classical "heroines" (e.g., Dido to Aeneas, Medea to Jason, Ariadne to Theseus), whose agency is not acknowledged in textural representation, or female characters such as Héloïse, Pamela, and Clarissa, many of whom, in epistolary fiction, in Altman's words, are "locked into erotic dramas that turn primarily around the agency and power of entrepreneurs on whom their destiny depends" ("Graffigny's Epistemology" 173), Thúy somehow takes an active role in agency and claims a gendered authorship. And unlike other female characters in conventional epistolary narratives around "'what he did to me,' 'what will he do next?' or 'what I am doing as a consequence of his action'" (Altman 174), Thúy, an educated bilingual writer of upward mobility, develops an equal exchange with the male counterpart, who also writes as a bourgeois traveler with shifting global perspectives. Their global perspectives proffer a Bakhtinian dialogic not simply on domestic trivia, love, and sentiment confined to the private sphere, but also on sensitive issues (e.g., war, racism, history) usually discussed in the public sphere.

In *À toi* Thúy uses letters as a kind of dialogical emancipation to show how writing itself could be a form of agency to liberate her from the constraints of life as a woman and as a foreigner. The exile and traveling also allow her and Janovjak to circulate different cultural vistas through the epistolary form. Writing to a friend or to the self enables the writers to articulate these complexities and contradictions. Women's epistolary practice as a genre also produces a subjectivity that carries the writers and the heroines beyond the constrained immediacy of their daily lives. The particular epistolary genre scrutinized in this essay is also based on the intimacies, despite its longstanding "essentialist" scholarship and assumptions, between "feminization" and "epistolarity" (including letters and diaries) already expounded by many established feminist scholars (see Schor; Juhasz; Hampsten; Gallop). A common but cogent argument by these scholars is that epistolary documents—"lacking a sense of the architectonics of shape or plot, non-teleological—[are] somehow feminine" (Hogan 96).

Nevertheless I contend that while following conventions established in Montesquieu's *Lettres persanes* and other novels of the period, *À toi* attempts to challenge these generic limits and diverge from these conventions beyond the nonteleological architectonics. In *Lettres persanes* Usbek, master of a seraglio in Ispahan, who undertakes in 1711 the long trip to France, exchanges letters with his young friend Rica, and the symbolic journey also frames two opposing cultures, Asian and European, and two conflicting religions, Muslim and Christian. Very akin to the Usbek-Rica correspondence, the Thúy-Janovjak email exchange evokes multiple comparative perspectives about inside/outside, exile/settlement, and Asian/American/European dialectics. Read as a modern version of *Lettres persanes,* the narrative of *À toi,* with a more expansive global coverage, more compressed temporal differences, and faster digital responses, provides a similar subtext about *l'autre,* but an "other" construed and constructed as far more complicated in the global, digital era. Both writers engage in questioning and redefining the "self-other" dialogic. Janovjak, for example, writes about himself from ghettoization (i.e., "ex-centricity"):

> Bien après le cocon de l'enfance, j'ai souvent eu l'impression de vivre dans des bulles. Celles de la différence: être slovaque en Suisse, Suisse en France, français ailleurs, expatrié en Asie, riche parmi les pauvres. Habitant

à Ramallah, dont on dit souvent que c'est une bulle, car la vie y est plus facile qu'ailleurs en Palestine, et la Palestine elle-même, un ghetto, insérée dans un pays qui lui-même dans le souvenir obsédant d'autres ghettos. (45)

(After leaving the childhood cocoon, I've often got the impression of living in bubbles, bubbles of difference: as a Slovak in Switzerland, a Swiss in France, a French abroad, an expatriate in Asia, a rich one among the poor. Living in Ramallah, often said to be a bubble, because life there is easier than outside of Palestine, which itself is a ghetto, inserted in a country confined to a haunting memory of other ghettos.)

If Montesquieu's work has been interpreted as an exercise in, or commentary on, Enlightenment Europe's encounters with "the other" through the Persian travelers in France, where they exchange letters about French society and the Arabs or Berbers, the twenty-first-century emails by Thúy and Janovjak deliberately participate in a post-Enlightenment social critique of the global public with their global readers and with a much more widely circulated market of readership. In the modern e-epistolary version, the restrictive *l'autre* (Usbek or Rica) is complicated and multiplied by an open dialogic *à toi* (to you—*you* conceptualized as a site of possibilities or a medium to unidentified addressees) in that both writers represent the ex-centrics, writing from the border and writing against the mainstream. In this precise sense, the epistolarity that goes beyond the feminine, beyond the private, and beyond the form becomes a powerful tool of public participation for dialogic reciprocality, which, according to Christine Lorre, relies on "the principles of uprooting and displacement as ways to open the mind to new truths" (272). Several passages on displacement and uprooting—also resonating with Hutcheon's ex-centricity—are constantly brought up between Thúy and Janovjak, thereby reiterating the central question in French epistolary novels such as *Lettres persanes,* in which "perspectives are reciprocal, and one is always somebody's outsider" (Lorre 273). Participating in the global public, the epistolarity in *À toi,* through dialogic reciprocality, reshapes each correspondent's worldview and intervenes in generic characteristics in conventional epistolary writing.

If epistolary documents, pinpointed by the scholars (e.g., Schor; Juhasz; Hampsten), lack stylistic architectonics, email letters even more so debilitate the formality of this genre. These email letters, in fragmentary narratives in a digital form devoid of the materiality and physicality of letters, present a (neo)epistolary genre that compresses and transcends the national, temporal-geographic, and cultural borders between Thúy and Janovjak, whose collaborative work mingles epistolarity and correspondence across six different time zones. The narrative forms the "dialogue de deux êtres vivant entre deux/plusieurs cultures au sujet de l'identité, du métissage culturel et de la poéticité du quotidien" (the dialogue of two living beings between two/several culures about identity, cultural métissage, and everyday poetics [Yang 253]). As mentioned earlier in the background of epistolary writing, Thúy addresses in her writing these detours and contours through the renovations of nineteenth-century French and Quebecois genre writing (e.g., Jean-Jacques Rousseau, Laure Conan), while inheriting French/Quebecois feminist traditions (e.g., Simone de Beauvoir, Nicole Brossard), adopting emancipatory narrative writing (e.g., Hubert Aquin, Jacques Godbout), and aligning herself to minority cultures and écritures *migrantes* (e.g., Dany Laferrière, Hédi Bouraoui). It is crucial to contextualize these Francophone conventions implied in her narrative and her disruptions from such literary conventions because through these inheritances and evolutions, we also see a new form of epistolary practice in which the ex-centric subjects engage in everyday consumption, the global economy, and technological revolution. Through corresponding with an ontological "you" and through this public participation and circulation of discourse, the narrative shows how the world is constructed to serve new needs in new ways that are material as well as discursive.

I want to underline the *poéticité du quotidien* (everybody poetics) of epistolarity as a kind of tactical consumption in Michel de Certeau's *The Practice of Everyday Life* (1984). Certeau sees the production of culture as a form of Foucauldian power and a mechanism of discipline, that is, a Gramscian negotiation between the ruling class and subordinate groups. Everyday consumption is employed to resist ruling structures and powers in consumer culture, where ordinary people appropriate images, products, and space for their own interests. By focusing on the everyday practices (e.g., cooking, shopping, reading) of consumers, Certeau recasts consumers of mass cultural productions as counter producers. In the Certeauean cultural production, the consumer is not just a passive recipient but an active participant in the creation of meaning: "To a rationalized, expansionist and at the same time centralized, clamorous, and spectacular production corresponds another production, called 'consumption'" (xii). Certeau's influence also enables new, self-conscious forms of cultural practice to emerge, to coalesce, and to collaborate in the network of artists and activists. An important tactic in these procedures is the "reuse of products" in conjunction with social situations and power relationships, and such double work of consumption and production "articulates conflicts and alternately legitimizes, displaces, or controls the superior force. It develops in an atmosphere of tensions, and often of violence, for which it provides symbolic balances, contracts of compatibility and compromises, all more or less temporary" (xvii). In other words Certeau elevates these acts to a political dimension: "The tactics of consumption, the ingenious ways in which the weak make use of the strong, thus lend a political dimension to everyday practices" (xvii).

The subject matter of Thúy and Janovjak's correspondence encompasses Certeauean quotidian practices (e.g., walking, traveling, and cooking), which construct and connect the epistlers' logic and space. Thúy's narrative space, fraught with everyday realities in Canada and remote memories in Vietnam, produces "wandering lines" (Certeau xviii)—lines for the other interlocutor (or producer) to read, to respond to, and to produce his trajectory of everyday realities in Switzerland and memories in the Middle East. In one poetic passage, from an email time-stamped 18:20 on November 1, Thúy reminisces about a restaurant in Saigon associated with a woman's perfume, her lines exhibiting procedures and ruses of interests and desires for Janovjak to follow and expand:

> La chef a tenté de me persuader que, sans l'ajout de sa cuillerée habituelle de glutamate monosodique, mon bol de soupe tonkinoise ne goûterait que ma salive. Moi, je voulais la convaincre que ses quelques filaments de feuilles de lime kaffir suffisaient pour habiller les vermicelles de riz, de la même manière que les quelques gouttes de parfum vaporisées dans le cou d'une femme dessinent déjà tout un paysage sur sa peau. (120)
>
> (The chef tried to persuade me that, without adding her standard spoon of MSG, my Tonkinese soup would taste only my saliva. I wanted to convince her that simply a few filaments of lime kaffir leaves would suffice to season the rice vermicelli, same as just a few drops of vaporized perfume on a woman's neck already permeated through the entire landscape of her skin.)

At 13:22 on November 2, Janovjak, picking up on these wandering lines, responds immediately with his memories of olfactory and visual images:

> Je ne crois pas que je saurais apprécier le parfum de la fleur de lait, et j'ajouterais sans doute une cuillère de glutamate dans ma soupe tonkinoise. . . . Des senteurs éthérées que tu décris j'aime l'idée, et l'image—et j'avoue que le mélange d'effluves lourds qui flottent dans certaines parfumeries françaises m'insupporte aussi, beaucoup plus que la puanteur de la station d'épuration bombardée qui m'a accueilli la première fois à Gaza, ou que celle de la grande tannerie à l'ouest de Dhaka. (121)
>
> (I don't think I would appreciate the smell of mozzarella, and I would certainly add a spoon of glutamate in my Tonkinese soup. . . . Ethereal scents that you describe, I like the idea, the image, and I admit that I too can't stand the mixed heavy smells flowing in some French perfumeries, worse than the stench of the bombed treatment plant that greeted me for my first arrival in Gaza, or the stink of the big tannery in western Dhaka.)

Odors, images, associations, memories, places—everyday practices and consumptions—adapt the imposed order to the interests of users/consumers (i.e., the two writers), who create a narrative space for the ordinary to deflect the normal functioning of the dominant structures in the "insignificant" everyday practice of email writing. Certeau believes in the strength of the ordinary and silence. Such power of ordinary and quotidian silence as production and as writing, hidden in its utilization, is confirmed in Janovjak's words: "Ce que j'aime dans notre correspondence, c'est cet étrange silence des messages, qui ressemble au faux silence des déserts" (100; What I like in our correspondence is the strange silence of messages, which resembles the deceptive silence of the deserts). These ordinary practices of consumption insinuate silently but bring infinitesimal transformations in their lives and in their views of the world. The dialogue about the banal, ordinary realities of the everyday life, seemingly "deceptive silence," somehow develops in an atmosphere of tensions in the epistolary tactics to enable potent hidden forms, like silent deserts, of energy and production.

▶ Global Public

The correspondence is remarkable as it is exchanged between two global writers, both writing and reflecting upon their similar hybrid cultural backgrounds in colonization, in war, in migration, in expatriation. The email exchange opens with Janovjak's personal memory about the war in Iraq and Israeli colonization: "Ce jeudi-là marquait le début de la guerre en Irak, le premières frappes sur Bagdad" (7; That Thursday marked the beginning of the war in Iraq, the first military strikes in Bagdad). It is immediately followed by Thúy's recollections about her last dance in Hanoi: "La dernière fois que j'ai dansé, c'était à Hanoi sur la scène d'un vieux théâtre transformé en club" (9; The last time I danced, it was in Hanoi in an old theater transformed now to a club). The personal memory is expanded to the collective realm by Janovjak's notion of colonization that "la colonisation israélienne n'est pas une colonisation classique, façon Indochine française, puisqu'il s'agit d'occuper des territoires sans annexer des populations" (27; the Israeli colonization is not a classic type of colonization, like French Indochina, since it involves territorial occupation without annexing the populations). Janovjak's concept of Israeli colonial history forms a different view about colonization from Thúy's ambivalent feeling about French colonization and Vietnamese people's ambiguous relationship with the former colonizer.

This dialogical exchange about the world shifts back to their own cultural origin and self-other differences. Janovjak's exilic experience in Jordan, Lebanon, and Bangladesh leads him to recount the genealogy of his Slavic name—"Janovjak est un nom slave que l'on trouve encore sur une colline, en Slovaquie" (25; Janovjak is a Slavic name that we can still find on a hill in Slovakia)—and Thúy, in response, delves into the more complicated origin of name/naming of a former colonized country in relation to its colonizer: "Tu m'appelles Kim, comme tout le monde, alors que je m'appelle Thúy. Pendant longtemps, j'ai envié les Françaises de pouvoir porter le nom de leur époux, comme une nouvelle peau" (26; You call me Kim, just like most people, whereas I call myself Thúy. For a long time I envied the French for being able to carry their spouse's name just like a new skin). Janovjak replies right away: "J'aime penser que pendant que tu enviais les Françaises et leur nom, elles enviaient ton visage. . . . Je continuerai à t'appeler Kim, si tu veux bien. Sinon tu deviendrais une autre" (27; I like to think that while you were envying the French and their names, they were envying your face. . . . I will continue to call you Kim, if you agree. If not, you would become another person).

Starting with their initial encounter in Monaco, the correspondence becomes a textual (or rather "virtual") site of their global traveling from Dhaka to Jordan, from Hanoi to Quebec, as well as their own inner wanderings. The email exchange jumps back and forth and revolves from national identity/destiny to personal identity/destiny, from the private sphere to the public sphere, and from one locality to several globalities. At many symbolic levels, Thúy and Janovjak articulate their global identity and distinct visions in the writing appropriated to a public project and to a grander transnational multitude. Concerning their (dis)placement, Thúy conceptualizes her place in the world: "Et, symboliquement, à quarante et un ans, j'ai fermé les yeux pour sauter dans la profondeur de ce bleu si mystérieux, si menaçant, si nouveau, et y rencontrer les plus grands poissons de la Terre. Comme prévu, ils étaient impressionnants de par leur taille" (56; And symbolically, at forty-one years old, I closed my eyes to jump into the deep blue, so mysterious, so threatening, so new, and met the biggest fish on earth. As expected, they were impressive in their size). In response to displacement, Janovjak compares his "itinérance bien plus confortable" (60; much more comfortable roaming) with his father's forced exile—"un jeune homme de vingt-cinq ans, qui avait quitté son pays, sa famille, avec une petite valise contenant trois chemises et deux livres" (59; a young man of twenty-five years old, who had left his country, his family, with a little suitcase of three shirts and two books). In their private experience in the emails, the correspondence somehow makes legible and public certain national and international histories about the Communist regimes in Eastern Europe and Southeast Asia in the sixties and seventies. Thúy's Vietnamese diasporic experience in the seventies is juxtaposed with Janovjak's father's expatriation from Slovakia in the late sixties. Both writers employ epistolarity to highlight the ambivalent crossing between the private sphere, "the sphere of the family" (Habermas 55), and the public sphere by blending "critical debate in the world of letters, about experiences of their subjectivity or whether private people in their capacity as owners of commodities communicated through rational-critical debate in the political realm, concerning the regulation of their private sphere" (Habermas 55–56). Read and understood in the Habermasian context, the private sphere in *À toi* constructs an engendering space for the two "owners of commodities" to communicate and circulate their political concerns open to the public, global sphere.

At this point, despite different transnational locations from which they think and write, both writers participate in what Habermas calls the "public sphere" constituted "in discussion (*lexis*) and in common action (*praxis*)" (3). In *The Structural Transformation of the Public Sphere: An Inquiry into a Category of Bourgeois Society,* Habermas claims that in the apparatus of the modern state, bourgeois people (e.g., scholars, writers) are the "real carrier of the public, which from the outset was a reading public" (23). Part of my reading is that the two writers employ epistolarity to circulate both *lexis* and *praxis* to envision a kind of public sphere that also reacts to certain postcolonial realities and neoliberal globalizations. Epistles conventionally reveal private feelings, but with writers as public figures, the correspondence is dispersed across the public sphere and across the global public. Habermas proposes "critical publicity," where a mediation is made through informal opinions channeled into the circuit of opinions. In a way epistolarity in digital forms as the Habermasian critical publicity mediates these "categories" (e.g., private vs. public spheres, local vs. global perspectives, and generic formality vs. informality) and articulates the contradictions of the private communication exposed to the public readership. In other words as mediation—the medium to circulate discourses and to negotiate these differences—plays a crucial role in critical publicity, the digital form in epistolarity as the medium resonates with the Derridean genre that plays the role of "resemblance, analogie, identité et différence, classification taxinomique, ordonnancement et arbre généalogique" while producing a paradoxical participation without belonging. Thúy consciously embeds the writing subjects (woman-man; Vietnamese Canadian–Slovakian Swiss; Canadian Francophone–European Francophone) into the epistolary practice in which both writers engage and intersect the writing with consumer culture in the global economy (e.g., publications for their targeted global readership) that defines the changing modes of contemporary Francophone writing. With an intention of publicizing their private talks to global readers and to a global market, both authors, apart from sharing with each other their private lives, write to another addressee outside their private sphere. In other words the receiver of their messages is not just one or the other but also the invisible reader, unknown to both, and this open space to the global readers is a public sphere.

According to Catherine Kerbrat-Orecchioni, letter receivers can be divided into *allocutaire* and *non-allocutaire* (23), the former an intended direct addressee and the latter the public and the indirect addressee. In sharing their political criticisms and views on identity not just between themselves but with a global readership in mind, *À toi* (to you, to the reader, to the *non-allocutaire*) registers in another sense: it invites another party and participates in a new discourse of public opinions, the new Republic of Letters.[4] Their correspondence with the participation of the intended invisible third party (*non-allocutaire*), that is, the reader, fits in Habermas's elaboration of critical publicity in the public sphere: "An opinion that is public in the strict sense however can only be generated in the degree that the two domains of communication are mediated by a third, that of critical publicity" (248).

The major argument of this essay concerns the global, the public, and the digital, as well as the intersectionality of the three axes. My analysis starts with gendered tactics and the Certeauean tactics of everyday consumption and continues to examine how the discursivity of epistolarity staged as a site of the global public tackles such thorny issues as immigrant writing, national literature, global citizenship, and cultural production. In a nutshell the interplay of several theoretical frameworks underpins the analysis of generic reconfigurations of epistolarity in relation to letter writing as a form of participation and engagement: from the postmodern ex-centric standpoint, from a Certeauean perspective, and from Habermas's critical publicity.

First, writing from/within the margins allows the writers seen by their society as *l'autre* to provide insights into both the center and margins of location, history, and movement, and in this precise sense, such an agency constitutes acts of possibilities and resistance formed from the ex-centrics. Reading Thúy and Janovjak's epistolarity on the off-center as generic renovation, as feminist practice, as transmigrant writing, and as Quebecois writing counteracts the conventional epistolary genre, male-dominated literature, mainstream ethnic writing, and mainstream Anglophone and continental French writing. This kind of tactical writing leads the epistlers to use "difference" to operate within the challenging cultures as well as against the defining dominant cultures. They generate a multiplicity of narrative movements to a commonly perceived situation of marginality and ex-centricity.

Second, these possibilities and resistances, understood as Certeauean everyday practice and consumption, enable the epistlers to reuse an old form to circulate commodity and consumption and enact this active "user language" by the users/consumers, "whose status as the dominated element in society (a status that does not mean they are either passive or docile) is concealed by the euphemistic term 'consumers'" (xi–xii). Both interlocutors employ epistolarity—particularly everyday emailing as a tactical medium for cultural consumption and production—to transcribe invisibility to visibility, the private sphere to the public sphere, and the regional/national realm to the global setting. If, for Certeau, these acts entail political gesturing and symbolic coding, both epistlers' email writing, acting as an expressive participation in new media, also forms a kind of "multitude of democracy"[5] that redefines global citizenship vis-à-vis cultural production and consumption.

Third, as these practices attempt to render invisibility and silence legible to the public sphere, the epistolary is a textual creation that gives the speaking voices of the ex-centrics a certain agency to express publicly their thoughts, emotions, and experiences. The e-epistolarity can be seen as a remapping of the Habermasian public sphere; digital epistolarity, the porous character of the letter morphed into a compression of time, space, and speed, acts as an expediting medium to circulate a network society. Based on numerous informal email exchanges, the final production in a book form (or e-book) suggests a strong political act of creating a "publicity work" to be made through "communification" (Habermas 201). In transforming this literary genre (is the book a novel? a collection of emails? several vignettes of self-confessions in a diary form?), the generic innovation of turning the private sphere to a global public not only signals their resistance to a fixed ethnic, racial, or national identity but also points to an open critical publicity of technological, personal, and contextual changes. As my argument moves toward its conclusion, it will become clear that in circulating a multitude of *lexis-praxis* modes in the two writers' views of the world through epistolarity for cultural consumption and production, Thúy and Janovjak also practice consumption as a "secondary production" that entails a transformation of cultural practices (e.g., letter writing) in global hybridization. The past materiality of epistles, paper, or documents now is rendered as "virtuality" or "digitality" as a direct result of technological advancement and altered utilization, and the critical publicity is now multiplied in their mediation and reception in the cross-cultural consumption, dissemination, and production, now annexing the global public.

▶ Digital Public

The correspondence in the narrative expounds and expands the conventional public sphere to a broader global setting and to a wider participation and reception of readership. What differs from traditional letter writing is the utilization of new media in their narrative vignettes. The concurrent exchange via electronic media deterritorializes and detemporizes location-bound and time-bound restrictions in traditional epistolary correspondence characterized by long waiting for messages to arrive and delayed, anticipated reciprocation. At 23:38 on October 16, Thúy sent her email and got a reply almost immediately (given the time difference of six zones apart) from Janovjak at 13:36 on October 17. They talk about differences (here "time" as an example) between the East and the West. Concerning different concepts of time, Thúy takes the lead: "En Amérique du Nord, tout est chronometré, noté, calculé. Les invités à une soirée arrivent presque toujours en même temps parce que tout le monde respecte l'heure prévue à *la minute près*" (86; In North America, everything is timed, marked, calculated. The guests to a party arrive almost always on time because everybody respects the expected time almost right to the minute). In turn Janovjak proffers his definition with a different observation:

> Mais j'y ai gagné un aperçu sur d'autres conceptions du temps. Un temps plus ample, plus souple, un temps multiple, qui ne se mesure pas à la vibration du quartz ou aux minutes qui s'égrenènt. Le temps occidental est lineaire, comme tu dis: un evenement en suit un autre, et les journées du Robinson de Tournier sont toujours penchées en avant, les unes menent aux autres, dans le source permanent du future. (87–88)
>
> (But I've gained some insight into the sense of time, which is looser, more flexible, and multiple, not measured by the vibration of quartz or the ticking minutes. Western time is linear, like what you say: an event is followed one after another, and the days of Robison Crusoe in Tournier's fiction are always leaning forward, and one thing results in another in the permanent point of the future.)

In such dialogical exchange, the digital form becomes even more immediate and interrogative in its request for a timely response, that is, temporality and spatiality compressed in digitality. In their discussion about an issue, the exchange also exposes differences about seeing the other, thus generating a multitude and a spectrum of multiple views facilitated through electronic mediation: the West looking at the East, the East looking back, the Westernized East looking at the East, and the Easternized West looking at the West.

We might pause here and ask several questions. In the postmillennial digital era, do people still exchange letters? Do people write letters or simply email or blog? Do people still read at all? If so, when the reader's interest or habit shifts from perusing long fiction to skimming short epistolary narratives, thereby influencing writers' style and concern of production today, what is the significance of the research on this old genre with new forms? *À toi* is a text that can further elaborate a newly coined term, *neo-epistolarity,* proposed by Emma de Vries, who, based on the epistolary studies by Altman and Derrida, looks at the (re)form of neo-epistolarity: "contrary to traditional letters, neo-epistles are no longer written out of need (the confinement of medial scarcity) but out of artistic deliberation (the freedom of abundant alternatives)" (6). The letter in the digital era is a dying art, but today, the epistolary genre takes new electronic forms: emails and other social media (e.g., Twitter, Facebook). Notwithstanding the different communicative forms in the epistolary art, the "reciprocality" remains unchanged in epistolary exchange, "whereby the original you becomes I of a new utterance" (Altman, *Epistolarity* 117), and where all mail implies the possibility of a response from the addressee and more exchanges afterward. Electronic media also overcome the temporal-geographic limits and delays of the letter. *À toi,* written sometime between October 3 and December 26 of a year (perhaps 2010?), was published in 2011, at a time when actual letter exchange and delivery had largely disappeared from people's daily lives. This "email novel" somehow revitalizes the dynamic of electronic epistolarity, associated with artistic exchanges about "the power of emotional disclosure in these electronic conversations" (Strenski).

The assemblage of various subgenres (i.e., e-writing, epistolarity, diary) is not simply a generic evolution but also epistolarity in the digital age and, in the era of media and fast information circulation, can reveal many philosophical implications of convergences and divergences. More than two decades ago, John L. Brown had already noticed that "[in] this agitated and uncertain time of rapid and dramatic change, the decline, indeed the demise of the letter constitutes one of the . . . signs that we are entering, or have entered, a new 'electronic' phase of world history, [where] we no longer have time to write letters, or by extension, to establish and maintain the long-term human relationships of which they are an expression" (220). From Altman (1982) to Garfield (2013) on epistolary evolution and transformation, de Vries's neo-epistolarity theory offers certain refreshing insights into new generic aesthetics. The epistolary medium is pervasively rehabilitated in our everyday practice and consumption, and neo-epistolarity has permitted mass, unregulated dialogue between individuals across the globe. What accompanies the new epistolary writing communities is mail art and reinvented epistolary narratives in a profusion of texts and visuals. Neo-epistolarity inquires into media-technological change and its cultural implications, and Thúy's work reconfirms these changes while challenging the *je-crois-te-parler* (in Kauffman's phrasing) in epistolary narratives in Francophone literature. In line with how other new migrant writers in Quebec continue to enlarge these dialogic frames of reference by the deconstructionist practice of writing the "opposite" and the "other," Thúy's collaborative work with Janovjak also repositions Quebecois writing in a digital forefront, in a broader public sphere, and in a global setting.

Not only does neo-epistolarity point to the generic evolution, circulating textuality almost simultaneously between the epistlers in more dispersed digital flows, but this new genre also redefines epistolary fiction in a consumer culture. Jean-Christophe Agnew looks at modern consumption, a kind of "cultural work" from "cultural capital," as part of a community through the accumulation of goods (30). According to Agnew, precisely in cultural capital and labor in consumption, the world of letters, like the world of goods, creates a space of community and solidarity based on a sense of belonging of cultural commodities. According to Agnew, in consumption the world of letters, like the world of goods, creates a space of community and solidarity and "a sense of longing and belonging" (30). Agnew's concept further cements the Certeauean correlations between epistolarity and consumption; Certeau's "tactical" powers reconfirm this minority woman's writing in a dominant language, French, rather than in her mother tongue, Vietnamese. Thúy appropriates letter writing as "everyday practices" in dominant genres in Canadian national literature through which the "weaker" sex and race use the stronger language to claim the tactical power in the face of predominant English writing and production. In the Certeauean *lexis* and *praxis* of "everyday practices," paradoxically, correspondence (that between celebrities, artists, and writers) is published and circulated more widely and read by a public less attracted to fiction than to (auto)biography and personal revelations. Neo-epistolary practice and consumption in a digital world expedite the production and profusion of these personalized narratives and create a multitude of democracy through digital media technologies that engage with multiple causes of economic consumerism and production and changing patterns of political participation.

In the digital age, technological changes and advancements make us redefine epistolary writing: Is an email considered a literary text? Is it a disposable message? Traditional epistolary writing is often declared dead[6] or technologically reincarnated in email and social media. In the email exchange, transcending—or rather "compressing"—time and space, unlike the ancient letter delivery and reception with time lapse and spatial restriction, I argue, neo-epistolarity traverses the prism of dialogism in *la mise en récit* of the reality-fantasy, of the hopefulness-desperation, and of the aspiration-exploration beyond autoethnographic writing. Finally, read in the Anglo-Franco literary polemics in the Canadian national context, *À toi* also redefines from another perspective the classic Canadian psyche with its "two solitudes."[7] Instead of aligning the collaborative work with Hugh MacLennan's Anglo-Franco friction and alienation so deeply ingrained in the Canadian mentality, I wish to propose that epistolarity reifies the "two solitudes," originally borrowed from the German poet Rainer Maria Rilke's famous quote: "Love consists of this: two solitudes that meet, protect and greet each other." This love then goes beyond any border and truly reveals the universality of literary value. Still gaining little critical endorsement and scholarly attention, *À toi* is certainly not a deliberate attempt in the interest of textual de- or re-territorialization; rather the neo-epistolarity is an epistemological reconfiguration of center and margin, self and other, individual and community, private and public, regional and global. And in this definitional context, Thúy's emails with Janovjak evoke multiple reincarnations and transmigrations across, between, and at the interstices of genres in Francophone literature. This new paradigm probably responds directly to the critical inquiry of this collection on the intersection of digitality, literature, philosophy, and globality by acknowledging digital mediations and reincarnations in the fluid networks and the untranslatability while writing transnationally.

Notes

1. This essay is a partial fulfillment of my research project funded by the Ministry of Science and Technology, "La Neige Vierge: Epistolarity in the Works of Two Asian Franco-Canadian Writers" (104–2410-H-002–135-MY2). In its draft form, the paper was presented at M@king It New in English Studies: Fourth International Conference, Slovene Association for the Study of English (SDAŠ) in September 2016, and later, with a revised version, it was presented at the trilateral joint symposium organized by National Taiwan University, University of South Carolina, and Ewha Womans University, "Literature and the Global Public: A Transnational Symposium," held at NTU in October 2016. My deep appreciation goes to Prof. Allen Miller for his insightful comments on my paper as well as his incredible leadership in materializing this collaborative project to be copublished by both prestigious university presses. A big bucket of thanks also goes to the unequivocal feedback from my colleagues: Chi-she Li, Jerry Weng, and Mou-Lan Wong, who are always there to encourage and support the team. Unless otherwise indicated translations in this essay are my own.

2. From the 1930s to the 1950s, Quebec languished in a "dark age," during which the Cold War, McCarthyite paranoia, and the dictatorial Catholic Church led to kinds of state censorship. Premier Maurice Duplessis allowed seizure of property belonging to "suspected" Communists, which shadowed Quebec society in church-controlled dictatorship. It is against this backdrop that young artists began to gather at informal meetings to discuss art, literature, and the need for intellectual and religious freedom. Up until the election of Jean Lesage in 1960, Quebec was still an Anglo Canadian–dominated territory, and the following Quiet Revolution throughout the sixties launched the notion of Quebecois identity and of French Canadian language and cultural pride. Within a few years of bloodless internal revolution, Quebec gained its sovereignty with its own tax system, pension plan, and educational system (CBC Digital Archives).

3. The famous English and French epistolary novels, as exemplified by *Clarissa* by Samuel Richardson and *Les liaisons dangereuses* by Pierre Choderlos de Laclos, were not considered to be serious literature at their time of publication. Charles E. Kany's 1937 study, *The Beginnings of the Epistolary Novel in France, Italy, and Spain,* offers numerous examples of the genre's development and traces the use of letters in the novels of fifteenth-century Spain to dispel the impression that the epistolary novel was the sole purview of late seventeenth- and eighteenth-century England and France. In addition to *Les liaisons dangereuses,* the most famous French epistolary novels are *Lettres persanes* (1721) by Montesquieu and *Julie, ou la nouvelle Héloise* (1761) by Jean-Jacques Rousseau.

4. See, for example, Susan Dalton's detailed analysis in *Engendering the Republic of Letters* on the epistolary exchanges of famous salon women in France and the Venetian republic in the late eighteenth century, who experienced the pivotal events that changed Western civilization: Julie de Lespinasse, Marie-Jeanne Roland, Giustina Renier Michiel, and Elisabetta Mosconi Contarini.

5. This term derives from Michael Hardt and Antonio Negri's debate of globality and globalization in *Multitude,* where Hardt and Negri argue that the multitude of democracy dismantles the barriers within the mass of disenfranchised laborers, citizens, and refugees and that such a multitude is "an alternative" to imperialistic rule as "the set of all the exploited and the subjugated, a multitude that is directly opposed to Empire" (393).

6. See, for example, Liz Stanley's "Death of the Letter?," in which she argues that despite the disappearing letter, new digital forms of communication are enabling the expression of epistolary intent in a wide array of ways, with "letterness" taking new forms around the time/space compressions involved.

7. In 1945 Hugh MacLennan published the Canadian classic *Two Solitudes,* which won a Governor General's Award. The metaphor of "two solitudes"—the inability of communication between the Anglophone Canadians and Francophone Canadians—has addressed an inherent Canadian psyche of bicultural friction. The metaphoric invocation of the Anglophone-Francophone context within Canadian nationalism and regionalism has also generated debates ever since World War II over whether Canada has a unified national identity.

Works Cited

Agnew, Jean-Christophe. "Coming Up for Air: Consumer Culture in Historical Perspective." *Consumption and the World of Goods.* Ed. John Brewer and Roy Porter. London: Routledge, 1993. 19–39.

Altman, Janet Gurkin. *Epistolarity: Approaches to a Form.* Columbus: Ohio State UP, 1982.

——. "Graffigny's Epistemology and the Emergence of Third-World Ideology." *Writing the Female Voice: Essays on Epistolary Literature.* Ed. Elizabeth C. Goldsmith. Boston: Northeastern UP, 1989. 172–202.

Berrouët-Oriol, Robert, and Robert Fournier. "L'Emergence des écritures migrantes et métisses au Québec." *Québec Studies* 14 (1992): 17–22.

Brière, Eloise A. "Quebec and France: *La Francophonie* in a Comparative Postcolonial Frame." *Postcolonial Theory and Francophone Literary Studies.* Ed. Adlai Murdoch and Anne Donadey. Gainesville: UP of Florida, 2005. 151–74.

Brown, John L. "What Ever Happened to Mme de Sévigné? Reflections on the Fate of the Epistolary art in a Media Age." *World Literature Today* 64.3 (1990): 215–20.

CBC Digital Archives. "The 'Dark Age' of Quebec." http://www.cbc.ca/archives/entry/the-dark-age-of-quebec.

Certeau, Michel de. *Practice of Everyday Life.* Trans. Steven Rendall. Berkeley: U of California P, 1984.

Corcoran, Patrick. *The Cambridge Introduction to Francophone Literature.* New York: Cambridge UP, 2007.

Dalton, Susan. *Engendering the Republic of Letters: Reconnecting Public and Private Spheres in Eighteenth-Century Europe.* Montreal: McGill-Queen's UP, 2003.

De Vries, Emma. "On Phoenixes and Dying Swans Neo-Epistolarity, or Letter Writing in a Digital Age." n.p., n.d. 10 Dec 2016. http://www.inter-disciplinary.net/at-the-interface/wp-content/uploads/2014/02/Draft-paper-Emma-de-Vries.pdf.

Derrida, Jacques. "La loi du genre." *Parages.* Paris: Galilée, 1986. 251–87.

Dupuis, Gilles. "Transculturalism and *écritures migrantes.*" *History of Literature in Canada: English-Canadian and French-Canadian.* Ed. Reingard M. Nischik. Rochester, NY: Camden House, 2008. 497–508.

Gallop, Jane. "Annie Leclerc Writing a Letter with Vermeer." *The Poetics of Gender.* Ed. Nancy K. Miller. New York: Columbia UP, 1986. 137–56.

Garfield, Simon. *To the Letter: A Journey through a Vanishing World.* Edinburgh: Canongate, 2013.

Goodman, Dena. *Becoming a Woman in the Age of Letters.* Ithaca: Cornell UP, 2009.

Grant, George P. *Lament for a Nation: The Defeat of Canadian Nationalism.* Ottawa: Carleton UP, 1982.

Green, Mary Jean. *Women and Narrative Identity: Rewriting the Quebec National Text.* Montreal & Kingston: McGill-Queen's UP, 2001.

Habermas, Jürgen. *The Structural Transformation of the Public Sphere: An Inquiry into a Category of Bourgeois Society.* Trans. Thomas Burger with Frederick Lawrence. Cambridge: Polity, 1989.

Hampsten, Elizabeth. *Read This Only to Yourself: The Private Writings of Midwestern Women, 1880–1910.* Bloomington: Indiana UP, 1982.

Hardt, Michael, and Antonio Negri. *Multitude: War and Democracy in the Age of Empire.* New York: Penguin 2004.

Heidenreich, Rosmarin. "1608–2008: The Time In-Between: Major Trends in French- and English-Canadian Prose Fiction." *Zeitschrift für Kanada-Studien* 28.2 (2008): 101–13.

Hogan, Rebecca. "Engendered Autobiographies: The Diary as a Feminine Form." *Prose Studies: History, Theory, Criticism* 14.2 (1991): 95–107.

Hutcheon, Linda. *The Canadian Postmodern: A Study of Contemporary English-Canadian Fiction.* Toronto: Oxford UP, 1988.

——. *A Poetics of Postmodernism: History, Theory, Fiction.* New York: Routledge, 1988.

Juhasz, Suzanne. "Towards a Theory of Form in Feminist Autobiography: Kate Millet's *Flying* and *Sita;* Maxine Hong Kingston's *The Woman Warrior.*" *International Journal of Women's Studies* 2.1 (1979): 62–75.

Kany, Charles E. *The Beginnings of the Epistolary Novel in France, Italy and Spain.* Berkeley: U of California Press, 1937.

Kauffman, Linda S. *Special Delivery: Epistolary Modes in Modern Fiction.* Chicago: University of Chicago Press, 2007.

Kerbrat-Orecchioni, Catherine. *L'énonciation de la subjectivité dans le langage.* Paris: Librairie Armand Colin, 1980.

Lorre, Christine. "Ying Chen's 'Poetic Rebellion': Relocating the Dialogue, In Search of Narrative Renewal." *Asian Canadian Writing beyond Autoethnography.* Ed. Eleanor Ty and Christl Verduyn. Waterloo: Wilfrid Laurier UP, 2008. 267–95.

Mackenzie, Catriona, and Natalie Stoljar. "Introduction: Autonomy Refigured." *Relational Autonomy: Feminist Perspectives on Autonomy, Agency, and the Social Self.* Ed. Catriona Mackenzie and Natalie Stoljar. New York: Oxford UP, 2000. 3–31.

McPherson, Karen. *Archaeologies of an Uncertain Future: Recent Generations of Canadian Women Writing.* Montreal & Kingston: McGill-Queen's UP, 2006.

Schor, Naomi. *Reading in Detail: Aesthetics and the Feminine.* New York: Methuen, 1987.

Soron, Anthony. "*Ru* de Kim Thuy ou l'alchimie de l'épreuve." n.p., n.d. 10 Dec 2017. http://www.msha.fr/msha/recherche2011–2015/transformation/antony_soron/alchimie_epreuve.pdf.

Stanley, Liz. "The Death of the Letter? Epistolary Intent, Letterness and the Many Ends of Letter-Writing." *Cultural Sociology* 9.2 (2015): 240–55.

Strenski, Ellen. "Epistolary Art." n.p., n.d. 15 Nov. 2015. http://wac.colostate.edu/rhetnet/rdc/strenski2.html.

Thúy, Kim. *Ru.* Montreal: Libre Expression, 2009.

Thúy, Kim, and Pascal Janovjak. *À toi.* Montreal: Libre Expression, 2011.

Ty, Eleanor, and Donald C. Goellnicht, eds. *Asian North American Identities: Beyond the Hyphen.* Bloomington: Indiana UP, 2004.

Yang, Ziyan. "Pour désorienter une autoethnographie orientale: Une étude des representations identitaires chez quatre écrivains québécois d'origine asiatique." Diss. Dalhousie University, 2014.

Wagner in China

Negotiating the National, the Universal, and the Global

Nicholas Vazsonyi

I begin by quoting from the opening remarks given by Hansen Liang, chair of the Chinese Association for Stage Film Production, at a 2016 conference on Chinese stage film held at the campus of the University of South Carolina. Talking in general about traditional Chinese opera and the preservation of this cultural heritage, he remarked: "Nostalgia lies in everybody's heart, while Chinese opera film brings to that heart the voice of home. When a Chinese person hears the sound of huqin and the music of Chinese opera, no matter where he is, his longing and respect for home will undoubtedly be aroused."

In 1911 the Austrian Jewish author Stefan Zweig traveled to America. His visit included attending a performance of Richard Wagner's last opera, *Parsifal,* at New York's Metropolitan Opera. Remarking on the meaning of the event for himself and his fellow German-speakers that night, he wrote: "The Germans over there in America have no home other than their music. . . . Never have I felt more keenly . . . how much Wagner means for Germany, how much he embodies Germany, is Germany, the most penetrating symbol of his nation and age" (Zweig 56).

In other words, even if the specific artwork in question might be different, its significance and meaning dependent on one's cultural background, the idea that the artwork per se can evoke a feeling of home or of coming home seems to be both timeless and universal or—to use a term more in vogue today—global. Though, on second thought, there is surely a difference between the terms *universal* and *global.* The suggestion that certain ideas or values might be universal is largely the product of the philosophical idealism of the eighteenth and early nineteenth centuries. It is a concept conceived in Western Europe, albeit also exported to the United States of America. In addition to some fundamental principles, like those of human rights, the notion that certain works of art, though produced within a particular culture and at a particular time, would nevertheless speak to all peoples of all times extended the concept of the universal to the sphere of the aesthetic.

Global, by contrast, is a term of more recent vintage. It carries with it a more practical, dare I say, mercantile meaning that suggests that certain products might have a market worldwide. It is by now established that certain products are purchased by consumers globally and the companies that sell them have a global reach. Although these products may also have their origins in a specific culture and time, they have been found to appeal to people globally. The American hamburger, specifically ones marketed by McDonald's, would be an example. Italian coffee and its derivatives marketed by Starbucks would be another. There are countless examples, from cell phones to cars, blue jeans to T-shirts. While these products are sold and purchased worldwide and thus can be termed "global," one might also nevertheless claim that they have "universal" appeal, meaning that there is something inherent in them that human beings in the main find attractive and satisfying on an emotional and psychological as well as a practical level. In other words consumer objects can be simultaneously both global and universal; in fact maybe they ultimately cannot be one without the other.

The question this essay asks is whether or not the same can be said of aesthetic products and, specifically, music. In other words, while music may be marketed globally, can it also have a "universal" appeal, significance, and meaning? And do we need to draw a distinction between "appeal," on the one hand, and "significance" and "meaning" on the other?

The two quotes I initially presented, articulated at different times and places by two very different people and about two very different types of work, established that perhaps no art form has a more universal ability to evoke that feeling of home than does music, with its sounds, rhythms, forms, and instrumental combinations often so distinctive that they instantly convey their place of origin. Home, in this context, does not refer to just a geographic location, though this is of course crucial, but also to a psychological complex of ideas, feelings, memories, and sensations that constitute something I prefer to call a "spiritual home," because it can be recalled anywhere and at any time. While the power of music as such to evoke such feelings might be universal, the question I ask is whether the reach of any one particular piece of music is perhaps much more local. In other words, to give a concrete example: If Beethoven's Ninth Symphony is performed in Berlin and Tokyo, do these performances produce fundamentally different experiences for their respective audiences? Phrased differently, can we talk meaningfully about universal music and thus of global music?

The conference for which the current book was the basis posed the question "How can a global culture allow meaningful dialogue not only between localities but also between histories and traditions?" It is an important question, in part, because localities, histories, and traditions are being brought face to face with one another with an intensity and immediacy that seems to grow almost daily. Dialogue is possible only when people can exchange ideas with each other using a mutually intelligible communication system and, further, when there is some common basis for sharing thoughts and feelings. If we consider the case of the artwork, how are such works experienced by different people in different places and at different times? Is there a difference between "understanding" a work intellectually and having a deep emotional response to it? If yes, what are the criteria for "understanding" versus "feeling"?

This forum asked an additional question: "How does the digital, which makes possible the dream of a global culture, not devolve into uniformity and the eradication of difference?" First of all, again, what do we mean by "global culture" and, secondly, why would this be a "dream" at all? What are we dreaming of? And perhaps more to the point, are we just talking about "global access to cultural products," or do we mean something deeper and more significant? What do we mean by "uniformity and the eradication of difference" or even "universal translatability"? What do such concepts mean when we look at actual people and actual situations? Again, I am not talking about the fact that one can buy Gap jeans in New York and Taipei or the fact that there seems to be one design for airports wherever one travels in the world.

In the essay in the present collection by Alexander Beecroft, he addresses the phenomenon of global literature, meaning in his case works written recently with the principal objective of selling internationally. One of the qualities he observes in such works is a sort of leveling that eliminates local particularities from the text, leaving only the generic that can be understood and identified with broadly. The same can be said of world music or even the pop music industry, which churns out formulaic songs designed to be top-forty hits. In the following, however, I will not be thinking about works conceived recently and with a potentially global market in mind. Rather I am more concerned with music created before the global market as we understand it today came into existence, though it is music that was nevertheless conceived to have a universal reach.

Focusing specifically on German music of the nineteenth century, I will explore the questions of "universal" versus "global." I begin with some basic concepts of the universal articulated by Germans in the eighteenth century and, after talking about the specific case of Beethoven's Ninth Symphony, will end with a discussion of a "global" project I co-organized in 2013 that marked the two-hundredth anniversary of the birth of the composer Richard Wagner.

The arguably Romantic idea of universality has its roots in the German Enlightenment of the eighteenth century and its utopian assertion of the existence of universal reason and the aspiration for its realization. An offshoot of this project, specifically a certain discourse about music—meaning in particular German instrumental music—was formulated around the year 1800. Already starting around 1760, German-speaking music critics began reacting against the dominant aesthetic classification of instrumental music, that is, music with no verbal text attached, as the lowest of all art forms, because such music had no discernible meaning. For Germans this was especially frustrating, because the French and Italians dominated the world of vocal music, in particular the genre of opera, in part because they, especially the French in Paris, had financial resources to support opera that German courts could never match. So, starting around 1760, in articles appearing in journals such as the *Allgemeine deutsche Bibliothek* (Berlin), German music critics began to mount a counterargument, that instrumental music was actually superior to vocal music because it was usually more complex both in terms of form and harmonic structure.[1] Comments abounded about the "Mißgeburten seichter Italiäner" (monstrosities of shallow Italians), which evoked "Ekel" (disgust). Such opinions were contrasted with proclamations about showing "Ausländern einen Beweis von dem Talente unserer Landsleute" (foreigners proof of our countrymen's talents), where German music was characterized as "männlich" (manly) and full of "gute[n] Harmonie und rührende[r] Melodie" (good harmonies and moving melodies) (Morrow 259). The prime musical examples that proved the argument were the nonvocal works of Johann Sebastian Bach as well as the orchestral works by Joseph Haydn and Wolfgang Amadeus Mozart, composers who approached the composition of purely instrumental music with unprecedented command, creating works that were both intellectually challenging and at the same time deeply satisfying emotionally. This line of argumentation fed the concurrently developing discourse that the French and Italians as a people and a culture were superficial and shallow, whereas Germans were genuine and deep, a discourse with its roots in the tension between Catholicism and Protestantism.

What had originally begun as a budding nationalist discourse was inflated a generation later during German Romanticism. If instrumental music started out merely demonstrating German intellectual superiority and emotional depth over their Latinate neighbors to the south and west, German authors of Romanticism, the first among them E. T. A. Hoffmann, proclaimed the transcendent and thus universal potential of (German) instrumental music. The prime example was now Ludwig van Beethoven. Precisely because instrumental music is not bound by the limitations of language, it simply bypasses the problem or even the need for "universal translatability" and is by definition a universal language of sound that addresses all humans of the globe on the level of emotions that we all share—in theory, at least. Except that it was the Germans who were uniquely able to create such music. In other words, from a German Romantic perspective, whereas Indian or Chinese music that is purely instrumental would be considered an example of ethnic and regional culture, German instrumental music is a mode of universal communication. The fact that sound itself might be culturally specific and bounded had not occurred to these thinkers. So by around 1800, Romantic critics claimed that an artwork could be simultaneously national and universal (meaning it did not require translation to be understood).

To illustrate this claim, I point to a poem fragment by Friedrich Schiller drafted in 1801 but never published. In the poem, subsequently titled "Deutsche Größe" (German Greatness), Schiller made just such an attempt to synthesize the universal aspirations of the Enlightenment with the national mission of German culture.[2] Even though Schiller emphasized that the "Germans' greatness does not entail conquering with the sword," his text clearly articulated imperial zeal. Applying the familiar notion of the German "Kulturnation" (nation of culture), he located Germany's greatness "in the culture and in the character of the nation, which is independent from its political fate." German national identity, for Schiller, was inseparable from spreading the blessings of German culture and enlightened reason to the world: "He [the German] is destined for the highest, and just as he finds himself in the middle of Europe, so is he also the core of humanity. . . . He has been chosen by the world spirit to work on the eternal edifice of the development of humanity." According to him, the German language was the primary tool to carry out this project. Like German music, it was seen as a universal cipher that simultaneously reflected and expressed the German national character: "Language is the mirror of a nation, and when we look into this mirror, we see a magnificent image of ourselves" (Schiller 432; my translation).

In becoming a universal medium of reason and self-enlightenment, Schiller's German language produced a world of enlightened citizens who overcame conflict and national difference. Unlike other national languages and cultures, it was the German language that could and should serve as a universal platform of understanding and self-transformation, or as Schiller unabashedly and somewhat alarmingly formulates it, "Unsere Sprache wird die Welt beherrschen" (Our language will rule the world) (Schiller 432). This is the moment at which the universal and emancipatory aspirations of the Enlightenment became, with all the best intentions, threatening and hegemonic.[3]

The universal ambitions of German culture found no more emphatic a statement than in the last movement of Beethoven's last symphony, the famous Ninth, where the grandest of all purely instrumental forms—the classical symphony—gets reunited with sung text, specifically a poem by Schiller titled "An die Freude" (Ode to Joy). The poem imagines a utopian moment of global reach in which "alle Menschen werden Brüder" (all people will become brothers). This is not the place to discuss the complexity of Beethoven's gesture both musicologically and ideologically except to say that it has indeed become the anthem reproduced around the world to convey the idea of universal brotherhood.[4] So is Beethoven's Ninth an example of global culture? Probably yes, in the sense that it is ubiquitous, the default music for certain occasions. It is global also in the sense that it has experienced the leveling to virtual meaninglessness that is the fate of all things global, robbed of its specificity and, potentially, of all its meaning, save for the most basic and simplistic, an example of exactly what Beecroft describes in his essay. In the process of becoming a piece of what can be called world music, has it not become devoid of its specific Germanness? Put more tangibly, when played, can it evoke that feeling of home anymore? Just to be clear, I am not talking about the rest of the Ninth, just that part which has become a "top-forty hit," for want of a better label.

The significance of Beethoven's Ninth was not lost on Richard Wagner, who was born a generation later. For Wagner, Beethoven's last symphony was a work whose immense meaning and significance could be mined for his own aesthetic purposes. In the end Wagner extracted—or perhaps better said, projected—a set of meanings onto the symphony that in effect set the basis for his own compositional project and career.

Wagner's stated project was in the first place one with a national objective: to create an operatic form that would be distinctly German and in no way equivalent to products from either Italy or France. He was so intent on producing something different that he refused to even use the term *opera* to describe what he was doing. Because he was committed to a musical-dramatic form, he argued that instrumental music had already exhausted its maximum potential with Beethoven, a contention Beethoven had even tacitly adopted himself, Wagner claimed, as proven by his unprecedented move to add text in the last movement of his last symphony.

However, as nationalistic and as linguistically specific as Wagner's project was, he also never gave up on the bid for universal relevance. Hence his decision to base his dramatic works in mythology, with the following rationale: "The incomparable quality of myth is that it is always true, and its content in concentrated form is forever inexhaustible."[5] While the return to a musical-dramatic genre reintroduced the need for language and thus raised once again the problem of translatability apparently so deftly eliminated with language-free instrumental music, the application of myth, which addresses situations and emotions that are essentially human and thus emotionally universal, reduced the burdens placed on the task of translation. This is the argument at the core of Wagner's premise.

Beyond the work itself and its distinctive content, there was an additional dimension to the Wagner project that would focus on its mode of presentation. This is what sets him apart from his contemporaries and makes him a figure who anticipates the stakes of the music business in the twentieth and twenty-first centuries. Not content solely to be a composer, Wagner was as committed to ensuring the ideal circumstances of the performance of his works as he was to the creation of those works. His idea was to re-create a form of communal artistic event, reminiscent of the dramas in Ancient Greece, which would be performed on a series of days that would be declared public holidays and which the entire community would attend free of charge. On the face of it, this was an entirely antimodern, anti-capitalistic idea, underscored by the fact that the location Wagner conceived for this event was to be far away from the metropolis, thus forcing the audience not only to travel a distance and endure a certain degree of hardship to attend but also, more important, to be forced to take time off from work so that they might devote themselves entirely to the artistic experience.

After many years of trying and several false starts, Wagner managed to have his dream theater built in Bayreuth, a small town in Upper Franconia that he ended up taking over completely. This theater, opened in 1876, still stands today and is used for the exclusive performance of Wagner's works during a summer festival that lasts from July 25 until the end of August. People still travel there, by now from all over the world, and, in so doing, leave their jobs and daily routine temporarily to devote themselves exclusively to the artistic experience. Not only is the Wagner festival in Bayreuth the longest-running theatrical event in Europe, it boasts a ten-year waiting list for tickets.

During the many years it took to build the theater and found the festival, Wagner penned essays explaining his goals and intentions. Bayreuth would represent the opposite of Paris, which, in Wagner's mind, stood for the worst that the world metropolis had become: a place where fashion ruled, where the bored and moneyed elite sought frivolous and empty entertainment after a long day in the office, where daily discourse was steered by journalists in search of the latest scandal (usually fueled by gossip), all financed by shady banks run by a consortium of international Jewry.[6]

However, for all his stated intentions of founding a festival that would be located far from the madding crowd, an event that would be of national significance all the more because it was steeped in distinctive local color and off the beaten track, this is in the end not what happened. Not unlike Paris, the Bayreuth venture needed money in order to be built and to function. As much as Bayreuth was to be a gesture in opposition to commercial modernity, it depended no less on the modernity it rejected in order to come into being and be sustained, from injections of capital to an up-to-date transportation system to ferry audience members to and from their mostly metropolitan homes.

Along with the effort to build the theater, which added an entrepreneurial dimension to Wagner's artistic enterprise, the story of its financing unintentionally introduced the global element. While Wagner did have one very wealthy and powerful patron, King Ludwig II of Bavaria, he was compelled to launch a scheme whereby smaller stakeholders could buy certificates to fund the construction of the theater. Each certificate would entitle its holder to all three runs of the four-part *Ring of the Nibelungen,* the seventeen-hour work written with the theater and the idea of a festival in mind. When word of the patron certificate scheme got out, one merchant in the town of Mannheim came up with an idea that would enable people of extremely modest means to participate. In 1871 he founded an organization that came to be called the Wagner Society, whose members would pay very reasonable dues. From those dues certificates would be purchased, and the chance to get the tickets to attend the festival would be decided by lot for dues-paying members. This idea caught on rapidly, and within a couple of years, there were Wagner societies all over Germany and then Europe, with Bayreuth serving as a sort of hub. Thus, as part of the project to build a theater in Bayreuth, dedicated exclusively to the performance of his own works, Wagner oversaw the founding of countless societies in a network that spanned the globe. These were both fundraising societies as well as places for Wagner fans to gather and share their enthusiasm. By 1876, when the festival first opened its doors, there were Wagner societies in New York, Boston, Cairo, and even Istanbul. During Wagner's lifetime, in other words, the Wagner empire became a global concern, perhaps the first tangible moment when the German idea of universal music was fused with the more contemporary notion of the global. Today, while there are none in China, Asia has Wagner societies in Tokyo, Singapore, and Bangkok, and there are a total of 132 chapters worldwide.[7]

All of which brings us to the 2013 bicentennial of Richard Wagner's birth and the project called WagnerWorldWide 2013 (www2013), which was initiated at the Institut für Musiktheater at the University of Bayreuth. The objective of the project was to take stock of Wagner both in scholarship and in the theater in the second decade of the twenty-first century. The rationale for the global perspective of the project lay both in the universal reach of Wagner's music and in the global dimension of Wagner's entrepreneurial undertaking already during his own lifetime. By the time the project began in earnest, three additional institutions from around the globe had joined the effort: the University of Bern, the University of South Carolina, and the Shanghai Conservatory of Music. While the Universities of Bern and South Carolina each mounted a conference, the Shanghai Conservatory of Music scheduled a series of talks and workshops that took place over two consecutive summers in 2012 and 2013. The workshops were conducted by the team of Anno Mungen, director of the Institut für Musiktheater, and myself, based at the University of South Carolina. The topic of the masterclass was to explore differences in approaches to the interpretation and staging of, in this case, Wagner's drama *The Mastersingers of Nuremberg*. Two well-known performances, available on DVD, were examined side by side: one of them a traditional rendition from the Metropolitan Opera House in New York, and the other, a radical reading of the work performed at the Bayreuth Festival in 2008.[8] I will describe the experience of teaching these workshops, which goes directly to the topic of this chapter, but first an introduction to the story of Wagner in China.

Starting around 1875, traveling troupes from Europe, initially Italy and England, brought European opera to China and specifically Shanghai at regular intervals. Such performances were offered primarily to the expatriate European community, and only slowly did the local Chinese population begin to attend, growing steadily in numbers during the first half of the twentieth century. The repertoire was mainly Italian and French fare, and it was 1905 before excerpts of Wagner were first performed, the same year the Shanghai Operatic Society was formed. More slowly Chinese opera was also brought to the West. Indeed the interactions and interconnections between Western and Chinese opera have grown significantly in recent decades, as has the influx especially of Chinese students studying at music schools and conservatories in the West. There has also been a certain cross-pollination between Eastern and Western styles. Wagner's full *Ring of the Nibelungen* was performed at the Shanghai Expo in 2010 to the wildly enthusiastic acclaim of the normally more restrained Chinese audience, which, according to reports, clapped for a solid twenty minutes at the conclusion of the four-day performance. Since the 1970s Chinese students have been coming to European and American centers of learning to gain technical mastery in performing the Western canon and to be honed in the subtleties of understanding and interpretation. Since that time Western artists have also been traveling to China regularly in order to bring that same knowledge and expertise to students in China.

In this sense the workshops offered by Mungen and myself were nothing unusual, just one more example of the active and ongoing cultural transfer between West and East. Nevertheless I was interested to see the degree to which Wagner seemed to be an example of a foreign culture to the students and whether the notion of universality was at all evident. So to start out, I asked the class of perhaps between thirty to forty men and women, with a slight preponderance of the latter, why they were interested in Wagner or what they liked about him. One particularly eager male student raised his hand immediately and gave a mini-lecture about the peaks of Western history—Galileo, Newton, Mozart, and Beethoven—which he concluded by saying, "The West is very successful, and I want to understand why." I found this to be quite a stunning answer, and it took me a moment to collect myself. While doing so I looked around and asked if there were any other answers. Another male student raised his hand, described the orchestration Wagner often used, and explained that he found the sound of the trumpets to be very exciting. While the second answer at least addressed the music, however superficially, neither answer struck me as anywhere remotely responding to the artwork spiritually or identifying it as having become part of their being. Certainly nothing close to the way the huqin and Chinese opera are described in the quote at the beginning of this essay. After we talked a little bit about the two answers, and in the absence of additional offerings from the students, we moved on to the meat of the workshops—an introduction to and analysis of the two radically different stagings of *The Mastersingers.* At first, and following my expectations, the class was able to connect with the traditional staging of the Metropolitan Opera and was put off by the provocative and, by comparison, disrespectful interpretation of the Bayreuth production. This response was reinforced by their professor, who sat at the front of the class and was often the first to offer a comment. But gradually, and with some encouragement from Mungen and myself, the students started to break free from the hold their professor—and quite possibly their own cultural training—had on them and to start engaging with the provocative staging, which itself was an attempt to break free from expectations and from a staging tradition that has been viewed as oppressive and closed-minded. In other words the students began to enact within their own context the rebellion that was the Bayreuth staging.

On the one hand, then, our efforts at cultural transfer worked. Through a process of education and understanding, the students not only were able to connect in some way with the Wagner opera but also were able to appropriate the lesson they learned from an interpretation of the work and to adapt it to their own situation. On the other hand, I doubt that the experience transformed them deep down into having them sense that *The Mastersingers* was somehow a work that would evoke a feeling of their own spiritual home. Of course, absent such a relationship already being there at the outset, it is doubtful an intense connection could be established as the result of one workshop anywhere. On the other hand, one might ask what I would have wished for as an answer to the question I posed the Chinese students. I imagine students in the West might also offer a variety of responses, maybe some of them disconnected from the artwork itself. But given the perceived role of the arts and humanities in the West nowadays, I would also expect a student, brave and single-minded enough to devote themselves to a course of study that did not guarantee significant or even any financial rewards, to explain their decision as stemming from some emotional or spiritual need they had to spend their time with works of art. This would be as true of a graduate student in English literature as it would be of someone pursuing art history, that is, not just limited to Wagner or music per se.

So to return to my opening question, while opera in general and Wagner in particular is now more available in China than it was a century ago, is this all we mean when we talk about a global culture? Is there some kind of quantitative threshold that needs to be passed in order for a cultural product to qualify as global? And, putting that question aside, are we claiming that the experience of Wagner for Chinese people is today qualitatively different from a hundred years ago? In other words, does Wagner seem less foreign, or indeed, does his music maybe even evoke a feeling of being at home? Does his music, in other words, elicit a deep emotional and spiritual response, as it does for some but certainly not all people in the West? Maybe we should ask the question in reverse: is Chinese opera global? According to a recent article by Barbara Mittler, a leading Sinologist, it is. She cites as proof the playful citation and incorporation of Chinese opera in contemporary Western works and the citation of Western opera—including specifically Wagner—in recent Chinese opera. But is anyone actually listening to these works? And, more broadly, do people in the West in any appreciable number listen to Chinese opera on their sound reproduction devices at home or in the car the way that Chinese people listen to Western classical music at home? Mittler also addresses the issue of Wagner now being "understood" by Chinese audiences. She cites Chinese media expressing uncertainty and anxiety about whether upcoming performances of Wagner will be understood, which she counters with emphatic claims of audiences who clearly "all exhibited a thorough understanding of the art of opera" (101). But I wonder what *understanding* means. Does the use of the word by a Western academic when talking about the Chinese audience not still carry with it the echo of condescension, however unintended?

Put differently, do we want to draw a distinction between understanding a work of art, meaning some sort of intellectual comprehension based on knowledge of the historical and cultural circumstances of its creation as well as an appreciation of its formal qualities and content, and having an emotional connection to it, based on the degree to which it has some fundamental and deeply personal meaning? The former, understanding, was demonstrated abundantly by the students in the workshop; the latter, emotional feeling and connection, less so.

Wagner had something very specific to say on this matter: he argued that understanding (*Verstand*) of his works is achieved through feeling (*Gefühl*)—what he calls "die Gefühlswerdung des Verstandes" (the transformation of understanding into feeling) (Wagner 78). True to Romanticism, Wagner privileges emotion over reason, a gesture of anti-intellectualism that rhetorically returns art to the people (*das Volk*) and preempts sophisticated dissections of his works by trained critics, since educated responses to his artwork represent a misunderstanding:

> The artist addresses the heart, and not the mind; if a response comes from the mind, that is as much as to say that he has not been understood. Our critics do nothing but admit to their non-comprehension of the artwork, which can only be understood through feeling" (Wagner 232).[9]

By Wagner's definition the students in the Shanghai workshop had not actually understood the work, because it had not evidently registered at the level of the heart. Is it an intellectual decision that drove them to devote their studies to Western classical music, or is there indeed something deeper that motivated their choice? Were I to have another opportunity to conduct such a workshop, I would now be more assertive about asking questions and more probing in my efforts to glean what they are thinking and feeling.

Can art really be talked of in global terms the same way that a manufactured piece of technology like a car or a mobile phone is a global product? I mean serious art, not works created according to some generic formula that is calculated to have some appeal globally. Or to return to the question I asked at the outset, how do we negotiate between the goal of spreading art throughout the world while also reserving that special role of art to evoke the feeling of home?

I would like to end with an anecdote from Barbara Mittler's article: A group of singers from the United States were touring China. When they visited a factory, the workers spontaneously began singing the "Factory Hymn," which was none other than the melody of Beethoven's "Ode to Joy" from the Ninth (Mittler 114–15). So maybe the Germans were right after all, and there is such a thing as a universal language of music. Or maybe the "Ode to Joy," extracted from the context of the complete symphony, is nothing more than an early example of a generic tune that barely qualifies as art for the very reason that, like a chameleon, it can adapt itself to any purpose where uplifting sounds are needed.

Notes

1. See Mary Sue Morrow's groundbreaking study, *German Music Criticism in the Late Eighteenth Century.* See also Morrow, "Building a German Identity through Music."

2. For debate on when the poem was drafted and why Schiller never completed it, see Müller and the apparatus of the *Nationalausgabe.*

3. Theodor W. Adorno made this connection between Germany and the ominousness potentially embedded in Beethoven's Ninth Symphony when he wrote in 1942, "Hitler and the Ninth Symphony: Be encircled, all ye millions" (77), a macabre twist on the line from Schiller's ode: "Seid umschlungen, Millionen" (Be embraced, all ye millions), which is sung at a particularly exposed moment in the last movement of

Beethoven's last symphony, exposed in the sense that we hear voices only with no orchestral accopaniment.

4. The literature on the Ninth Symphony is vast, but specifically in the context of this chapter, see Höyng.

5. "Das Unvergleichliche des Mythos ist, daß er jederzeit wahr, und sein Inhalt, bei dichtester Gedrängtheit, für alle Zeiten unerschöpflich ist" (Wagner 64).

6. See my "Bayreuth: Capital and Anti-Capital."

7. For a listing of all the countries with chapters, see the homepage of the Richard -Wagner-Verband International: http://www.richard-wagner.org/rwvi/de/.

8. The Metropolitan Opera's version of *Die Meistersinger von Nurnberg* was conducted by James Levine and directed by Otto Schenk (Deutsche Grammophon, 2005); the Bayreuth Festival's version was conducted by Sebastian Weigle and directed by Katharina Wagner (Opus Arte, 2011).

9. "Der Künstler wendet sich an das Gefühl, und nicht an den Verstand: wird ihm mit dem Verstande geantwortet, so wird hiermit gesagt, daß er eben nicht verstanden worden ist, und unsere Kritik ist in Wahrheit nichts Anderes als das Geständniß des Unverständnisses des Kunstwerkes, das nur mit dem Gefühle verstanden werden kann."

Works Cited

Adorno, Theodor W. "Beethoven." *The Philosophy of Music: Fragments and Texts.* Ed. Rolf Tiedemann. Trans. Edmund Jephcott. Stanford: Stanford University Press, 1998. Originally, "Hitler und die IX. Symphonie: Seid umzingelt, Millionen." *Beethoven: Philosophie der Musik.* Frankfurt: Suhrkamp, 1993.

Hoffmann, E. T. A. "Beethovens Instrumental-Musik." *Kreisleriana. Phantasiestücke in Callots Manier (Part 1).* Vol. 2 of *Sämtliche Werke.* 6 vols. Ed. H. Steinecke and W. Segebrecht. Frankfurt: Deutscher Klassiker, 1993. 1:52.

Höyng, Peter. "'The Gospel of World Harmony' or Beethoven's Transformation of Schiller's *An die Freude* into World Music Literature." *Modern Language Quarterly* 74.2 (2013): 261–76.

Mittler, Barbara. "Wagner Goes East (and Back Again . . .): Operatic Performance between Europe and China." *Music Theater as Global Culture: Wagner's Legacy Today.* Ed. Anno Mungen, Nicholas Vazsonyi, Julie Hubbert, Ivana Rentsch, Arne Stollberg. Würzburg: Königshausen & Neumann, 2017. 91–117.

Morrow, Mary Sue. "Building a German Identity through Music." *Searching for Common Ground: Diskurse zur deutschen Identität 1750–1871.* Ed. Nicholas Vazsonyi. Cologne: Böhlau, 2000. 255–68.

——. *German Music Criticism in the Late Eighteenth Century: Aesthetic Issues in Instrumental Music.* Cambridge: Cambridge University Press, 1997.

Müller, Joachim. "Schillers Gedichtentwurf 'Deutsche Größe': Zum Problem der Kulturnation in der deutschen Klassik." *Wissenschaftliche Zeitschrift der Friedrich-Schiller-Universität* 2.3 (1952–53): 97–109.

Schiller, Friedrich. "[Deutsche Größe]." *Nationalausgabe,* vol. 2, pt. 1. Weimar: H. Böhlaus Nachfolger, 1983. 431–36.

Vazsonyi, Nicholas. "Bayreuth: Capital and Anti-Capital." *Other Capitals of the Nineteenth Century: An Alternative Mapping of Literary and Cultural Space.* Ed. Richard Hibbitt. New York: Palgrave Macmillan, 2017. 205–22.

Wagner, Richard. *Sämtliche Schriften und Dichtungen,* Vol. 4. Leipzig: Breitkopf & Härtel, [n.d. 1911].

Zweig, Stefan. "*Parsifal* in New York." *Der Merker* 2.19/20 (July 1911): 55–56.

Part Two

Going Global

Digital Popular Culture

Right to the City

The Metropolis and "Gangnam Style"

Julie Choi

First uploaded on July 15, 2012, Psy's "Gangnam Style" was the first YouTube video ever to reach one billion and then two billion views.[1] Gangnam, as everyone in the world now knows, is the glitzy area south of the Han River in Seoul. Born into a family in Gangnam and educated in America, Park Jaesang (a.k.a. Psy, a nickname he derived from *psycho*) grew up with all the privileges of the newly moneyed class in South Korea. The video's status as a truly global phenomenon invites us to consider why it became the most widely successful song and dance hit of its moment. The parody videos that rapidly followed revealed that reenacting its mood and moves generated a particular happiness with seemingly universal appeal.[2] The visual content of the video and the lyrics to the song are decidedly indifferent. The famous horse dance was described by Psy himself as "cheesy."[3] But in its digital moment, Psy had created indifferent content that touched on a universal chord. This essay examines how and why such a mediocre product succeeded in speaking to and for so many in its time.

Psy's "Gangnam Style" is best understood as a multimedia, digital representation of the metropolitan experience, a cityscape. The idealized landscape of a pastoral or sublime natural setting, which had long held a prestigious place in artistic representation, has been replaced in preeminence by the metropolitan experience at the core of modern life, demanding new parameters of representation (Gelley 255). Disrobing the mystique of privileged spaces, "Gangnam Style" engages in a calculated contestation of Gangnam spaces such as its riverside, glass towers, and stables—the lifestyle symbolizing the horse-riding set. Psy's horse dance is a tasteless parody of such "class." He explodes the ideal of aristocratic privilege and reveals that the pastoral is neither an achievable dream nor a desirable destination. If the traditional pastoral represents a yearning to flee to the country to escape the alienation of the city, Psy's song and dance is an invitation to re-create an alternative pastoral in the city. Psy is not content merely to offer a memorial to the spectacle of the city. His work is both a representation and an obfuscation, a participation and an intervention, a celebration and a defamation of the experience of the city not as theme but as the paradigmatic condition of modern existence, a text that defies easy articulation. Different city locations are reinterpreted as spaces for play and use value, while productive time is suspended by the rambunctious energies of the horse dance imitated and enjoyed en masse in cities across the globe.

In "The Right to the City,"[4] Henri Lefebvre reflects on how the domination of space as private property, upheld by the state and other forms of class and social power, contributes to the permanent loss of the absolute qualities of place as locus or oeuvre when exchange value comes to override any potential use value. The psychedelic spectacle that denominates itself "Gangnam Style" offers up a rich and colorful array of metropolitan experience that starkly distinguishes itself from the monotony of the rational workday. Psy presents himself as a party crasher who appropriates the city and uses its spaces without consideration for the exchange values they represent. Daily life is transposed into leisure as festivity becomes possible in city spaces planned and developed for entirely different purposes. The perfectly synchronized horse dance performed by Psy and the citizens he encounters in his journey across the metropolis provides the core content that appealed to the global masses. In the tradition of the modernist flaneur, Psy narrates the city from the perspective of the scavenger or ragpicker making his way through the glorious detritus of contemporary commodity culture.

Carnival, mass ornament, flaneur—these are the tropes I borrow from classical cultural studies to examine the different facets of engagement with urban issues in "Gangnam Style." I begin by setting up my argument within the framework of Mikhail Bakhtin's carnivalesque. I then turn to the mechanical system and rigor of the choreographed dance that complicates the energy of carnival, aided by Siegfried Kracauer's observations on the mass ornament and factory production. Kracauer foresaw that consumption would become the necessary correlate of rationalized production, and I seek to show how the mass ornament of the digital era represents not only factory production but also consumption itself as the new labor. The cheesiness of the horse dance, however, and Psy's outrageous fashion undermines the logic of rationalized action, introducing the possibility of a knowing self-distancing from the system of exploitation. I then trace in Psy's gestures and antics the dandyism of Walter Benjamin's flaneur, who seeks to distance himself from the rationale of capitalist production but is ultimately doomed to become a consumed commodity himself. In the concluding section, I return to Lefebvre's manifesto, supplemented with observations made by Jacques Rancière on the distribution of the sensible, to argue that it is ultimately through the expansion of the aesthetic through play that "Gangnam Style" manages to recuperate the right to the city.[5]

▶ Carnival and the World Upside Down

The carnivalesque Gangnam of the hit tune is represented as a place where folk humor prevails in the form of festive laughter. M. M. Bakhtin's work on the carnival in *Rabelais and His World* (1965) foregrounds the opposition of the official and the unofficial, folk culture and institutions of power. The physical materiality of the human body represented through grotesque exaggeration contests the official order through laughter and celebration of the communal body.[6] And indeed it is this spirit of the carnival, which "does not acknowledge any distinction between actors and spectators" (198), that we most readily witness in the spontaneous horse-dancing flash mobs that materialized across the globe in 2012. The grotesque realism of the carnival tradition works through its vulgar, emphatic language and rhythms that function almost as incantation. The phrase "Oppa'n Gangnam Style" achieved the status of an obnoxious lingua franca in the months following the song's release, mouthed by prisoners in the Philippines, brass bands in the United States, and even leftist intellectuals such as Noam Chomsky in an unending series of parodies that celebrated the rambunctious energy of the horse dance.

The modern metropolitan subject is trapped in the net of money, space, and time in ways that inevitably feel like exploitation and domination, and Psy's "Gangnam Style" can be approached in the first instance as a utopian bucking of such limitations. This sentiment is best expressed in the song's refrain: "the guy who runs, but above him the guy who flies." In colloquial Korean "the guy who flies" signals extreme competence and a willingness to break the rules, connoting both power and pleasure. In contrast the guy who runs signals the exemplary citizen driven by the proper work ethic in a society that promotes hard work, discipline, and obedience to the rules. The dandy in shorts and tux with the sunglasses that mirror back the world exemplifies the aggressive bravado of one who would be the flying man.

The motif of flying opens the video in the shot of an airplane reflected in what turns out to be Psy's sunglasses. The little plane is flying an ad banner that reads in inverse GANGNAM STYLE, which serves as a visual clue: Gangnam style backwards, in reverse, upside down. The tacky advertisement for his own tune in the form of the flying banner captures the many ironies and paradoxes of the ultimate consumer who proclaims his power to go against the flow of time and money in an urban setting strictly driven by the logic of capital. As the camera draws back from the close-up of the image of the plane in the sunglasses, we are treated to the physique of Psy, a plump, short Asian man in perfect dress, lying on the beach. A longer take reveals that his bottom half does not match the top. Shorts and rubber slippers complete the outfit of the man soaking in the rays in a sandpit. Instead of the luxurious beachfront property in a world where nature has become the choicest real estate, the camera pans out onto a children's playground in an apartment complex of ordinary and identical middle-income housing units. The first-person narrator masquerading under the self-bestowed title *Oppa* is not the Gangnam guy in any sense except the parodic.

The playground sequence, which features a child dressed as an uncanny miniature of Psy and performing the horse dance in a sandbox, abruptly gives way to the stables of an exclusive private riding club on the outskirts of Seoul. Suited up in a tuxedo and bowtie, Psy defiantly strides past stalls of thoroughbreds but never mounts a real horse. Rather he engages in the now famous horse dance on an imaginary steed amid an anonymous crowd. The ensuing video is a collage of different urban locations where the character Psy, dressed in variations of outrageous, deconstructed formal attire, flaunts his ability to master the varying urban terrain through song and dance. Psy encounters his "sexy lady" on the subway, and their romping takes place in the glimmering caverns of an underground station. The encore-worthy performance of the famous reality television star Yoo Jae-suk, who, dressed in a neon-yellow suit, emerges from a scarlet sports car in a parking garage to challenge Psy, in blue, to a dance-off, serves as candied icing on a visual spectacle that celebrates the riotous and euphoric overthrow of proper boundaries of place and time.

The garish use of color in the video flouts the colorlessness of the city. In his highly regarded work on the urban experience, David Harvey invokes Georg Simmel's thesis on the colorlessness of money that reduces every value into the same system to illustrate the reduction of both time and space into abstract units in modern life.[7] Profitable production and exchange over space made it possible to tighten the chronological net around daily life, and as time became the measure of capitalist value and productivity, space too "came to be represented, like time and value, as abstract, objective, homogeneous, and universal in its qualities" (176–77). Space and time were thus both reduced into freely alienable parcels that could be bought and sold on the marketplace. As Harvey notes, efforts to overcome the repressive constraints of "intersecting spatial, chronological, and monetary nets" almost always attempt to portray "different modes of operation in time and space from those that have increasingly come to dominate all aspects of social life" (180).[8] By adopting the figure of the garish dandy, Psy presents himself as heroic party crasher. The co-opting of upper-class codes such as riding and formal attire marks a suspension of hierarchical precedence, much like in carnival time celebrated by Bakhtin. By breaking dress codes, Psy generates distinction amid the sameness that goes by the name of taste. Liberation from ordinary norms of etiquette and decency create the space for festive laughter.

In one of the more tasteless scenes of the video, bathroom humor prevails, with Oppa, in formal dinner jacket and seated on a toilet, pants down, defiantly gesticulating that he is the "man who flies." The obscene gyration of the celebrity comedian Noh Hong-chul[9] in the hotel elevator over the recumbent figure of Psy marks the climax in crassness of a video that openly revels in the vulgar. These scenes place the defecating, sexual body unequivocally center stage. Bakhtin reads the celebration of the grotesque as the triumph of the communal body over the individualized body: "the essential principle of grotesque realism is degradation, that is, the lowering of all that is high, spiritual, ideal, abstract; it is a transfer to the material level, to the sphere of earth and body in their indissoluble unity" (205). The lowest denominator here is not money but the human body that will eventually be brought down to earth. Sexuality, like defecation, is celebrated as part and parcel of the human experience, not to be policed and hidden. Psy's defiance is lubricated by an abundance of self-mockery that informs the spirit of carnival. As Bakhtin emphasizes, carnival laughter is directed not least at the participants themselves: "it is gay, triumphant, and at the same time mocking, deriding. It asserts and denies, it buries and revives. Such is the laughter of carnival" (200). Much of Psy's bravado derives from his clear glee in making a mockery of himself.

Psy, as master of self-deflation, is both defiant and bathetic. Oppa, loosely translatable as "Big Brother," is both an appropriation of power and a ventriloquizing of the enemy. Mark Greif comments that the sublimity of pop relies at least partially in internalizing that which threatens to destroy you, "the drawing of the inhuman into yourself; and also a loss of your own feelings and words and voice to an outer order that has come to possess them" (111). We could say of Psy what Greif says about Radiohead, whose "song turns into an alternation, in exactly the same repeated words, between the forces that would defy intrusive power and the intrusive power itself, between hopeful individuals and the tyrant ventriloquized" (112). The pathos of the powerless ventriloquist merges with the strident dissonance of he who would defy his dehumanization to create a refrain infinitely translatable across all borders.

▶ Mass Ornament and the Logic of Consumption

In stark contrast to the breaking down of everyday rules of carnival, the extremely precise and synchronized dance moves of K-pop mark a mechanical sublime that needs to be explored in contradistinction to the world turned upside down. Kracauer describes the phenomenon of the mass ornament of the early twentieth century, epitomized by the symmetrical movement of the legs of the Tiller Girls,[10] as the mirroring of hands in the factory joyously affirming the progress of rationalization. He views in the spectacle of the mass ornament a perfect mirroring of the rational process of production:

> Community and personality perish when what is demanded is calculability; it is only as a tiny piece of the mass that the individual can clamber up charts and can service machines without any friction. A system oblivious to differences in form leads on its own to the blurring of national characteristics and to the production of worker masses that can be employed equally well at any point on the globe.—Like the mass ornament, the capitalist production process is an end in itself. (78)[11]

There is no attempt to convey any spiritual content in the mass gymnastics of the Tiller Girls, whose legs parallel the hands in the factory, which reflect "the aesthetic reflex of the rationality to which the prevailing economic system aspires" (79). The order and abstraction of movement in the dance rip apart any false sense of organic unity or individuality in the modern world. The popular appeal of the mass ornament is an undeniable source of its power, though it may only be a crass manifestation of an exploitative logic. For Kracauer intellectuals who privilege more elite forms are not superior to the masses, who at least have the virtue of acknowledging the reduction of reason to the bare rationality imposed by the prevailing economic system. Kracauer is interested in such "surface-level expressions" of the culture, which, "by virtue of their unconscious nature, provide unmediated access to the fundamental substance of things" (75). By paying close attention to popular culture, he seeks to achieve a more accurate diagnosis of the contemporary condition, without reverting to archaic myths of power such as "the organic connection of nature with something the all too modest temperament takes to be soul or spirit" (86). Comprehensive and romantic meta-narratives cannot help us understand the broken nature of the modern experience.

If Kracauer found the movement of the Tiller Girls to reflect the regulated bodily movements of the factory line, the perfectly synchronized routines of K-pop choreography can be comprehended as incorporation of the additional compulsion of consumption as the new labor. Writing a century ago, Kracauer already saw consumerism as the enforced result of a system of production that "spews forth" commodities (78). Consuming, like producing, is subsumed in a rational system whose logic is endless profit without any commitment to any value beyond that of exchange. More recently Jean Baudrillard brilliantly exposes the character of the *Ego consumans* as the epitome of modern exploitation. Consuming is the new labor, and it must be performed in no less rigorous and scientific a manner than the Fordism of yore. Baudrillard comments that the "rationalist mythology of needs and satisfactions is as naive and helpless as traditional medicine when faced with hysterical or psychosomatic symptoms" (76). The field of desire itself has become "a *function of production* and, hence, like all material production, not an individual function, but *an immediately and totally collective one*" that is imposed as "both a morality (a system of ideological values) and a communication system, a structure of exchange" (78). No longer bound by the fiction of fulfilling needs, objects are freed to signify other values such as prestige, indifference, exclusivity. Such is the object's liberation into the field of consumption proper. Objects and needs are not bound by any rational logic but rather float freely in a field of hysterical lack and desire. Desire is imposed by a system of production that properly renders consumption a matter not of choice but of compulsion, in itself exclusive of enjoyment, "the *duty* of the citizen" who "regards enjoyment as an obligation; he sees himself as an enjoyment and satisfaction business" (80).

Having a good time Gangnam style, then, is at least in part to be on top of the business of consumption as prescribed and enforced "pleasure." Passion and action, discipline and desire fuel the boss, the guy who flies if not the guy who merely runs very fast. The hyperactivity demanded by the new "fun morality" presents itself guilelessly as an opportunity to fulfill one's potential. The psychotic frenzy of Psy exemplifies the intensity required to succeed in the new competition. If the horse dance seemed to mark liberation from traditional constraints, it simultaneously reveals that utopia is not so easily achieved. Affluence and consumption do not represent a new freedom from production but rather a more advanced stage in the same process whereby the laborer is forced to consume all the products of his or her own labor. Baudrillard finds it difficult to imagine consumers generating any sense of solidarity, because consumption is atomizing and consumer objects produce distinctions and status stratification.

The mass ornament in the renewed context of digital culture, however, can be read as a manifestation of a newly imagined solidarity of consumers who mobilize their bodies in syncopated order to demonstrate their communal power despite their subjection to the forces of production. One of the most memorable aspects of K-pop events around the world is audience participation. Girls in Europe and America, but also across Southeast Asia and the Middle East, were entranced by groups such as Girls Generation and spent inordinate amounts of time and energy reproducing their fashion and dance moves. Fashion allows a subject to adopt a new and more confident persona without abandoning the security of the general trend.[12] Euphoria stems from complete mirroring of idols as fans perfectly reproduce the scripted and choreographed routines in the imagined community of the "idol republic."[13] However derivative, imitation is experienced as an empowering act of agency in the disciplined performance of a desired identity. K-pop groups speak to the disenfranchised, to whom they seem to give voice and a sense of active participation.

Elite audiences were baffled by the popular pleasure felt by the crowds in response to the spectacle of the Tiller Girls in the stadium images of a century ago, just as they were taken aback by the horse dance that took the world by storm in 2012. Kracauer claimed that the mass ornament was superior to anachronistic attempts to sustain an older, more "noble" aesthetics that no longer have any connection to lived reality. Similarly there is truth in a phenomenon such as "Gangnam Style" that exceeds any elite theory of cultural value. There is in the gesture of the mass ornament an attempt to express power, pleasure, and control—to speak, not merely to make noise. No figure in cultural theory more accurately captures the bathos of such ambition than Walter Benjamin's flaneur, who begins by seeking to establish his distinction from the crowd but ends up becoming a mere commodity himself. Oppa's translation of *flânerie* is explored in the next section.

▶ *Flânerie* and Fashion

Benjamin's exploration of the paradigmatic modern man, the flaneur, is central to his uncompleted Paris Arcades project, a study of nineteenth-century Paris, which preoccupied him for well over a decade until his death in 1940. In 1938 he published a part of this work as *The Paris of the Second Empire in Baudelaire,* which was to be the middle of three sections of a book on Baudelaire. The middle chapter of this work, "The Flâneur," was rewritten based on Adorno's critical comments and republished as "Some Motifs in Baudelaire" in 1939.[14] Benjamin recognized in the figure of the flaneur a modern Odysseus navigating the modern metropolis. He read in the self-positioning of the flaneur a self-proclaimed challenge to the masses and mass production, the rigorous efficiency of Taylorism. Although the flaneur would eventually succumb to the commodity, it is in his role as collector of trivial pieces—the very essence of the Arcades project—that he can view things freed from the compulsion of being useful:

> His leisurely appearance as a personality is his protest against the division of labour which makes people into specialists. It is also his protest against their industriousness. Around 1840 it was briefly fashionable to take turtles to walk in the arcades. The flâneurs liked to have the turtles set the pace for them. If they had had their way, progress would have been obliged to accommodate itself to this pace. But this attitude did not prevail; Taylor, who popularized the watchword 'Down with dawdling!' carried the day. ("Flâneur" 55)

The flaneur sets himself apart by his dress and his attitude, and he makes a deliberate point of flaunting his disregard for the time and space constraints of productive labor. The elegant fashion of taking a turtle on a walk is a memorable cameo.

Benjamin claims that the enjoyment of the spectacle of the crowd worked as a kind of narcotic on the flaneur. He quotes Baudelaire in the notes for the Arcades project celebrating the flaneur as an incognito prince who is spectator and partaker of the ebb and flow of the metropolitan multitude:

> The lover of universal life enters into the crowd as though it were an immense reservoir of electric energy. We might also liken him to a mirror as vast as the crowd itself; or to a kaleidoscope endowed with consciousness, which with each one of its movements, represents the multiplicity of life and the flickering grace of all the elements of life. (Baudelaire, "Le Peintre de la vie modern," qtd. in Benjamin, *Arcades* 443)

The image of the "kaleidoscope endowed with consciousness" is particularly powerful and provides a valuable lens through which we can survey Psy's own representation of his movement through the crowd. Benjamin claims that though Baudelaire was intoxicated by the crowd, he was never blinded by the "horrible social reality," and this is why "in Baudelaire the big city almost never finds expression in the direct presentation of its inhabitants" ("Flâneur" 59), unlike in earlier writers on the city such as Percy Shelley ("Hell is a city much like London"). The "unfeeling isolation" of the big city decried by a provincial such as Engels in his famous exposition of the alienating experience of the bustle of London was experienced by the flaneur as a charged isolation of strangers.[15]

One of the most remarkable moments in Benjamin's remarks on Baudelaire occurs in his reading of "A une passante," a sonnet from *Les Fleurs du Mal:*

> Far from experiencing the crowd as an opposed, antagonistic element, this very crowd brings to the city dweller the figure that fascinates. The delight of the urban poet is love—not at first sight, but at last sight. It is a farewell forever which coincides in the poem with the moment of enchantment. Thus the sonnet supplies the figure of shock, indeed of catastrophe. But the nature of the poet's emotions has been affected as well. What makes his body contract in a tremor—*crispé comme un extravagant,* Baudelaire says—is not the rapture of a man whose every fibre is suffused with *eros;* it is, rather, like the kind of sexual shock that can beset a lonely man. ("Some Motifs" 125)

The last line of the sonnet reads, "O toi que j'eusse aimé, o toi qui le savais" (Oh you whom I could have loved, oh you who knew it too; my translation). Though they will never meet, the shock of their momentary encounter is suffused with a fantasized recognition of the kindred spirit. The "Oh, sexy lady!" refrain of "Gangnam Style" is a manifestation of this very theme.

The episode on the subway where Psy finally encounters the sexy lady is strongly reminiscent of Benjamin's tragicomic love-at-last-sight account of Baudelaire's poetic encounter with the woman in the crowd. In the song's lyrics, the Oppa persona characterizes his lover as "warm and human in daytime, knowing how to luxuriate over a cup of coffee, but a heart burning with passion at night, the kind of woman who knows how to transform herself." Meanwhile, he is the "sana-i," who is "as warm and sweet as you in daytime, but can down his coffee in one shot while it's hot and whose heart explodes when day turns into night" *Sana-i* connotes the machismo of the manly man. Psy's physique and his antics undercut the sheer effrontery of his boast; in this he is reminiscent of that other urban dandy lover, Prufrock, who measures out his life with coffee spoons. Psy's prurient fantasy goes wild in the second verse as he envisages the girl "letting down her hair when it's time, modestly covered but more sexy than those who bare their skin," while he is "the guy who looks reserved but knows when to play, the one who goes crazy when it's time, and whose ideology is more impressive than his muscles."

The line about his ideology being more muscular than his physique pokes fun at the exaggerated bravado of "Oppa." *Oppa* is the word for an older brother to a younger sister within a family but is now more often used as the word of choice for men who wish to play the role of protector to their lover. *Oppa* carries many of the connotations of desired masculinity in a society where men are no longer viewed as quite so powerful and able as in more comfortably patriarchal times. "Eh, sexy lady, the guy who runs, and above him, the guy who flies, baby baby, I'm someone who's got a clue, Oppa'n Gangnam style." This is the refrain that brings the song to its close. The sexy lady and Psy never actually embrace. They miss each other at last glance as each is lost in the crowd that separates and makes them one again in the electric energy of the carnivalesque communal horse dance. The final group dance takes place in an anonymous, empty, warehouse-like interior filled with crowds dressed as representing a wide variety of professions including nurse and taekwondo instructor. At the center are Psy and the sexy lady dancing in parallel but not in any direct relation to each other. Like Baudelaire's sonnet and T. S. Eliot's "The Love Song of J. Alfred Prufrock," this song can only have been written in a big city that produces works that "reveal the stigmata which life in a metropolis inflicts upon love" (Benjamin, "Some Motifs" 125).

Benjamin quite correctly predicted that the flaneur could not forever keep his distance from the crowd. He cannot avoid the fate of being reduced to imitating "both the machines which push the material and the economic boom which pushes the merchandise," the "feverish pace of material production" ("Flâneur"

53). The crowd becomes a kind of opiate for those condemned to live under these new conditions, and as one abandoned in the crowd, the flaneur "shares the situation of the commodity. He is not aware of this special situation, but this does not diminish its effect on him and it permeates him blissfully like a narcotic that can compensate him for many humiliations. The intoxication to which the *flâneur* surrenders is the intoxication of the commodity around which surges the stream of customers" (55). Just as the commodity is fetishized and can be imagined as prostituting its soul to the many who are willing to love it and take it home, "empathy is the nature of the intoxication to which the flaneur abandons himself in the crowd" (55).

The jerky moves of the horse dance approximate the automatization of production as also suggested by Kracauer with respect to the mass ornament, and the enjoyment of the crowd is mirrored in the mass dance. The promiscuity of the commodity as love object is a quality that the Psy as flaneur demonstrates in abundance: he is quick to break out into the love dance, not only with the sexy lady but also with random men in parking lots and older ladies on tour buses, even cuddling up to a tough guy in a sauna. Quoting from Baudelaire, Benjamin comments: "that which people call love is quite small, quite limited, and quite feeble" compared with "that holy prostitution of the soul which gives itself wholly, poetry and charity, to the unexpected that appears, to the unknown that passes" ("Flâneur" 56). The exuberant promiscuity of the horse dance participates in the prostitution of the soul that bathes in the exhilaration of adoption by the crowd.

Benjamin predicted that the flaneur's final destination would be the department store. He would become himself the ultimate object for sale, fanning the desires of the masses to partake in a mutual pleasure of empathy: "Empathy with the commodity is fundamentally empathy with exchange value itself. The *flâneur* is the virtuoso of this empathy. He takes the concept of marketability itself for a stroll. Just as his final ambit is the department store, his last incarnation is the sandwich-man" (*Arcades* 448). The flying banner advertising his song reflected in Psy's sunglasses is a perfect reincarnation of the ad of the sandwich-man wearing a signboard for a product, unwittingly revealing that he himself is for sale. Can the man for sale, himself a commodity, also be a potential figure of redemption? Despite the indifference of his "message," his dance and song lay claim to the right to the city by temporarily suspending the everyday coordinates of time and space.

▶ The Right to the City

The familiar transformed into the unfamiliar, the unfamiliar translated back into the everyday. The disjunctive scenes of "Gangnam Style" can be read as a deliberative montage of urban pastoral, a travel to a city reimagined as inhabitable, partaking in an older ethos of the oeuvre, or work of art to be lived and appreciated, overriding the tyranny of spatial practices that "restrict time to the time of productive work and reduce lived rhythms to rationalist and localized gestures in the division of labour" (Lefebvre 49). The song and dance allowed audiences across the world to take a break from their uncanny daily routines to transform themselves for the moment into the ludicrous persona of Oppa, the man who flies. The ability to participate and to celebrate that participation through uploading of parody videos from all corners of the globe then became part of the "Gangnam Style" phenomenon, which is first and foremost one of participation.

Jacques Rancière takes up the topic of Plato's artisans, who cannot take part in the community of citizens, "because they do *not have the time* to devote themselves to anything other than their work" (*Politics of Aesthetics* 12). For Rancière *le partage du sensible* is the "distribution of spaces, times, and forms of activity that determines the very manner in which something in common lends itself to participation and in what way various individuals have a part in this distribution" (12). In "Gangnam Style" we have the promise of the redistribution of space and time and an invitation to all those who "do not have the time" to share in the good life, the free life, by taking charge of what should be common to everyone. If, as Rancière believes, "politics revolves around what is seen and what can be said about it, around who has the ability to see and the talent to speak, around the properties of spaces and the possibilities of time" (13), "Gangnam Style" is indeed entirely political. Its contents may be distinctively lowbrow, mediocre, even cynical, but that is almost beside the point. The indifference to message or ethos is the mark of its democratic appeal. Psy's indifference to message shares similarities with what Rancière describes as Gustave Flaubert's "refusal to entrust literature with any message whatsoever" as "evidence of democratic equality," because "the equality of all subject matter is the negation of any relationship of necessity between a determined form and a determined content" (14). Just as the novel as genre once brought indifferent content to the eyes of all, breaking down the hierarchies of representation and establishing a new community of readers "only by the random circulation of the written word" (14), the Internet has established itself as the decisive medium for circulating indifferent digital content to a universal global audience.

For Rancière egalitarian promise is everything and perhaps the very precondition of aesthetics as politics, not as the fascist theatrical staging of power and mass mobilization but rather as a renewal in the way space and time are partitioned, as those formerly without voice are allowed to make speech rather than merely noise:

> Politics occurs when those who "have no" time take the time necessary to front up as inhabitants of a common space and demonstrate that their

> mouths really do emit speech capable of making pronouncements on the common which cannot be reduced to voices signaling pain. This distribution and redistribution of places and identities, this apportioning and reapportioning of spaces and times, of the visible and the invisible, and of noise and speech constitutes what I call the distribution of the sensible. ("Aesthetics as Politics" 24)[16]

Psy invites the masses to take over urban spaces that elude them, where they are not invited, and to make themselves at home in these newly pastoralized loci. The utopian task at hand is to restore the right to the city, as concrete rights. Lefebvre wished to restore to the working class its right to *inhabit* lost to rules of production, exchange value, and private property:

> Among these rights in the making features the *right to the city* (not the ancient city, but to urban life, to renewed centrality, to places of encounter and exchange, to life rhythms and time uses, enabling the full and complete *usage* of these moments and places, etc.). (179)

Lost to private appropriation and tourism, the city demands its own reaffirmation as "right to urban life" of the masses who must claim the city as oeuvre. Only those who inhabit can replace the "Olympians of the new bourgeois aristocracy," who no longer inhabit but "go from grand hotel to grand hotel, or from caste to castle, commanding a fleet or a country from a yacht. They are everywhere and nowhere" (159).

In the tradition of the greatest flaneurs, Psy manages to turn the streets of the city into an *intérieur.* Benjamin cites Baudelaire on the ability of the flaneur to make himself at home in the most unlikely of spaces: "être hors de chez soi, et pourtant se sentir partout chez soi" (to be outside one's home, and yet to feel everywhere at home) ("Flâneur" 37).[17] The playground is his living room and the parking garage his ballroom; the neighborhood bathhouse his swimming pool and the embankment his private gym where he can ogle the most attractive people. The public toilet is his throne, and the bus full of tourist ladies his traveling harem. The emotional highlight of the song, the encounter with the sexy lady, happens exactly at midpoint in the video, most logically on the subway, in that subterranean underworld the modern Odysseus must navigate to come back home. The kaleidoscopic juxtaposition of mundane spaces reflects contemporary urban life in which being jolted is the norm. The deep interiority of the bourgeois subject is an outdated model. Outside and inside no longer remain distinct, much less surface and depth, reality and phantasmagoria. Psy's signature sunglasses, which mirror back the world rather than allow a personal interchange of gazes, proclaim a refusal to be subjected to the nostalgia of aura.

For Rancière the aesthetic opens up a field beyond both the ethical and the realm of representation (mimesis): aesthetic indifference and free play are a break from the sensorium of domination. Such play opens up an aesthetic regime of art that can construct forms for a new collective life:

> If aesthetic "play" and "appearance" found a new community, then this is because they stand for the refutation, within the sensible, of this opposition between intelligent form and sensible matter which, properly speaking, is a difference between two humanities. ("Aesthetics as Politics" 31)

In its refusal to read the difference between two humanities of intellect and bare life, aesthetic play produces a revolution of sensible existence itself, bypassing the question of forms of state, investing rather in the autonomy of a new form of sensory experience that promises "the germ of a new humanity, of a new form of individual and collective life" (32). If Psy's "Gangnam Style" succeeds, it does so by proffering just such a challenge to the capitalist division of different humanities.

The startling fad of "Gangnam Style" flash mobs in public plazas and prison yards around the globe was strangely exhilarating if ephemeral. Centers of decision-making and public authority were temporarily yielded to different publics suddenly transformed into mass ornaments. In October 2012 dissident artist Ai Weiwei posted his version of the song and danced with handcuffs to deride the Chinese regime. Ai's video was quickly blocked in China, but in a gesture of solidarity, Anish Kapoor posted from London a tribute featuring hundreds of artists, actors, and dancers horse-dancing handcuffed. For both Ai and Kapoor, Psy's video served as a platform for participating in political parody with global outreach.[18] It was a fashion that could not endure, and yet as *Erfahrung*, experience that exceeds the merely lived-out, its traces endure in recesses that are still being reset to emerge as the future. Rancière points to the essential contradiction whereby the artwork's promise of emancipation is achieved at the moment it becomes part of the "living tissue of experiences and common beliefs in which both the elite and the people share" ("Aesthetics as Politics" 37). Pop, Greif writes, "encourages you to hold on to and reactivate hints of personal feeling that society should have extinguished" (114). The pop song, like poems, fashion, and fairy tales, is extinguished the moment it participates in the construction of the festivals of the future.[19]

▸ Coda

After this essay was nearly completed in 2016, flash mobs took on new meaning in Korea. At Ewha Womans University, where I teach, students and faculty protested, among many perceived wrongs, the admission of a horse-riding student, alleged to have received special favors through the influence of former South

Korean president Park Geun Hye. The central campus area (ECC) was lit up by thousands holding up the flashlights on their mobile phones. Students occupied university headquarters for three months, during which they released a "Gangnam Style" parody titled "Unni'n Bonkwan [Main Administration Building] Style." The female students satirically replaced *oppa* with *unni* for "older sister." The protests at Ewha built up to nationwide demonstrations ending with the ousting of the president after months of peaceful mass vigils that often felt like festivals lit up by mobile phones in the central public spaces of Seoul. Crowds have always enjoyed representations of themselves, and the televised images of these scenes were conveyed around the globe. In some secret way, the flickers of Psy's horse dance and the fashion for flash mobs may have helped light the way for these festivals of the future. It is no small irony that "Gangnam Style" had been performed in the central plaza of Seoul at the personal invitation of the former president at her inauguration. The lesson we take away is that festivals are too easily manipulated for political purposes, and so the way forward is precarious indeed.

Notes

This work was made possible through the generous support of a 2013 Ewha Global Top 5 Grant from Ewha Womans University. An earlier version of the article was presented at the joint National Taiwan University, University of South Carolina, and Ewha conference held at NTU in the fall of 2016. It is reprinted here with the kind permission of *Korea Journal* (Vol. 59 No.2) published by the Academy of Korean Studies.

1. In three days the video was getting one million hits per day, and it reached nine million hits per day two months after its release. It broke the YouTube counter for keeping track and forced the company to devise a new way to count how many times a video was viewed. To date (September 2018), the video has been viewed more than three billion times.

2. Flash mobs of tens of thousands gathered in prominent public places such as the Eiffel Tower in Paris and the Piazza del Popolo in Rome, and 2013 was rung in at New York's Times Square with Psy and M. C. Hammer singing and horse dancing together. Over a million viewers participated through video streaming, and masses of people joined them on site and online to form a giant cultural event. As a skit on the 2012 season premiere of *Saturday Night Live* demonstrated, for some reason the horse dance made people crazily happy.

3. Psy described the ethos of "Gangnam Style" to Britney Spears as "dress classy, dance cheesy," on *The Ellen DeGeneres Show,* NBC, September 11, 2012.

4. Lefebvre's manifesto, written to mark the centenary anniversary of Marx's *Capital,* serves as a guiding light for my reading of "Gangnam Style."

5. "But my spirit and my agenda is play," Psy professed in a *New York Times* interview from October 2012 ("His Style Is Gangnam, and Viral Too").

6. Bakhtin's celebration of the carnivalesque has been vulnerable to the criticism that it is perhaps overly utopian, especially because the objects of carnivalesque laughter could be the powerless and marginalized as much as those in positions of authority and power. For an overview of discussions of the impact of his work on the carnivalesque, see Pam Morris's introduction to *The Bakhtin Reader.*

7. See Harvey, "Money, Time, Space, and the City," for his explanation of how the interconnected abstractions of money, space, and time combine to create interlocking and repressive sources of social regulation that "precludes liberation from the more repressive aspects of class-domination and all of the urban pathology and restless incoherence that goes with it" (165). Harvey's insights throughout his work are greatly indebted to the writings of Georg Simmel, in particular *The Philosophy of Money* (1900).

8. Piet Mondrian's signature grid of primary color blocks can be read as an intellectual modernist grappling with such a reduction. Psy's colorful metropolis is an attempt to crash through the grid itself.

9. Both Noh and Yoo Jae-suk are stars with a global following, as documented in their respective Wikipedia entries. Korean popular entertainment has gained an impressive foothold in the universe of nonsensical, reality-style entertainment. Noh's famous pelvic-thrusting dance is his trademark and is officially known as "jeo-jil dance," signifying low-class dancing.

10. The Tiller Girls were highly trained precision dancing troupes who enjoyed great popular success starting at the end of the nineteenth century. John Tiller of Manchester had the idea of matching the girls by height and training them to link arms and kick high to create the effect of the machinelike precision of the mass ornament. They performed in many locales, including the Folies Bergère in Paris and the London Palladium.

11. "The Mass Ornament" is the title piece in a self-collected edition of Kracauer's early Weimar works published in 1963. Levin's introduction provides a fine overview of Kracauer's career and a good analysis of the importance and brilliance of the early work. A student of Simmel and friend of Benjamin, Kracauer made it to the United States to join friends and former colleagues from the Institute for Social Research including Theodor Adorno and Max Horkheimer.

12. Simmel's "The Philosophy of Fashion" (1905) provides a strong analytical framework for understanding the new social formations of individual and group identity that are mobilized through fashion.

13. See Kim, "Idol Republic." Kim remarks that "in the current global convergence, fans do not merely want the interpretive appreciation but, rather, a whole world in which they can immerse themselves and perform and recreate the codes and practices their idols embody" (338).

14. Both of these essays were collected in *Charles Baudelaire: A Lyric Poet in the Era of High Capitalism* (1997). I will also refer to the scattered notes published for the first time in full in English as *The Arcades Project* (1999), which covers materials from

volume 5 of Benjamin's *Gesammelte Schriften* gathered under the title *Das Passagen-Werk.*

15. Benjamin quotes extensively from Engels's *The Condition of the Working-Class in England in 1844* (1845) to convey the difference between the experience of the city of a newly arrived outsider and one who is at home in the crowd. A long quote is crowned by the final sentence: "The brutal indifference, the unfeeling isolation of each in his private interest, becomes the more repellent and offensive, the more these individuals are crowded together within a limited space" ("Flâneur" 58).

16. This reformulation is taken from the more recent piece, "Aesthetics as Politics," in *Aesthetics and Its Discontents* (2009), translated by Steven Corcoran.

17. The street becomes a dwelling for the flaneur; he is as much at home among the facades of houses as a citizen is in his four walls. To him the shiny, enameled signs of businesses are at least as good a wall ornament as an oil painting is to a bourgeois in his salon.

18. Louise Gray wrote on the *New Internationalist* blog: "Kapoor is quoted as saying: 'Our film aims to make a serious point about freedom of speech and freedom of expression. It is our hope that this gesture of support for Ai Weiwei and all prisoners of conscience will be wide-ranging and will help to emphasise how important these freedoms are to us all.' And it's interesting to see how a Korean pop song with banal lyrics about sexy ladies and knowing men, that invokes the name of a high-class Seoul district, has pressed people into action."

19. Rancière comments, "Even Mallarmé, the pure poet par excellence, assigned to poetry the task of organizing a different topography of common relations, of preparing the 'festivals of the future' . . . the poem has the inconsistency of a gesture which dissipates in the very act of instituting a common space, similar to a national holiday fireworks display" ("Aesthetics as Politics" 33–34).

Works Cited

Ai Weiwei. "Ai Weiwei does Gangnam Style." YouTube, uploaded by Triplenickel, 15 Oct. 2012, https://www.youtube.com/watch?v=n281GWfT1E8.

Bakhtin, M. M. "Folk Humour and Carnival Laughter." *The Bakhtin Reader: Selected Writings of Bakhtin, Medvedev, Voloshinov,* edited by Pam Morris, Routledge, 1994, pp. 194–206.

Baudrillard, Jean. *The Consumer Society: Myths and Structures.* Translated by Chris Turner, Sage, 1998.

Benjamin, Walter. *The Arcades Project.* Translated by Howard Eiland and Kevin McLaughlin, Harvard UP, 1999.

——. "The Flâneur." *Charles Baudelaire: A Lyric Poet in the Era of High Capitalism,* translated by Harry Zohn, Verso, 1997, pp. 35–66.

——. "Some Motifs in Baudelaire." *Charles Baudelaire: A Lyric Poet in the Era of High Capitalism,* translated by Harry Zohn, Verso, 1997, pp. 107–54.

Gelley, Alexander. "City Texts: Representation, Semiology, Urbanism." *Politics, Theory, and Contemporary Culture,* edited by Mark Poster, Columbia UP, 1993, pp. 237–60.

Gray, Louise. "Video: Going Gangnam for Ai Weiwei." *New Internationalist,* 23 Nov. 2012, https://newint.org/blog/2012/11/23/gangnam-style-ai-weiwei-amnesty-anish-kapoor/. Accessed 18 Mar. 2013.

Greif, Mark. "Radiohead, or the Philosophy of Pop." *Essays against Everything.* Pantheon Books, 2016, pp. 99–117.

Harvey, David. "Money, Time, Space, and the City." *The Urban Experience.* Johns Hopkins UP, 1989, pp. 165–99.

Kapoor, Anish. "Art world goes Gangnam Style made in solidarity with Ai Weiwei. mp4." YouTube, uploaded by wxou gr, 21 Jan. 2013. https://www.youtube.com/watch?v=qmbomoq_DxY.

Kim, Yeran. "Idol Republic: The Global Emergence of Girl Industries and the Commercialization of Girl Bodies." *Journal of Gender Studies,* vol. 20, no. 4, 2011, pp. 333–45.

Kracauer, Siegfried. "The Mass Ornament." *The Mass Ornament: Weimar Essays,* translated by Thomas Y. Levin, Harvard UP, 1995, pp. 75–86.

Lefebvre, Henri. "The Right to the City." *Writing on Cities,* translated and edited by Eleonore Kofman and Elizabeth Lebas, Blackwell, 1996, pp. 61–181.

Levin, Thomas. Introduction. *The Mass Ornament: Weimar Essays,* by Siegfried Kracauer, translated by Thomas Y. Levin, Harvard UP, 1995, pp. 1–30.

Morris, Pam. Introduction. *The Bakhtin Reader: Selected Writings of Bakhtin, Medvedev, Voloshinov,* edited by Pam Morris, Routledge, 1994, pp. 1–24.

Psy. "Psy-Gangnam Style M.V." YouTube, uploaded by Officialpsy, 15 Jul. 2012, www.youtube.com/watch?v=9bZkp7q19f0.

Rancière, Jacques. "Aesthetics as Politics." *Aesthetics and Its Discontents,* translated by Steve Corcoran, Polity, 2009, pp. 19–44.

——. *The Politics of Aesthetics: The Distribution of the Sensible.* Translated by Gabriel Rockhill, Continuum, 2004.

Ryzik, Melena. "His Style Is Gangnam, and Viral Too." *The New York Times,* 11 Oct. 2012, https://www.nytimes.com/2012/10/14/arts/music/interview-psy-the-artist-behind-gangnam-style.html?_r=0. Accessed 29 Mar. 2013.

Simmel, Georg. "The Philosophy of Fashion." *Simmel on Culture,* edited by David Frisby and Mike Featherstone, Sage, 1997, pp. 187–206.

SNL. "Saturday Night Live—Gangnam Style." *YouTube,* uploaded by ComedyCentral India, 27 Sept. 2012, https://www.youtube.com/watch?v=bMUsOJmRcrc.

The Ellen DeGeneres Show. "Surprise! Britney Learns 'Gangnam Style' from Psy!" *YouTube,* uploaded by TheEllenShow, 10 Sept. 2012, https://www.youtube.com/watch?v=QZmkU5Pg1sw.

The Garden of Living Paths

Interactive Narratives in Global Geek Culture

Mou-Lan Wong

I see it as something living and growing. I think of the world's literature as a kind of forest, I mean it's tangled and it entangles us but it's growing. Well, to come back to my inevitable image of a labyrinth, well it's a living labyrinth, no?

Jorge Luis Borges, in Richard Burgin, *Conversations with Jorge Luis Borges*, 1967

To Borges, literature is a living, intertextual labyrinth that continues to grow and expand with the involvement of both its readers and its writers.[1] The image of such a labyrinth, which constantly emerges in his work, is a key theme in Borges's seminal short story "The Garden of Forking Paths." This study attempts to survey the exterior living labyrinth of popular interactive narratives in order to unravel the tangled intertextuality of Borges's interior labyrinthine "Garden." According to his ideal of "the world's literature," Borges's living garden has never solely resided within his short stories. The intertwined intertextual elements of "Garden" actually propagate an outward living garden that further realizes Borges's infinite labyrinth paradigm. Rather than recognizing how much intertextuality is reflected and refracted outside of "Garden," critics have more often been "entangled" to explore only the inner garden by wading through the nuances in different editions and translations of Borges's story.[2] Yet within any single version of "Garden," the facade of polyphony, fabricated by multilayered intertexts, readily forces the reader to formulate intertextual connections.

In only a handful of pages, Borges's short story manages to be sinuously serpentine. The plot starts with an initial exposition that leads to a confession written by a professor of English, Yu Tsun, to explain a certain inconsistency on page 22 of B. H. Liddell Hart's history of World War I. Yu Tsun, Chinese in nationality, is actually an unwilling German spy who has discovered the secret location of a British artillery camp near the French town of Albert. He tries to communicate the location to Germany while being pursued by an Irish inspector, Richard Madden. Yu Tsun decides to expose the location in a newspaper headline by murdering Stephen Albert, whose name he has acquired from a telephone directory. Upon finding Albert, Yu Tsun is caught off-guard by the fact that Albert is a sinologist who has been studying a work titled *The Garden of the Forking Paths,* an unappreciated masterpiece by a defamed ancestor of Yu Tsun's. Albert produces a letter written by the ancestor, Ts'ui Pên, as a key to deciphering *Garden,* a book that attempts to narrate all the possible outcomes of the protagonist's major decisions in life without a specific registry or index. Following Albert's deliberations, Yu Tsun comprehends that *Garden* is neither unintelligible nor inefficacious but is an innovative experimental model of nonlinear temporality. In *Garden* time seems to branch forever outward to create an almost infinite number of possible futures. Despite receiving invaluable insight with the potential to rehabilitate his family's maligned history, Yu Tsun shoots Albert and is later apprehended by Madden for his crimes. The story ends with an imprisoned Yu Tsun reading the news about the German bombing of Albert.

There are several intertwining fictional intertexts at work here: the exterior narrative that initiates the story; Liddell Hart's book cited by the exterior narrator; Yu Tsun's confession throughout most of the story; Stephen Albert's interpretation of Ts'ui Pên's *Garden* and letter; Ts'ui Pên's *Garden* and letter; the directory providing Stephen Albert's name and residence; and the newspapers communicating the location of the artilleries and confirming the German bombing. Beyond the kernel texts that sway the plot, some other relevant texts are also mentioned in "Garden": the *Annals* of Tacitus, *Hung Lu Meng, The Lost Encyclopaedia,* and *The Thousand and One Nights.*[3] These texts intercept, interweave, and cross one another so that the short story becomes an intertextual hub that compels the reader to unravel its convoluted web of significance. In this light Borges's "Garden" is in itself an interactive narrative, because the reader has to piece together a series of mental jigsaws to make sense of the narrative.[4] Much of the intertextuality and interactivity lies in Borges's attempt to generate multiplicity and malleability in the reader's concept of time. Borges's deliberate intertextual maneuvering can be detected right from the beginning of "Garden."

In an attempt to rewrite history (in other words, to change chronology), the exterior narrative of the story supplies Yu Tsun's confession to challenge the accuracy of Liddell Hart's historical work, but such a tactic is entirely ineffective since Yu Tsun's confession is not a piece of sufficient evidence. However, the confession does offer a simple remedy: the newspaper featuring the bombing of Albert. By simply quoting or referencing the date of the bombing from the newspaper without Yu Tsun's confession, the argument of the exterior narrative would be much more persuasive. However, to do so would obviously run contrary to the forking-paths temporal model at the crux of the story, as Yu Tsun's confession is provided as a "what if" scenario rather than a direct confrontation with Liddell Hart. The fact that the exterior narrative never returns to close up the story further enhances the effect of the fiction's open-endedness. In the *Labyrinths* version of "Garden," this is reinforced by missing quotation marks that should signal the end of Yu Tsun's confession (29).[5] Furthermore it would be very unlikely for page 22 of Liddell Hart's history to chronicle the events of the Second Battle of Albert, which occurred toward the end of the second year (July 1916) in a four-year war (1914–18). If the events in 1916 were chronicled on page 22, Liddell Hart's entire book would contain roughly fifty pages—making it unlikely to have chronicled the postponement of artillery deployment of a single battle, given the book's brevity. In the translation of "Garden" in *Ficciones,* the page number provided is 212 rather than 22, and the title provided for Liddell Hart's book is *A History of the World War*—much more faithful to the title of the actual work than *History of World War I,* as *Labyrinths* has it.[6] In any case neither of the pages cited contains the relevant passage under scrutiny by the exterior narrative, but since the theme of "Garden" revolves around possible futures and alternate histories, there might be a timeline where Liddell Hart actually titled an edition of his book *History of World War I* and references the incident in question on either page 22 or 212. In this light the intertextual citation of Liddell Hart becomes apt initial legerdemain for Borges to generate polyphony in his forking-time garden.[7]

Although "Garden" is widely praised for its innovative concept of branching time, Borges's intertextual sleight of hand has not gone unnoticed by critics. For example Jeffrey Gray surmises that the structure of Borges's "Garden" is surprisingly linear given its polyphonous ideas, since "the story's convergence—in one physical place and historical moment—of individuals, crimes, thoughts, and events performs the opposite of forking" (35). Robert L. Chibka also has observed that "Garden" in effect "has only a single, relentlessly chronological plot . . . in a medium that is incontrovertibly finite and unremittingly linear, both temporally and spatially" (116–117). While Chibka does entertain the idea that a library that contains varying translations and errors between editions of "Garden" could be somewhat forking, he concludes by arguing that "[l]anguage may win a battle, but time wins the war" and that Borges's work only "enforces the irrevocable, heartbreakingly finite nature of life" (118). Chibka is correct if we examine Borges's "Garden" exclusively within the text and medium (the printed page) of his short story. However, the limitation of the medium is perhaps not lost to Borges, as his vision of the literary living garden elevates the intertextual "Garden" away from the confinement of the printed page. In fact, with its multilayered inner intertextuality, the story has managed to branch out into the academic field of hypertext studies.

The presence of Borges's "Garden" in the hypertextual realm corresponds to the emergence of digitization in the last few decades. David Ciccoricco observes that "digital technology has radically foregrounded the dynamic process that Borges explores metaphysically, mathematically, and poetically in his texts" (77). This is evident in how Stuart Moulthrop and others at the turn of the twentieth century attempted to create working hypertext fiction. Experimental works such as Michael Joyce's *Afternoon: A Story,* one of the earliest published hyperfictions, and Moulthrop's *Victory Garden,* which uses a map for navigation instead of plain hyperlinks, generated enough academic interest for scholars Noah Wardrip-Fruin and Lev Manovich to publish a collection in 2003 titled *The New Media Reader,* which features "Garden" as one of the first chapters (30–34). *The New Media Reader,* faithful to its theme, comes with an interactive CD-ROM and has crisscrossing labels in the margins that lead to cross-referential markers along the edge of the page, and it also features discussions on video games and comics alongside computer programming and the Internet. Perla Sassón-Henry, in her *Borges 2.0,* discusses exhaustively the progression from Borges's fictions to the genesis of hyperfiction through "points of contact among literature, science and digital narratives" (72). However, pure text-based adventures and hyperfictions have been rarely discussed or even academically pursued, and Sassón-Henry also acknowledges the fact that "the quickly evolving digital and virtual technologies will almost indefinitely pave the way for novel interpretations of Borges's futuristic ideas" (113). Hypertext has now been combined and incorporated into other media expressions to create multimedia experiences particularly in video games and other formats, yet little research has been done on the relation between Borges and these newfangled media. This study will attempt to update the scholarship by demonstrating how "Garden" anticipates various interactive pop-culture narratives from printed texts to digital and cinematic media.

The following survey into popular interactive narratives first hones in on how the choose-your-own-adventure books that utilize the forking-paths concept actually foreground a convergent-paths model already preconfigured in Borges's "Garden." This section mainly compares the printed and digital interactive narratives from choose-your-own-adventure books to video games. The second part of the survey explores the idea of experiencing multiple timelines through the looping effect of rereading branching narratives. Each self-enclosed converging path can be proliferated through different incarnations of its existence across countless possible worlds. Here the emphasis shifts to the cinematic medium, where the themes of possible worlds and time looping have become prominent features. The concluding section revisits the advantages of recognizing Borges's intertextual living garden in popular culture and how this garden satisfies, at least in part, Borges's riddle on time inscribed in "Garden."

▶ Choosing Your Convergent Adventures

Borges's idea of a book containing multiple narrative paths was widely adopted by entrepreneurs, and it culminated in a boom of choose-your-own-adventure books in the 1970s and 1980s. Most of these titles adopt a second-person narrative that is rarely utilized in literature.[8] In these books, typically aimed at adolescent readers, the reader can make key decisions that might alter the outcome of the story. Most titles feature narratives on espionage, science fiction, high fantasy, or Indiana Jones–style adventures. Others entertain wildly different tropes by combining popular themes from crime fighting and mythology to orientalism. The application of the second-person point of view and the ability to control some of the decisions of the protagonist generated huge interest across its intended readership. There was something thrilling about the capacity to exercise limited decision-making in a traditionally passive medium. The level of immersion created for young adults in the early days of choose-your-own-adventure books might not seem impressive in this era of virtual/augmented reality programs, but these guided narratives certainly entertained many a child with dreams of high adventure across multiple worlds. Due to their mass juvenile appeal, these books are often referred to as game books and perceived as works without literary merit. The writing in early game books is indeed quite inferior in their literary value, even when compared to other juvenile literature of their time. These books, however, do anticipate one of the current trends of reexamining second-person narrations elaborated in such critical works as Jarmila Mildorf's 2016 article "Reconsidering Second-Person Narration and Involvement" and Leon de Bruin, Michiel van Elk, and Albert Newen's "Reconceptualizing Second-Person Interaction" in 2012. However, none of these studies focuses on game books or even acknowledges their existence, which is surprising given that both studies discuss the immersion and interaction from the second-person perspective that proliferates in the choose-your-own-adventure genre.[9]

Outside of academia, owing to their initial fandom and reception, choose-your-own-adventure books became increasingly complex and intricate as they developed alongside tabletop role-playing games such as *Dungeons & Dragons* and *GURPS* (Generic Universal Role Playing System). Series such as Steven Jackson and Ian Livingston's *Fighting Fantasy,* Joe Dever's *Lone Wolf,* and Dave Morris and Oliver Johnson's *Blood Sword* apply a very rudimentary rule set to allow for combat and skill tests, determined by dice rolls. In fact, to emulate character progression in a standard role-playing game, some series (e.g., *Grey Star* and *Tunnels and Trolls*) allow readers to bring their characters from book to book.

Although they did not die out entirely, the game books gradually faded to the background at the turn of the twentieth century under an onslaught of other forms of entertainment such as video games and mobile phone applications. In recent years, however, there has been a minor resurgence of game books, some of which have tried to go through the normal publishing route with varying degrees of success. According to its official website, the publisher Chooseco relaunched the *Choose Your Own Adventure* series in 2006 and has sold more than ten million copies. Writers such as Michael J. Ward reenvisioned *Fighting Fantasy*–style game books more geared toward adults in his *DestinyQuest* series from 2013, while James Schannep adopted the choose-your-own-adventure model for a pulp adventure novel series called *Click Your Poison* beginning in 2012. Nicholas Bourbaki[10] published *If* in 2014 as an attempt to engage readers by presenting a protagonist without a fixed identity who interacts with an antagonistic childhood bully designated with the first-person *I*. Bourbaki's *If* offers twenty-two possible life-choice endings, with one alluding to Borges's "Garden"—albeit a twisted version of it (246–56). A similar theme of life choices had already been attempted by Kim Newman in the mature branching-narrative fiction *Life's Lottery* (1999), where the reader starts out pre-birth and has the decision of taking the first breath or not (9–11). But one of the most extraordinary and unique forms of game book adaptation is the autobiography published in 2015 by the actor Neil Patrick Harris, titled *Neil Patrick Harris: Choose Your Own Biography,* which bills itself as "an exciting read that puts 'u' back in 'aUtobiography,'" ostensibly involving the reader in creating or re-creating Harris's life.

Attempts to reproduce the choose-your-own-adventure experience in a different format have recently resurfaced in the realm of board-gaming. For example, the 2009 edition of *Tales of Arabian Nights* expands upon the 1985 classic of the same name but offers a much more streamlined set of rules and refined components and graphic art. As the title suggests, players assume the role of characters on a map of the ancient Middle East, encountering djinns and efreets among other mystical creatures in more than two thousand interrelated mini-narratives. Based on a matrix of locations and keywords, a certain narrative paragraph is read to the active player from a colossal "Book of Tales." The active player is given options on how to proceed with the narrative, and then the matrix player consults matrix tables to determine the next designated paragraph for the reading player to continue the narrative. Under this structure the players are engaged in the narrative creation akin to a multifaceted version of Bourbaki's *If* or Newman's *Life Lottery* by interspersing life-or-death decisions for surreal ancient Middle Eastern characters. In effect *Tales of Arabian Nights* intertextually establishes a forking-paths model that is uncannily Borgesian.[11]

Despite attempts to revitalize game books on paper, the most popular mode of reissuing them, however, is digitalizing classic titles. Joe Dever digitized part of his extensive thirty-two-book series as *Joe Dever's Lone Wolf* on mobile and computer platforms beginning in March 2013. Tin Man Games' digitization of the *Fighting Fantasy* series reached a new peak with their 2016 release of *The Warlock of Firetop Mountain,* a sentimental treat for game-book fanatics. This is so far the only reimplementation of game books to feature entirely three-dimensional renderings for the characters as well as their environments. What is surprising about these digitizations is not the evolution of their graphic renderings but the constant harkening back to their paper-based roots. Despite digital technology advancing far beyond the amount of data that a conventional book may contain, the mimicry of the printed page here seems to suggest a strong sense of nostalgia to the fundamental mode of reading and the need to interact with physical objects. In the case of *Warlock of Firetop Mountain,* the high-quality three-dimensional renderings could have easily been accompanied by texts floating on transparent bubbles or scribed by a magically invisible hand, but Tin Man Games opted for text to appear on torn scraps of paper that push each other out of the screen as well as traditional game-book illustrations in two dimensions to accompany the text. In a similar vein, Inkle Studio's digitization of the *Sorcery!* series enhances the sense of adventure by providing a map that charters the protagonist's journey. Furthermore *Sorcery!* adopts the effect of sewn pieces of parchment to frame the text as well as illustrations from the original books. All such reminiscences seem to pay inadvertent homage to how Ts'ui Pên's fictional *Garden* is experienced and explored by Stephen Albert in Borges's short story.

Not all the digitizations of forking-paths narratives emulate the choose-you-own-adventure book format. Telltale Games, a leading company in interactive narratives, employs fully animated and voice-acted sequences that require the player to make timed decisions in reaction to plot twists and character choices. Telltale's business model has always focused on producing parallel interactive narratives of popular franchises such as *A Game of Thrones, The Walking Dead, Jurassic Park,* and *Back to the Future.* These parallel narratives correspond to the forking-paths model and Borges's idea of the living garden of literature. While most game books do provide a sense of choice and dilemma in certain branching points, the timed choices, where players have a few seconds to modify the narrative before the game proceeds down a predetermined path, in Telltale games provide the player with a more comparable experience to the "swarming" effect described in "Garden." Two instances of the swarming effect occur in Borges's story: the first occurs after Albert explains to Yu Tsun the true nature of Ts'ui Pên's masterpiece, thereby in effect restoring his ancestor's name and respectability (*Labyrinths* 27); the second happens when Yu Tsun sees Richard Madden coming up the road to Albert's house (28). Both instances are key turning points where Yu Tsun could have decided to spare Albert. Yu Tsun does not encounter such swarming prior to Albert's explanation of Ts'ui Pên's ingenuity, which enables a person to penetrate the barrier of the linear timeline. He experiences the effect only after realizing his potential agency to redirect his own narrative. Coupled with the fact that Yu Tsun is pressed for time due to Madden's relentless pursuit, the swarming sensations he feels seem to parallel uncannily the experience of timed decisions in the Telltale series, in which players are also pressured with making narrative-altering decisions at "swarming" points.

Telltale's most celebrated title, *The Wolf among Us,*[12] set in the *Fables* comic universe, which recounts a story where fairy-tale characters have been forced out of their original habitat and are now living among humans using a form of magic called "glamour" to hide their true identities. Players reenact the role of Bigby, the Big Bad Wolf, who is now the sheriff of the "Fables" populating parts of New York. The multiple "swarming" points and a solid script full of twists, with easily identifiable fairy-tale archetypes in a bizarre detective noir setting, make *The Wolf among Us* a profoundly immersive experience. However, it is not without its flaws, because, ironically, the twists and elaborations in the plot provide little room for narrative branches that actually make a significant difference. For instance Bigby has the option of killing Tweedledum in episode 3, which should mark a major shift in the plot since the Tweedles are two of the main henchmen for the antagonist, the Crooked Man. But killing Dum has little effect on the outcome in the climatic showdown between Bigby and the Crooked Man in episode 5, where Dum's words and actions are simply assigned to another auxiliary character. This is true of most branching decisions in the game (with the exception of a handful of choices that alter the endings of some minor characters). Since virtually nothing the player does can substantially alter the main plot, the games published by Telltale have often been criticized for being too linear. Indeed the Telltale narratives do not branch out like traditional forking paths, as the branches fork off slightly and swerve swiftly back into the linear plotline.[13] These minor rejoining branches seem more like convergent paths in contrast to Borges's proliferating forking paths.

Although they might seem contrary to the forking time in Borges's "Garden," these convergent-paths narratives more faithfully portray Borges's concepts of swarming points and the forking-paths model than is initially apparent. For example, a sense of convergence can be found in the description of Yu Tsun's first swarming: "I felt about me and within my dark body an invisible, intangible swarming. Not the swarming of the divergent, parallel and finally coalescent armies, but a more inaccessible, more intimate agitation that they in some manner prefigured" (27). The key word *prefigured* suggests that Yu Tsun's choice is somehow predetermined. Moreover Yu Tsun, though forearmed with the knowledge of forking possibilities, seems still unable to diverge from executing his original plan to murder Albert. The tinge of predestination is even more pronounced in the next swarming sensation felt by Yu Tsun:

> Once again I felt the swarming sensation of which I have spoken. It seemed to me that the humid garden that surrounded the house was infinitely saturated with invisible persons. Those persons were Albert and I, secret, busy and multiform in other dimensions of time. I raised my eyes and the tenuous nightmare dissolved. In the yellow and black garden there was only one man; but this man was as strong as a statue . . . this man was approaching along the path and he was Captain Richard Madden. (28)

Upon seeing Madden, Yu Tsun cryptically states to Albert that the "future already exists" and proceeds to shoot him with his revolver (28). In this light *The Wolf among Us* works exactly in accordance with Yu Tsun's statement, as its main plot has already been written despite the facade of choices provided. In other words the narrative plot will always unfold in a set sequence where every deviation and variance somehow converges, whether through circumstance or choice, back to the main storyline.

The converging-paths model offers a sense of illusion of control that is popularly infused in video games, and its popularity highlights the fact that video gamers generally prefer linear narrative development. The model is widely employed in games such as *Stories: The Path of Destinies,* a hack-and-slash action computer game that begins with an animated sequence of opening up a storybook. *Stories* is pertinent to this discussion because between each of its action-oriented segments, the narrative is interrupted with options mimicking the choose-your-own-adventure format presented visually in the layout of a game book. Yet no matter what the player chooses in the first play through the game, the protagonist's death is unavoidable, which then forces the player to restart and repeat the game. The protagonist remembers his death, and the narrative is reset with an animation of the game book flipping back to the starting page. Subsequent runs through the game unlock new options and twists to allow the player eventually (with enough patience) to arrive at the happily-ever-after ending. In this light *Stories* offer another iteration of the converging-paths model entrenched in Borges's "Garden." In fact *Stories* is most aptly provided with the subtitle *The Path of Destinies,* because of the ultimately single narrative path that players are forced to experience no matter how many branching stories (or "destinies") are created in the process.[14]

Despite its advertising a "unique choice-based narrative," *Stories* is extremely conventional in that it embodies the typical traditional game books' one ultimate "good" or "true" ending. In a game book, the good ending can be achieved by being extremely lucky, by cheating, by bookmarking, or, more conventionally, by reading the book multiple times, which usually involves repeated gruesome deaths of the protagonist. The orthodox method creates a disparity in the level of comprehension between the reader and the characters, and each subsequent reading of the book further enhances the disparity. While the characters retain the same mind-set throughout each reincarnation, the sense of swarming for the reader is intensified with each respective reading. As Newman indicates, in his *Life's Lottery* the swarming creates a dramatic irony in that "the reader learns more from multiple paths than Keith [the main protagonist] ever does from his single experience" ("On *Life's Lottery*" 103). In fact Newman included time travel in the novel so that "people would get the message that they *could* go back and start again, or read in parallel sections that show different outcomes from choices" (100). It is unsurprising that Newman relies on time travel in his branching-narrative novel, since the concept of reliving an adventure repeatedly naturally inspires interconnected themes of time traveling and parallel worlds.

The converging-paths model embedded in Borges's "Garden" has generated criticisms focused on the finiteness and the linearity of the short story. However, while each converging branch is enclosed and limited, variations of each branch exist in numerous possible worlds. Hypothetically there may exist an interminable number of variations for each converging branch. A review of time manipulation and possible worlds in the cinematic medium reveals why the converging-paths model is feasible in Borges's grand forking-paths scheme.

▶ Traveling across Multiple Times and Worlds

The time-traveling theme in popular culture has prevailed because, to most people, the nature of time remains opaque. The cyclical mode of reading and rereading game books somewhat parallels experiencing time as recurring in the form of loops. The time-looping genre was inaugurated on screen by *Groundhog Day* (1993), where Phil Connors wakes up each morning to the same day no matter what he does, including suicide. After a span of depression and experimentation, Phil decides to make the best use of his newfound immortality and starts improving his life and others'. However, the optimism of *Groundhog Day,* in which the protagonist escapes his time-looping inferno by making the day and himself perfect, is gradually replaced by a more sinister tone where escaping the loop is either fraught with perils or simply impossible. In *Edge of Tomorrow* (2014), a sci-fi alien invasion thriller in the vein of *Groundhog Day,* William Cage repeats the day he is sent to the battlefield against an alien race invading Earth. In the loop Cage meets Vrataski, a battle-hardened former time-looper, and together they turn the tide of battle against the previously undefeatable aliens by employing their time-manipulation capabilities against them and killing the queen of the alien hive mind. Yet the source material on which *Edge of Tomorrow* is based, the Japanese novel *All You Need Is Kill* (2004) by Hiroshi Sakurazaka, has a more tragic ending. In the novel Cage is actually required to kill Vrataski, whom he has fallen in love with, to escape the loop. In *Edge of Tomorrow / All You Need Is Kill,* death is the one constant element permeating each text, as it both initiates and terminates the loop.

In another popular time-looping title, *Looper* (2012), the concept of time travel is completely centered on death. Time travel is officially banned due to its unpredictable rippling effect, but criminals use it to send people back in time to be murdered so as technically to refrain from committing murder in the future. The executioners who kill people from the future are called loopers, because when the government discovers a specific illegal time-traveling racket in the future, the mob boss will send the relevant loopers' future self back to be murdered by his present self, which is called "closing the loop." Joe, the protagonist of the movie, fails to kill his future self, and the future Joe escapes to hunt down the sociopathic mob boss, who is still a young boy at the time. In the end Joe realizes that the young mob boss only becomes mentally unhinged because of future Joe's actions. Thus before future Joe can do irreparable harm, present Joe commits suicide to erase his future self from existence. While this kind of death does not appear to match the game book model, the idea that death and time cycles are intrinsically linked still persists. The major logical inconsistency in *Looper* is that if the future Joe ceases to exist when the present one dies, the events that future Joe puts into place when he travels back in time (i.e. causing the present Joe to commit suicide) would never have happened in the first place. In an online interview, the director of *Looper,* Rian Johnson, claimed that there are "multiple time lines existing," and it requires the viewers to suspend their linear-timeline logic to "make sense" of them (Lussier).

Similar concerns and conundrums of time looping were already anticipated in Borges's "Garden" as Yu Tsun muses upon *A Thousand and One Nights:*

> I remember too that night which is at the middle of the Thousand and One Nights when Scheherazade (through a magical oversight of the copyist) begins to relate word for word the story of the Thousand and One Nights, establishing the risk of coming once again to the night when she must repeat it, and thus on to infinity. (*Labyrinths* 25)

Even without the "magical oversight," the plot of reading stories night after night offers a sense of repetition inherent to time-looping and reading choose-your-own-adventure books. This idea of cyclical time is soon expanded to the forking-paths model when Stephen Albert explains to Yu Tsun the inner workings of Ts'ui Pên's masterpiece:

> "'The garden of forking paths' was the chaotic novel; the phrase "the various futures (not to all)" suggested to me the forking in time, not in space. A broad rereading of the work confirmed the theory. In all fictional works, each time a man is confronted with several alternatives, he chooses one and eliminates the others; in the fiction of Ts'ui Pên, he chooses—simultaneously—all of them. He creates, in this way, diverse futures, diverse times which themselves also proliferate and fork." (26)

By claiming that all possible choices are viable, Ts'ui Pên's *Garden* delivers the premises of numerous parallel worlds that exist throughout time. The idea of multiple worlds obviously does not originate from Borges, as many ancient religions and philosophies, such as Buddhism, have always acknowledged that numerous other worlds exist alongside the present one. While the many-worlds interpretation of reality was formulated by Hugh Everett in 1957, sixteen years after the publication of Borges's story, Erwin Schrödinger devised his famous thought experiment involving a cat, which attempts to explicate a quantum superposition, in 1935, six years before "Garden" was published. In Western philosophy the idea of possible worlds can be traced back as far as Gottfried Wilhelm Leibniz in the seventeenth century, yet such theories did not "gain any real traction" until the 1960s, when they developed alongside modal logic (Menzel). Whereas philosophy adopted possible worlds to examine the value of fictional issues, literature thrives on fictionality and seeks to establish "a legitimate logical space for fiction" (Ronen 39). Although he was not the first to entertain the idea of possible worlds or to explicate its theoretical principles, Borges is widely attributed to be the first to have conceived of a feasible vehicle for possible worlds to be presented.[15] Perhaps in the future quantum theorists will finally be able to prove the existence of multiple worlds, but for the public these worlds already exist—not just in Borges's fiction but also in choose-your-own-adventure novels, games, movies, and other media. In other words Borges has inseminated the notion and logic of possible worlds in the popular spheres, allowing it to engender and foster other creative progenies in the cultivation of his living garden of forking paths.

One such progeny, *Steins;Gate* (2009), a Japanese visual novel, integrates time travel and parallel worlds to unprecedented levels of interactivity and complexity.[16] This interactive novel, which follows the format of choose-your-own-adventure model, is riddled with logical and temporal leaps and loops that force the reader to reconcile its increasingly twisted plot—even answering a simple text message in game might have drastic impact on the narrative, because the message could have come from the future. In one converging-paths narrative arc, the protagonist, Rintaro Okabe, attempts to save his childhood friend Mayuri Shiina from death, but no matter how much he tries to alter the timeline, she always dies at the exact same time, as if the whole universe conspires to ensure that future. Such a plot is reminiscent of Telltale's typical converging-paths strategy: at certain anchors in the narrative, no matter what decision is made by the individual, it is impossible to affect the outcome of the main plot. However, in the *Steins;Gate* animation series (2010), Okabe's progeny comes back from the future to explain how multiple worlds actually function:

> It might help to think of world lines [i.e. timelines for parallel world] like fibers in a rope. At first blush a rope looks like a single thing, but hone in and it's obviously made up of many interlocking threads. Now each thread is its own thing, independent of its neighbors, but they are all moving in the same direction—that's why it's so strong.

Thus to make fundamental changes to major pivotal or focal events requires an alteration radical enough to jump to not just another thread in the same rope but to another rope entirely. In this light *Steins;Gate* actually validates the converging-paths model that we see not just in the choose-your-own-adventure books but also in the linearity in Borges's "Garden."

Despite its allusions to multiple worlds and forking timelines, Borges's "Garden" is in fact linear. It is easy to overlook that more than ninety percent of the narrative in "The Garden of Forking Paths" is derived from Yu Tsun's incomplete confession that is supposedly written after he has been caught by Madden. The key parts of the confession, such as Victor Runeberg's being captured, Yu Tsun's boarding a train to Ashgrove, and Stephen Albert's being killed, should be accurate. These fixed events are unalterable, because Richard Madden is privy to the information by either observation or deduction. Other than these Yu Tsun, who often describes his thoughts with alarmingly psychotic logic, is potentially unreliable. Perhaps the more coincidental and magical moments, such as those involving Ts'ui Pên's *Garden,* are merely Yu Tsun's ultimate attempt to clear his ancestor's name as he sits in his cell incapable of influencing anything else. In essence reading Yu Tsun's confession is akin to reading a historical text, in which historians construct a history around focal points that are fixed by documented facts and artifacts. Since Yu Sun has already murdered Albert when he writes his confession, his enigmatic statement prior to shooting Albert that the "future already exists" makes perfect sense. The statement marks the murder as a major focal point that Yu Sun has no way of altering despite the bifurcating "swarming" effect. In addition it is no coincidence that Borges's short story begins by questioning an account in a history book attributed to Liddell Hart, a widely recognized contemporary historian. Although Yu Tsun's confession doesn't necessary invalidate Liddell Hart's account, its existence lends credibility to Ts'ui Pên's idea of the forking paths of time and the nature of history itself. In this light the creation of historical narratives or what one perceives to be history is surprisingly similar to the converging-paths model. In many cases historians labor to fit hypothetical narratives into the framework of particular nodes according to physical records or secondhand transcripts by creating their own living paths. A breakthrough in historical studies often involves finding another piece of an evidential node that alters the common hypothesis of what might have happened—which is essentially the overarching narrative structure of Borges's "Garden," where the narrator attempts to rewrite part of the history published by Liddel Hart. Returning to the vision of many worlds proposed in *Steins;Gate,* a future where Albert is not killed by Yu Tsun is not impossible; there simply needs to be a major shift outside of Borges's "Garden," a tightly structured rope that is particularly unyielding. Prior to the time of writing "Garden," Borges went through periods of happiness and depression (Williamson 244–59). One major source of both his joy and sadness was the romantic rejection of him by Haydée Lange, a childhood friend (244–45). In a timeline where Lange married Borges, it is possible Yu Tsun would not kill Albert, since "Garden" might not have been written at all.

What is so ingenious about Borges's "Garden" is not that it is incredibly perceptive of history but that it is so accurately perceptive of the future. By setting up the possibility of the multiplicity of time and history, the story has firmly established itself as one of the fixed focal points that all future texts about temporal anomalies refer to and refract from. The small seed of time looping planted in Borges's "Garden" is now in full bloom in popular culture. Time loops have become a staple trope that is recycled in many popular titles featuring fantasy and fiction, with at least two Hollywood blockbusters in 2016 incorporating time loops in their narratives: *Miss Peregrine's Home for Peculiar Children* and *Doctor Strange.* In 2017 *Happy Death Day* and *Naked* both recycled the *Groundhog Day* trope of repeatedly reliving a single day as their main premise. This goes to show exactly how comfortable viewers feel with the idea of time being fluid and malleable. Recent popular action movies, despite their plots' involving no time distortion or loops, more often than not feature slow motion or bullet-time moments, a technique perfected by the Wachowskis' *Matrix* trilogy. The audiences' acceptance of shifting gears in visual time can be partially attributed to advances in cinematography, but it is perhaps also in part due to exposure to the malleability of time in movies and other media stemming from the Borgesian branch. And although the fundamental inspiration for the alternate reality in *The Matrix* can be traced back to the philosophical inquiries of René Descartes, Plato, and

Zhuangzi, the effect of entering a virtual world at the turn of the twentieth century from a postapocalyptic future is much like time traveling across different possible worlds. In addition an allusion to time loops in the form of historical cycles is made in the second movie of the trilogy as the Architect (creator of the Matrix) reveals that Zion (the human resistance outside of the Matrix) and Neo (the savior who can alter the computer generated reality inside the Matrix) are simply part of the rebooting process of the Matrix, a necessary recurrent cycle in its history.

Unlike the cyclical *Matrix,* straightforward time travel drives the plot of *The Terminator* (1984). However, as each subsequent movie in that franchise has introduced more time travel (and actors/actresses), the plot has become more convoluted and illogical, since multiple strands of time travel are difficult to reconcile and justify. The most recent attempt to revitalize the aging Arnold Schwarzenegger, *Terminator Genisys* (2015), rebooted the franchise by erasing most of the plots from the previous movies and stating that the multiple time travels have caused the timeline to shift to a different rope (to use *Steins;Gate*'s term), so that "Judgment Day" (when artificial intelligence destroys the known world) is postponed and the main characters' faces and characteristics are transfigured. The explanation conveniently accounts for different actors and actresses playing the roles of Kyle Reese, John Connor, and Sarah Connor. Even the iconic T-800 model Terminators—mass-manufactured robots—are played by actors other than Schwarzenegger.[17] *Genisys* ends with the latest Reese stating that the "future is not set," which sounds suspiciously like a forking-paths bifurcation of Yu Tsun's converging-paths utterance, "The future already exists."

One pivotal Borgesian progeny that epitomizes the interlayering of narratives is Netflix's *Black Mirror: Bandersnatch,* which premiered on December 28, 2018. Marketed as an "interactive film" associated with the highly acclaimed dark sci-fi series *Black Mirror, Bandersnatch* allows viewers to choose the paths of a psychologically troubled protagonist, Stefan, with their remote controls from the comfort of their armchairs. With Netflix's successful push for producing interactive dramas, together with how popular the possible-worlds scenario is on the big screen,[18] Borges's "forking paths" concept is now more prevalent and pervasive than before and is literally in the living rooms of families all over the globe. The main plot of *Black Mirror: Bandersnatch* is about a young program designer trying to code a choose-your-own-adventure book, *Bandersnatch,* into a video game of the same name. The penetrating postmodern self-critique of the forking-paths model, already evident in the plot, is pushed further by characters becoming aware of the time loops, predicting the future, and even becoming aware of the viewers controlling them. According to *Variety* there are "over a trillion unique permutations of the story," with roughly five "real" endings, and most of the time the viewer will experience multiple endings before the final credits roll (Roettgers). When the viewer encounters a dead end (when things go horribly wrong), the film cuts into a montage of brief flashbacks to get the viewer up to a point where the choices can make a difference. Some of the "real" endings can be achieved only after several such trial and errors. This is the main method that the creators of *Black Mirror: Bandersnatch* use to provide their viewers with roughly similar viewing experiences despite the film's "trillion permutations."

Despite forking paths, interactive narratives discussed here appear invariably to follow the converging-paths model by featuring some form of conclusive ending.[19] While infinite futures might exist for human beings, we can live only one life, and our physical limitation prohibits us from experiencing true infinity. Yet these popular interactive narratives do offer a glimpse of possibility into the infinite. And the staggering number of such narratives produced year after year is overwhelming. The totality of all these converging branches, for a single human being, is perhaps as close to infinity as our minds can comprehend.

▶ Bifurcating the Intertextual Living Garden

During their discussion of Ts'ui Pên's work, Albert tries to explain the key factor in the novel:

> "In a riddle whose answer is chess, what is the only prohibited word?"
>
> I thought for a moment and replied, "The word *chess*."
>
> "Precisely," said Albert. "*The Garden of Forking Paths* is an enormous riddle, or parable, whose theme is time. . . ." (27)

In Borges's "Garden" the word *time* is repeated several times in the text, and yet very few readers can claim to have solved Borges's ultimate riddle. Perhaps this self-reflexive answer still remains enigmatic to most of its readers, since no one truly understands time (despite the fact that everyone is under its influence). As previously noted, critics argue against the practicality of the polyphonous concepts in "Garden." Indeed Borges is confined to the medium of the printed page, and a pure forking-paths model is nearly impossible to facilitate on paper. Logically Ts'ui Pên's *Garden* is an implausible contraption, since, according to Stephen Albert, Ts'ui Pên "chooses—simultaneously—all" choices and "creates, in this way, diverse futures, diverse times which themselves also proliferate and fork" (26). Such a contraption goes contrary to all the choose-your-own-adventure books in existence, as even the most proliferating ones only provide a handful of choices, and even then it is not humanly possible to experience all of the choices simultaneously. Thus Ts'ui Pên's *Garden* can be viewed as yet another red herring to mask the identity of the real garden.

While the story in "Garden" is indeed linear, the layering of the main narrative, a fictionalized version of Liddel Hart's account of World War I, Yu Tsun's fragmented confession, Ts'ui Pên's *Garden,* and Stephen Albert's interpretation of Ts'ui Pên are not simply glaring constructs that mimic the multiple-world hypothesis concocted by Albert and Yu Tsun, but are rather clues to the final riddle of the real garden. The last key is provided after the story in Borges's curt dedication to Victoria Ocampo (*Labyrinths* 29).[20] The three italicized words "*For Victoria Ocampo*" have not generated much attention; even Chibka and Gray do not engage much with this seemingly meaningless appendage. Indeed such dedications are not unique to "Garden," since Borges dedicated many of his short stories with similar stubs of text to various friends and people he admired. Yet the presence of this post-narrative dedication attached to a story centered around forking time and multiple worlds clearly alerts the reader to the fact that multiple realities already exist, that is, there is a reality outside of the fiction. Yu Tsun's apologetic "The future already exists" can be read not only as a defeatist predestined worldview, but also as an affirmation of the actual existence of fictional realities generated by authors around the world(s). Furthermore Ocampo is known for her achievements as the editor of *Sur,* an influential literary magazine published in Argentina, which in turn reviewed "Garden" favorably, claiming that it "invented a new genre" for fiction (Williamson 259). In this light Borges accomplished a similar potency to what Northrop Frye observed in Romantic poetry—bringing the reality of "Garden" into being through the structure of his fiction and his dedication.[21]

Ultimately Borges's "Garden" provides a riddle and an answer that cannot be examined within the short story alone. While Borges's real garden has already begun blossoming outside of the short story, it requires time to flourish into the complex and meandering labyrinth of collaboration. One must admire Borges for simultaneously revealing the answer to his riddle yet hiding it in plain sight. The key to creating the garden is indeed time—not the improbable forking time that does not exist in actuality for human beings, but the time to plant that germinating seed of such possibility in a fictional reality. This study has focused mainly on popular culture, one of the main living paths in Borges's garden, but surely other paths exist that develop self-perpetuating realities across multiple dimensions different from ours. Hence Borges's "The Garden of Forking Paths" is comparable to a garden sewn with seeds that has gradually come into fruition since its inception. The short story itself is the garden of forking paths, not because of the varying interpretations of its reading, nor the multiple jarring layers of embedded narratives, nor the infinite possibilities swarming Yu Shen's decisions, but because of the germination of a culture that continuously cultivates ever-diverging narratives in countless imaginary worlds. Borges's "Garden" is the kernel from which has grown the real garden, the collaborative garden that continues to fork and join, converge and diverge, and bifurcate and intertwine. Most important, Borges's living garden will continue to grow its forking paths and to generate different realities.

For Livvy Tsai

Notes

1. I would like to express my sincere gratitude to Prof. Allen Miller, whose tireless dedication made the entire volume possible. I also owe much to the support of Prof. Bennett Fu, Prof. Chi-she Li, and Prof. Jerry Weng in organizing the "Literature and the Global Public" symposium, where an early draft of this chapter was presented to the chagrin of the audience.

2. From its initial Spanish publication in 1941 to its first English translation in 1948 in *Ellery Queen's Mystery Magazine* and two subsequent translations in 1962 and 1998, critics have been trying to figure out the differences in each version of Borges's meandering fictional garden of symbols and ambiguities. Paula Rabinowitz, for instance, spends several pages debating why one of the key characters in the fiction, Dr. Stephen Albert, was originally named Stephen Corbie in *Ellery Queen's Mystery Magazine* (179–84). Rabinowitz suggests several possibilities ranging from referencing a Welsh town to invoking Queen Victoria and surmises that the change is likely due to "authorial instability" (184).

3. These texts are not alluded to at random: the *Annals* is mentioned before Yu Tsun learns of Ts'ui Pên's *Garden* to provide a sense of traditional linear history; *Hung Lu* [or *Lou*] *Meng* is a masterpiece of Chinese fiction that attempts to epitomize life by featuring the rise and fall of a family with more than four hundred characters; encyclopedias aim to contain all branches of human knowledge and experience; some stories in *The Thousand and One Nights* feature multiple layers of embedded narratives and share structural similarities with "Garden." In fact the last two have generated minor branches of Borges's living garden in academia: Haiqing Sun argues that "the simulation of a Chinese garden in an English residence, the imagined multi-universal garden, and the unity of labyrinth and text, all carry reflections of *Hong Lou Meng*" (20); and Evelyn Fishburn finds that *The Thousand and One Nights* "has a revelatory effect, allowing the sinologist Albert to decipher Ts'ui Pen's perplexing novel, and see it as a metaphor for our labyrinthine universe" (153).

4. Following Borges's example, the interactive narratives in this study are not limited to the traditional sense that the reader/user has to interact physically with the work. Thus while movies and television shows are generally not associated with the term *interactive,* since they traditionally feature little to no interaction between the viewer and the medium, the ones in this discussion are interactive on a more psychological or interpretive level, since they require the viewer to be actively engaged in mentally puzzling out the labyrinthine mystery presented on the screen.

5. Although it might signal the incompleteness of Yu Tsun's confession, the exterior narrative only states that the "first two pages of the document are missing" without commenting on the ending (19).

6. For a thorough investigation to the discrepancies in the translations referring to Liddell Hart, please see Chibka 107–111.

7. Translations or translated texts feature saliently in Borges's "Garden." Stephen Albert translates Ts'ui Pên's letter and *Garden* (at least in part) into English, and various oriental or historical texts are mentioned. Efraín Kristal argues in his *Invisible Work* that Borges's fictions "can be read as solutions to problems resolved in the process of translation or as responses to works he translated" (xvii), and the significance of translation can be observed in the fact that the "majority of Borges's short stories include at least one character who translates" (88). Sergio Waisman in *Borges and Translation* maintains that there is "no other writer for whom translation is as integral a part of his or her literary production as it is for Borges" (11). It is not surprising that Borges put so much emphasis in translation, as it is one of the most direct forms of creative intertextuality. Thus it is perhaps excusable for me to analyze a South American writer by only referencing his translated works in English.

8. A precursor series to *Choose Your Own Adventure* was called *The Adventures of You* (1976–77).

9. For example these studies never examine the most prominent and persistent "turn to page X" or "go to paragraph X" commands in choose-your-own-adventures that require the reader to interact physically with the game book and its narrative.

10. The author employs Nicholas Bourbaki as a pseudonym to pay homage to Nicolas Bourbaki, a collective alias for a group of mathematicians that originated in France, also known as the Bourbaki group.

11. The board-game branch of Borges's living garden continues to grow from *The Thousand and One Nights,* later adopted by Jason Maxwell in his 2012 *Agents of SMERSH* to feature international intrigue and espionage. Ryan Laukat appropriated the "Book of Tales" concept in his 2015 European strategy game *Above and Below,* which blends the trope of village building with branching narratives that directly influence the village construction. In its 2017 sequel *Near and Far,* Laukat provided a campaign mode where the narratives are more sequential and interlocking for individual characters. In fact two of the most popular titles according to *BoardGameGeek* in 2017 employ the game-book concept: *Gloomhaven,* where the players decide the progression of the campaign narrative after each tactical card skirmish, and *The 7th Continent,* where cards tiles are assembled procedurally to create a map with numbers corresponding to textual passages in the game book. At the end of 2018, *Tainted Grail,* a narrative-driven adventure game combining elements from all the above, which raised almost five million pounds on Kickstarter toward funding its publication in 2019–20, exemplified the perennial popularity and longevity of Borges's forking-path concept.

12. *The Wolf among Us* is highly regarded by the video gaming community, receiving

a 97 percent positive recommendation out of more than sixteen thousand reviews on the Steam platform.

13. However, this doesn't mean that the players have no agency in the game. The minor or supporting characters' reactions or fates, the availability of certain choices open to the player, and objects in the surrounding environment can actually be affected. In fact Telltale entertains the feature interactivity by tallying statistics of its players' major decisions after each episode. In the instance of Tweedledum, roughly 53 percent of the players decided to spare his life.

14. While the order of each segment of the narrative can change according to the players' choices, the players end up forced to experience all of the segments if they play the game to completion.

15. For a full discussion on Borges and a history of quantum studies, please refer to Floyd Merrell's "Jorge Luis Borges and Early Quantum Labyrinths." Merrell notes that a passage of Borges's "Garden" is employed as the epigraph of a Princeton University publication dedicated to explaining Hugh Everett's quantum theory (52).

16. The visual novel is a form of interactive fiction with animation and voice acting. *Steins;Gate* has reached cult status among fans, and the visual novel was later developed into a popular animation series in 2010. The fact that *Steins;Gate* has successfully convinced tens of thousands of players that a time-traveling device can be built out of a faulty old microwave oven is perhaps a testament to its immense influence.

17. *Terminator* is not the first franchise to employ Borges's "Garden" as a rebooting strategy; *Star Trek* (2009) also completely overhauled the 1965 original series that entertained millions of fans by having Spock time travel through a black hole and alter "history" forever.

18. For instance, in 2018 *Spider-Man: Into the Spider-Verse* explicated the theory of forking paths and possible worlds with less than one minute of screen time on an instructional video playing in the background when the protagonist sneaks into a classroom. The whimsical brevity of the explanation demonstrates the confidence of the scriptwriter that the audience would already be familiar enough with Borges's concept of forking paths to accept six spider-persons (and a pig, fittingly named Spider-Ham) in a parallel dimension where Dr. Octopus is a female and Kingpin kills Peter Parker. Yet to properly gauge the extensive influence of Borges's "Garden," it is perhaps more fruitful to look outside of the spheres of sci-fi and fantasy. The counterintuitive concepts of possible worlds and alternate timelines are so prevalent and accepted that even romantic musicals such as *La La Land* are appropriating these tropes. Toward the end of the movie, the two protagonists, now leading separate lives, are projected into a long dance routine featuring a "what if" situation where they end up together and raising a family. The fact that such device appears without explanation in a genre that does not feature killer robots and pointed-eared humanoids seems to suggest a much wider general reception of a Borgesian concept of infinite branching time.

19. Even the labyrinthine *Steins;Gate* has only six possible endings, with just one of them labeled as the "true" ending.

20. In *Ficciones* "To Victoria Ocampo" is printed at the start of the short story on page 89.

21. Frye in his discussion of Romantic poetry finds that "the emphasis is not on what we have called sense, but on the constructive power of the mind where reality is brought into being by experience" (207).

Works Cited

Above and Below. Designed by Ryan Laukat, Red Raven Games, 2015.

Agents of SMERSH. Designed by Jason Maxwell, 8th Summit, 2012.

All You Need Is Kill. By Ryosuke Takeuchi et al., VIZ Media, 2014.

Black Mirror: Bandersnatch. Directed by David Slade. Netflix, 2018.

Borges, Jorge Luis. *Ficciones.* Grove, 1962.

——. *Labyrinths: Selected Stories and Other Writings.* New Directions, 1964.

Bourbaki, Nicholas. *If.* Livingston, 2014.

Bruin, Leon de, Michiel van Elk, and Albert Newen. "Reconceptualizing Second-Person Interaction." *Frontiers in Neuroscience,* June 2012, www.ncbi.nlm. nih.gov/pmc/articles/PMC3368580.

Burgin, Richard. *Conversations with Jorge Luis Borges.* Holt, Rinehart & Winston, 1969.

Chibka, Robert L. "The Library of Forking Paths." *Representations* vol. 56, 1996, pp. 106–22.

Ciccoricco, David. "Borges, Technology, and the Same Infinite Substance as the Night." *Cy-Borges: Memories of the Posthuman in the Work of Jorge Luis Borges,* edited by Stefan Herbrechter and Ivan Callus, Bucknell UP, 2009, pp. 73–87.

Coherence. Directed by James Ward Byrkit. Bellanova Films, 2013.

Continuum. Reunion Pictures, 2012–15.

Dever, Joe. *Lone Wolf* series. Beaver, 1984–88.

Dill, Karen E. *How Fantasy Becomes Reality: Seeing through Media Influence.* Oxford UP, 2009.

Doctor Strange. Directed by Scott Derrickson. Disney, 2016.

Edge of Tomorrow. Directed by Doug Liman. Warner Bros., 2014.

Fishburn, Evelyn. "Traces of the *Thousand and One Nights* in Borges." *Variaciones Borges,* vol. 17, 2004, pp. 143–58.

Fringe. Bad Robot, 2008–13.

Frye, Northrop. *The Stubborn Structure: Essays on Criticism and Society Anatomy of Criticism: Four Essays.* Methuen, 1980.

Gloomhaven. Designed by Isaac Childres, Cephalofair Games, 2017.

Gray, Jeffrey. "Borges and the Legacy of 'The Garden of Forking Paths.'" *The Labyrinth,* edited by Harold Bloom, Bloom's Literary Criticism, 2009, pp. 29–36.

Harris, Neil Patrick. *Neil Patrick Harris: Choose Your Own Biography.* Three Rivers, 2014.

Jackson, Steven, and Ian Livingston. *Fighting Fantasy* series. Puffin, 1982–.

Joe Dever's Lone Wolf. Forge Reply, 29 Oct 2013.

Joyce, Michael. *Afternoon: A Story.* Eastgate Systems, 1987.

Kristal, Efraín. *Invisible Work: Borges and Translation.* Vanderbilt UP, 2002.

La La Land. Directed by Damien Chazelle. Black Label Media, 2016.

Liddell Hart, B. H. *A History of the World War: 1914–1918.* Faber and Faber, 1934.

Looper. Directed by Rian Johnson. Endgame Entertainment, 2012.

Lussier, Germain. "Ten Mysteries in 'Looper' Explained by Director Rian Johnson." *Slashfilm: Blogging the Reel World,* 28 Sept. 2012, www.slashfilm.com/ten-mysteries-in-looper-explained-by-director-rian-johnson.

The Matrix, The Matrix Reloaded, and *The Matrix Revolutions.* Directed by Lana Wachowski and Lily Wachowski. Warner Bros., 1999–2003.

Menzel, Christopher. "Possible Worlds." *The Stanford Encyclopedia of Philosophy,* edited by Edward N. Zalta, plato.stanford.edu/archives/win2016/entries/possible-worlds.

Merrell, Floyd. "Jorge Luis Borges and Early Quantum Labyrinths." *Science, Literature, and Film in the Hispanic World,* edited by Jerry Hoeg and Kevin S. Larsen. Palgrave Macmillan, 2006, pp. 49–73.

Mildorf, Jarmila. "Reconsidering Second-Person Narration and Involvement." *Language and Literature* vol. 25, no. 2, 2016, pp. 145–58.

Miss Peregrine's Home for Peculiar Children. Directed by Ransom Riggs. Twentieth Century Fox, 2016.

Montgomery, R. A., et al. *Choose Your Own Adventure* series. Chooseco, 2006–.

Moulthrop, Stuart. *Victory Garden.* Eastgate Systems, 1991.

Near and Far. Designed by Ryan Laukat, Red Raven Games, 2017.

Newman, Kim. *Life's Lottery.* Titan, 2014.

——. "On *Life's Lottery.*" *Second Person: Role-Playing and Story in Games and Playable Media,* edited by Pat Harrigan and Noah Wardrip-Fruin, MIT, 2007, pp. 99–103.

Rabinowitz, Paula. "'The Abysmal Problem of Time': Dubbing Borges's Garden." *Cy-Borges: Memories of the Posthuman in the Work of Jorge Luis Borges,* edited by Stefan Herbrechter and Ivan Callus, Bucknell UP, 2009, pp. 178–97.

Roettgers, Janko. "Netflix Takes Interactive Storytelling to the Next Level with *Black Mirror: Bandersnatch.*" *Variety,* 28 Dec. 2018, variety.com/2018/digital/ news/netflix-black-mirror-bandersnatch-interactive-1203096171.

Ronen, Ruth. *Possible Worlds in Literary Theory.* Cambridge UP, 1994.

Sassón-Henry, Perla. *Borges 2.0: From Text to Virtual Worlds.* Peter Lang, 2007.

The 7th Continent. Designed by Ludovic Roudy and Bruno Sauter, Serious Poulp, 2017.

Sorcery! Inkle Studio, 2013–16.

Spider-Man: Into the Spider-Verse. Directed by Bob Persichetti, Peter Ramsey, and Rodney Rothman. Sony Pictures Entertainment, 2018.

Steins;Gate: The Complete Series. Funimation, 30 Sept. 2014.

Stories: The Path of Destinies. Spearhead Games, 12 Apr. 2016.

Sun, Haiqing. "*Hong Lou Meng* in Jorge Luis Borges's Narrative." *Variaciones Borges,* vol. 22, 2006, pp. 15–33.

"Tainted Grail: The Fall of Avalon." Kickstarter, 5 Dec 2018, www.kickstarter.com/projects/awakenrealms/tainted-grail-the-fall-of-avalon.

Tales of Arabian Nights. By Anthony J. Gallela et al., Z-Man, 2009.

The Terminator. Directed by James Cameron. Hemdale, 1984.

Terminator Genisys. Directed by Alan Taylor. Paramount, 2015.

Triangle. Directed by Christopher Smith. Icon Entertainment, 2009.

Waisman, Sergio. *Borges and Translation: The Irreverence of the Periphery.* Bucknell UP, 2005.

Walrdrip-Fruin, Noah, and Nick Montfort, eds. *The New Media Reader.* MIT, 2003.

The Warlock of Firetop Mountain. Tin Man Games, 31 Aug. 2016.

Ward, Michael J. *DestinyQuest* series. Gollancz, 2013–.

Williamson, Edwin. *Borges: A Life.* Viking, 2004.

The Wolf among Us. Telltale Games, 11 Oct 2013.

Part Three

The Global Object World

Literature and Ontology in Late Capitalism

The Ontological Turn

A New Problematic for Literature and Globalization

Meili Steele

One of the key problems for the study of globalization and culture is coming up with a problematic that can perspicuously display the contribution of literature to normative debates about cultural values and economic forces. I say this because most Western theories of modernity and globalization are compromised by two fundamental philosophical mistakes that contribute to the mischaracterizations of the West and others. The first is the reduction of modernization to a process that subordinates the analysis of literature, culture, and normativity to some larger force, such as rationalization, secularization, the division of labor, or the movements of empire.[1] The second, which is sometimes combined with the first, I will call the "disengaged" understanding of reason, according to which we must abstract ourselves from culture and language in order to think through principles. We can see this most clearly in normative philosophy, where two disengaged strains of thought are dominant, moral/political constructivism and utilitarianism. Utilitarianism ignores how individuals are embedded in language and culture, and it reasons about the goodness of an action for individuals or collectivities in terms of quantities of benefit.[2] As Daniel Little says, utilitarian and materialist approaches maintain "that there is a significant core of human agency that is species specific but not culturally specific and the content of this description is sufficient, in many social circumstances, to generate good social explanation of social patterns."[3]

The other way of abandoning literature and culture as resources of reasoning comes from moral constructivism, which Carla Bagnoli defines as "the view that the moral principles we ought to accept or follow are the ones that agents would agree to or endorse were they to engage in a hypothetical or idealized process of rational deliberation."[4] When we seek clarity in matters of morality, politics, or aesthetics, we should try to detach ourselves from the confusions of history and think in the realm of pure concepts that we generate through a thought experiment, such as Jürgen Habermas's "ideal speech situation" or John Rawls's "original position."[5] When Kant—the foundational exemplar of this tradition—looked at history, he saw meaningless violence and chaos without a pattern; however, his historical confusion did not trouble his moral certainty when he came up with the categorical imperative. How did such clear normative concepts emerge from the bloody wars and messy ideologies of history, and why do they continue as the site of specious clarity about rights, justice, and other principles for the West that it then tries to export?[6] I think we can do better than this, by taking an ontological turn, a turn that will help display the changing shapes of a society's collective imagination through time and the role that individual works of literature play in the construction and revision of these collective structures.

I will develop my argument in four steps. First I will look at the work of Edward Said to illustrate the persistence of the unproductive Western assumptions about literature and world politics from a well-known thinker. I will then work through two forms of ontological investigation, a hermeneutic one proposed by Charles Taylor and a Foucauldian one developed by Talal Asad. In the third section, I show how the ontological turn enables us to discuss the globalization of religion with improved clarity because it permits us to analyze what sociologist Olivier Roy called "the exculturation of the religious." In the last section, I will rectify an important lacuna in the work of ontological thinkers, which is how individual works of literature can argue with and through the collective imagination.

▶ Said's Universe: Ideological Objects, Cosmopolitan Subjects, Constructed Principles

In Said's landmark work, *Orientalism,* he examines how Western literature and the social sciences invented an Oriental other for purposes of invidious comparison and political exploitation. In this view social scientific studies and aesthetic texts display Western fantasies of the Orient rather than depicting the societies under study.[7] In *Culture and Imperialism,* Said goes beyond *Orientalism* by adding the work of non-Western writers to his critique of the West. In this study Said adopts the contrapuntal strategy of juxtaposing stories of imperialism (chapter 2) with stories of "resistance and opposition" (chapter 3). He wants to expose the ways that the ideologies of Western imperialism and of those cultures that fought against it have locked the world into unproductive misunderstandings.

Said does not offer a theory of imperialism but an ethical/political reading of literature. As he says, "Imperialism and the novel fortified each other to such a degree that it is impossible to read one without in some way dealing with the other."[8] Said views the literature of the colonizer and the colonized as mystifications that have prevented us from seeing how power and cultural identity work together to carve up the world into competing islands. He hopes to reconnect these islands by telling their stories in a way that breaks down the imperialist and nationalist narratives: "My interpretive political aim (in the broadest sense) [is] to make concurrent those views and experiences that are ideologically and culturally closed to each other and that attempt to distance or suppress other views and experiences."[9]

By juxtaposing competing narratives, Said unmasks previous accounts of the relations between the West and the East; however, he is not interested in writing a more adequate historical account of these relations. His aim is not to place these texts in the context of historical forces or discursive systems but to point out with a short maxim the ethical/political shortcomings that historical actors rationalized: "What appeared to be detached and apolitical culture disciplines [depended] upon a quite sordid history of imperialist ideology and colonialist practice."[10] We get a series of moral judgments and not an account of the collective imagination that these texts are contesting and/or reproducing.

Said understands traditions and cultures only as ideological traps to be exposed rather than as resources to be reworked.[11] While he is, of course, eloquent on his empirical positionality—that is, his upbringing in Palestine, Egypt, and America—he says little about how he situates his thought in any traditions. Literature and "culture" are defined only negatively as entrapment.[12] Said is so concerned that any ethical/political shape will become a reified enclave that he gives no theoretical, ethical, or narrative space to the positive construction of identity, including the identity of his ideal community. In leaping to principles detached from history, Said is following the constructivist tradition, in which moral/political judgments are determined by principles that, to recall Bagnoli's words cited above, "agents would agree to or endorse were they to engage in a hypothetical or idealized process of rational deliberation."

For instance, in his remarks on Jane Austen's *Mansfield Park,* he brings out Austen's silence with regard to the colonial activities that support the ruling class at the same time that she devotes considerable space to the textures of life at Mansfield Park. He tells us that "the task [of the critic] is to lose neither a true historical sense of the first [imperial force], nor a full enjoyment or appreciation of the second, all the while seeing both together."[13] The truth of history is the imperialism in the text; what saves the text from being merely an instrument of oppression is its aesthetic dimension that we "appreciate." But such an appreciation in no way changes the way the text's ethical and political engagement with the social imaginaries of its time or ours.

These problems in Said's model are not addressed in his discussions of third-world writers such as Frantz Fanon and C. L. R. James. Said celebrates these thinkers because they anticipate his own empirical insight that "Western and non-western experiences" belong "together because they are connected by imperialism" and because of their methodologies, which have "nomadic, migratory, and anti-narrative energy."[14] Yet his discussion of James does not sort through the different strains in James's thought; instead Said praises him only for his ability to juxtapose discrepant experiences, praise that is all too thin. Instead of engaging the content of James's work, Said praises merely formal features, such as "heteroglot" or "hybrid" qualities. Why is heteroglot discourse per se a good thing regardless of the content or context?[15] In the same way, "contrapuntalism" evacuates interpretive judgment, for it simply urges us to juxtapose previously separated narratives and discourses without offering guidelines about how to read them, about what the ensuing dialogue might look like or what the consequences of this confrontation might be for each side. Said has called his approach a combination of the methods of Foucault and Noam Chomsky: "*Orientalism* is theoretically inconsistent and I designed it that way. I didn't want Foucault's method . . . to override what I was trying to put forward. The notion of a kind of noncoercive knowledge, which I come to at the end of the book, was deliberately anti-Foucault."[16]

However, Said is not Foucauldian in his historical readings or in his moral judgments. He presents the West's "orientalist" projections from Aeschylus to Henry Kissinger, without looking at the specific discursive systems in place at the time the texts manifesting Orientalism were produced, an approach that Foucault never adopted. Said pulls out distorted Western projections from selected texts and then shows "how all representations are constructed, for what purpose, by whom, and with what components."[17] Literature is always in the service of a misguided ideology whose claims should be criticized by principles that are detached from any culture. The ontological turn, by contrast, opens up the complexities of conflicting social imaginaries, providing new places for intercultural interrogation. I begin with Taylor on secularity.

▶ Taylor's Hermeneutic Ontology

The starting place for Taylor's, Foucault's, and Asad's problematics is their development of the Heideggerian notion of "thrownness" (*Geworfenheit*). In this view the subject should be understood as Dasein, thrown into language, practices, and social imaginaries that can never be fully thematized and objectified. Dasein has no power over its ground, for it is "never existent *before* its ground, but only *from it* and *as it.* Thus being the ground means never to have power over one's ownmost being from the ground up."[18] This problematic seeks to overcome the massive mistake of Western modernity, which is to conceive of the world as a collection of objects abstracted from the world. For Heidegger we find ourselves in a prestructured world of value, what Heidegger calls "care," a normative landscape and not a neutral space for performing analysis, as we see from Descartes to Kant.

For Heidegger and Taylor, it is important to read through these structures from the inside, from the point of view of Dasein or the subject, as well as to read them from the outside, as collective ways of being. Care is prior to reason, and we must understand ourselves phenomenologically before we can understand ourselves logically. Our thoughts, actions, and sentences do not spring from spontaneous, autonomous sources—as we saw in constructivism above. Rather utterances and actions depend on background of practices and imaginaries that are logically prior to choice and reflection. In *A Secular Age,* Taylor says, "We are in fact all acting, thinking and feeling out of backgrounds and frameworks which we do not fully understand. To ascribe total personal responsibility to us for these is to want to leap out of the human condition."[19] The subject should not be understood as a thinker standing over against the world. When we encounter a hammer, we don't see an object made available by Kantian categories. Instead we encounter a universe of structured meanings and activities that connect hammers to nails, to houses, and so on. Because this world precedes every individual thought or action, any politics or morality is inescapably built on norms that are already in place, on norms that are not constructed.[20]

In order to get historical nuance into Heidegger's notorious Olympian history, Taylor's *Modern Social Imaginaries* draws on the notion of social imaginaries to discuss the collective, transsubjective historical shapes that make up this background, such as the public sphere, popular sovereignty, and secularity. He says that

> the social imaginary is not a set of ideas; rather, it is what enables, through making sense of, the practices of a society. . . . [Thus] the notion of moral order goes beyond some proposed schedule of norms that ought to govern our mutual relations and/or political life. . . . The image of order carries a definition not only of what is right, but of the context in which makes sense to strive for and hope to realize the right.[21]

The social imaginary concerns the ways that "ordinary people 'imagine' their social surroundings and this is often not expressed in theoretical terms but in images, stories, legends, etc."[22] Here literary works are looked at not as individual works but for how they help to bring about collective changes that have normative importance. An example of this reading of literature can be found in Benedict Anderson's *Imagined Communities,* which analyzes how the novel and the newspaper helped change the shape of time and nationality in the Western collective imagination, not how particular works intervene in local debates, which I will address later.

Taylor is not making a sociological claim, such as Anderson's structural explanation, but a philosophical claim about the priority of social ontology to isolated facts or norms. We can clarify the ontological approach by contrasting it with others on the issue of secularity. Political and legal philosophers seek to adjudicate controversial questions, such as headscarves in school and the display of the Ten Commandments on state grounds, by constructing norms of mutual accommodation (Secularity 1). Sociologists may focus on gathering statistics about church, temple, or synagogue attendance as evidence of secularization (Secularity 2). But before these facts or norms can appear, they require a background of intersubjective meanings that lets them show up for us as phenomena (Secularity 3). These things show up not neutrally but as mattering or not. Secularity 3 concerns the shift in "the conditions of belief" or historical ontology. On this view the "shift to secularity consists of a move from a society where belief in God is unchallenged and unproblematic to one in which it is understood to be one option among others, and frequently not the easiest to embrace." In other words Taylor wants to examine the shift "which takes us from a society in which it was virtually impossible not to believe in God, to one in which faith, even for the staunchest believers, is one possibility among others."[23] Of course people can bring different ideas and attitudes to secularity,

> but what they do not bring into the negotiations is the set of ideas and norms constitutive of [secularity itself]. This must be the common property of society before there can be any question of [debate]. Hence, they are not subjective meanings, the property of one or some individual, but rather intersubjective meanings, which are constitutive of the social matrix in which individuals find themselves and act.[24]

What Taylor takes from Heidegger is an articulation of social embedding that is deeper than ideology, and that is something that he shares with those who work in a Foucauldian line despite their differences, for they too investigate the ontological furniture of society, an approach that is often called "the political" rather than politics, as we saw in Secularity 1. Chantal Mouffe makes explicit the Heideggerian background to the study of the political: "Political science . . . deals with the empirical field of 'politics,' [whereas] political theory . . . enquire[s] not about facts of 'politics' but about the essence of the 'political.' If we wanted to express such a distinction in a philosophical way, we could, following Heidegger, say that politics refers to the *'ontic'* level while 'the political' has to do with the *'ontological'* one. This means that the ontic has to do with the manifold practices of conventional politics, while the ontological concerns the very way in which society is instituted."[25] Taylor is talking about the shift from a world in which religion structures the society to one in which, as Marcel Gauchet says, "religions continue to exist but inside of a political form and collective order that they no longer determine."[26]

These historical changes in secularity are accompanied by changes in the ontology of subjectivity. Taylor speaks of the shift from a porous subject open to heavenly voices—for example, Joan of Arc—to the modern buffered identity in which the divide between the interior and exterior worlds is firm and a vocabulary of interiority is developed, as we see in writers from Montaigne to the Romantics and beyond.[27]

▶ Alternative Historical Ontologies

I will now show how historical ontologies can become a site of contestation, by examining a competing line of ontological argument forged by Michel Foucault. Although Taylor cites parallels to his analysis in Foucault, Taylor's hermeneutic approach to philosophical assumptions cannot assimilate the ways that Foucault looks at the social apparatuses, exposing the domination hiding behind the discourse of right and legitimacy.[28] For example Foucault looks at the notion of the modern individual not as a philosophical assumption or a moral shape, as we find in liberalism; nor does he see it as an ideological illusion, as we find in Marxism; rather the individual is a production of the system, whose reality does not depend on its philosophical or political coherence. As he says, "The individual is no doubt the fictional atom of the 'ideological' representation of society; but he is already fabricated by this specific technology of power that I have called discipline. . . . Power . . . produces reality; it produces domains of objects and rituals of truth."[29]

For my purposes here, Talal Asad's work is the most relevant in the Foucauldian line of ontological critique, since he speaks directly to Taylor's work on the secularity. In *Formations of the Secular,* Asad announces that he will distinguish the historico-ontological enterprise of studying secularity (Taylor's Secularity 3) from the narrowly focused debates on principle and policy (Taylor's Secularity 1): "It is a major premise of this study that 'the secular' is conceptually prior to the political doctrine of 'secularism,' that over time a variety of concepts, practices and sensibilities have come together to form 'the secular.' . . . I begin with a partial genealogy of that concept. . . . Genealogy is not intended here as a substitute for social history ('real history' as many would put it) but as a way of working back from our present to the contingencies that have come together to give us our certainties."[30] If he is like Taylor in his concern with modernity's misdescriptions of itself through time, he is less focused on the articulation of the conditions of possibility than he is on the power of these misdescriptions to shape the world: "The important question is therefore not to determine why the idea of 'modernity' (or 'the West') is a misdescription, but why it has become hegemonic *as a political goal,* what practical consequences follow from that hegemony, and what social conditions maintain it."[31] Asad shows how secularism continues its Christian origins, working itself into a grammar of modernity, including human rights.[32]

He explores exactly what Taylor's holism ignores: the relationship of secularism to domination, but domination as an ontological constitutive problem, not as an external political force. While Taylor thinks of the ontological as the unrecognized condition of possibility, Asad looks at the way this shared ontological background becomes a forced imposition on different positions. "Secularism," for Asad, "is not simply an intellectual answer to a question about enduring social peace and toleration. It is an enactment by which a *political medium* (representation of citizenship), redefines and transcends particular and differentiating practices of the self that are articulated though class, gender, and religion."[33] Asad's comparative critique puts pressure on Taylor's account not just to acknowledge aspects of the history that it has denied or left out; rather Asad is disclosing a deep ontological layering of the social imaginaries and of concepts that goes unnoticed by Taylor's construal of ontological history. Answering Asad's would require the inclusion of ignored encounters with others as well as a revision of Taylor's description of the structures of the imaginaries and the concepts of normativity that are bound up with them.[34]

Taylor's and Asad's ontological approaches to religion offer a kind of historical, anthropological, and normative richness that contrasts with Said's ideological approach to what he takes to be an unproblematic category. For Said *religious* is a pejorative adjective that he attaches to all forms of cultural identity, a term he contrasts with *secular*.[35] Religion obfuscates the plurality of identities and blocks a moral commitment to open, public discussion: "The importance of secularism is that it does leave open the space of discussion, whereas this is not true of the return to religion. . . . The secular at least gives one the opportunity to present, to talk, to discuss, and to change, which is the most important thing."[36] Getting different cultures to make themselves vulnerable to dialogue at the same table is indeed a crucial issue; however, the kind of questioning proposed by Taylor and Asad provides more possibilities for productive dialogue than calling upon a set of constructed ideals that purport to trump all historical cultural and religious understandings.

▶ Globalization, Fundamentalism, and the Separation of Religion from Culture

If Taylor and Asad study the ways in which religion and culture are interwoven over long periods of time, they do not address important features of globalization, such as the rapid movement of people and beliefs across borders. However, other ontological thinkers provide important insights into these global phenomena. To show that, I will briefly discuss the work of Olivier Roy, who also takes up the politics of religion and secularity.[37]

For Roy globalization unmasks the West's understanding of the secular as the site of unbiased neutrality from which religious accommodations are made. When non-Westerners examine secularity, they do not see the slow development of fair solutions to conflicts about morality, politics, and religion. What they see instead is that Western secularity employed a morality that was compatible with the Christian moral beliefs of the majority so as to pacify believers who resisted the move to a secular state. Secular morality was not neutral toward the religions of the world; it was simply independent of the church and faith. Even in France, the most aggressively secular of Western countries, Jules Ferry, the minister of education during the years leading up to the landmark law of 1905 that made "*laïcité*" the state policy, emphasized the continuities between secular morality and the Christian beliefs of the populace.[38] In his circular to teachers on November 27, 1883, Ferry said, "Ask yourself if the father of one of your students, even one, who was in your class listening to you could withhold his assent from what you would say."[39] In the United States, Protestant morality became part of what Robert Bellah has called "America's civil religion," the common ground underwriting the debate about religion in the public sphere.[40] Thus when the West touts its principles to support its treatment of religion, the social imaginary reveals a very different story about the transsubjective, collective imaginary that holds those principles in its grip.

But globalization has produced much more than epiphanies about Eurocentrism. Roy connects globalization to the rise of fundamentalism and the detachment of religion from culture. Fundamentalism—whether Salafism or born-again Christianity—turns against the ambient culture of the political community when this culture does not allow believers to recognize themselves in it. The establishment of such alternative communities is further enhanced by media that enable groups to form without regard to territorial boundaries. Because fundamentalism does not require a culture, it is the form of religion "most suited to globalization, because it accepts its own deculturation and makes it the instrument of its claim to universality."[41] Therefore we should not mistake the current prominence of religion around the world for a "return of religion." As Roy says, "What we call 'the return of the religious' is not a return but a new form of visibility, a visibility of rupture and not of continuity."[42] We make a serious mistake when we treat the religious under the rubric of multiculturalism, because these new forms of religion are distinguished by their detachment from culture.[43]

The ontological approach thus offers us a variety of possibilities for understanding the nature of conflicts. It can open up temporality so that we can see how conflicts emerge historically through the background imaginaries over long periods. It can also give us access to the wide of range of structures that make up the collective mind that we study. We are not limited to the study of ideas and beliefs present to the minds of historical actors, for the imaginaries show not only how ideas emerge through imaginaries but also how they are continuously revised through imaginaries. Literary discourse can explore different dimensions of these background imaginaries—the ways it sets up its world, its languages, its characters, its views of causality and consciousness, and so forth—as well as how the transsubjective institutions of a culture come into being, such as the institutions of modernity.[44] However, there is an important aspect of the problematic of the social imaginary that Taylor, Asad, and Roy ignore.

▶ From Social Imaginaries to Critical Utterance

What is missing in the work of all the thinkers examined thus far is the place of the utterance, particularly the literary utterance as an engagement with the social imaginaries and apparatuses of domination. In Taylor's work we saw how the understanding of normativity for a community at any given moment must be understood as the slow emergence of macro imaginaries—public sphere, popular sovereignty, and the like—an account that is done from great historical height with attention to longue durée. This view implies that imaginaries are simply the nourishing background for principles or the shared background that makes debate possible. In Asad's work we saw how the ontological approach reveals the slow secretion of structural oppression but not how the individual text can act on these structures. I will rectify this lacuna by reading a story that reveals structural oppression and makes a normative claim, but not by appealing to a constructed normative concept, as saw in Said's work.[45] My reading is a philosophical example, not an historical or literary reading.

In 1917 Susan Glaspell published a simple, straightforward short story, "A Jury of Her Peers," just before women got the right to vote in the United States. This text illustrates how the social imaginary can become a space of reasoning superior to that of conceptual reasoning dear to Western philosophers and legal theorists.[46]

Glaspell's tale begins when Mrs. Hale is called from her work in the kitchen to join her husband; the sheriff, Mr. Peters; and Peters's wife. Mrs. Hale, the center of focalization for the third-person narrative, learns that Mr. Wright, the husband of an old friend, has been killed. The sheriff suspects Mrs. Hale's friend Minnie has killed her husband. The group proceeds to the Wrights' home, where it splits up. The men go out to the barn to look for evidence that can establish a motive for Minnie, while the women wait in the kitchen. While sitting there, they encounter the "text" of Minnie's life—the dirty towels, the mishandled stitching on her quilt, and so on. The dominant tradition that the women bring to Minnie's house, a tradition that they share with their husbands, forms pre-understandings that do not help them reconstitute the self-understanding of the text. The men have called Minnie "mad," and the women at this point can articulate no other reading, even though they sense that more is at stake here for them.

Slowly the women start to put together an explanation of the strangeness of Minnie's text—the systematic psychological torture to which her husband subjected her, a torture that culminated in the strangulation of Minnie's double, her pet bird. The process of coming to this explanation forces them to transform the understandings of their own lives and indeed the gendered imaginaries of the time. Minnie's text asks them disturbing questions, not just the other way around. They discover that Minnie's husband was not just "a cruel man" but also a typical one and that Minnie's response differs only in degree, not in kind, from the ones they have had but repressed. It is important that Mr. Wright committed no actionable offense. He merely brought into relief the norms that are already there, that inform the actions within many marriages. The story's off-stage narrator shows their complex interaction with the text—sometimes it grabs them, and sometimes they push it away—that is rarely made explicit in their consciousness or in dialogue. The women are not exchanging claims in discursive dialogue in which they use the constructed political concepts to unmask ideology. They are experiencing a rupture in the very medium that constitutes them—that is, Glaspell is arguing through the imaginary in displaying this rupture. The context of their reading—their moments of isolation interrupted by their husbands' condescending remarks about the triviality of women's occupations—helps foster their transformative reading. The women come to understand that the values and textures of their own lives are neither read nor recognized by their husbands and that the forces that drove Minnie mad operate around and within them as well. The women discover the anger that they have been socialized to ignore.

The women are ambivalent about this knowledge that their reading is bringing about. The boundaries of their selves have been unraveled as Minnie's text speaks not only to them but for them: "It was as if something within her not herself had spoken, and it found in Mrs. Peters something that she did not know as herself." Interpretation in this story is dramatized as an event undergone by the interpreters, not as their act. When Mrs. Peters discovers the strangled bird, she does not just solve a detective's riddle; she must rework the fabric of her memory and identity. As she recalls and revises the story of what a boy with a hatchet had done to her cat many years ago, she gets back the rage of the past moment: "If they hadn't held me back, I would have. . . ."[47] Minnie's text forces them to see themselves and their husbands in a way that requires a new language, one that gives distinctiveness and worth to their lives and that goes unread by the dominant culture. The women do not "empathize" with Minnie by learning the particulars of her life. Nor do they learn to apply a principle of nondomination or antidiscrimination. Instead Minnie's text forces them to recognize patterns and articulate the violence toward women that has been systematically silenced by the structures of the imaginary. These structures are both realistic and normative, since they make possible what world is available and the assessment of this world.[48] Normative argument relies on bringing aspects of the world into view, not only on the application of principles.[49] Unlike Minnie they are able to create a way of speaking that unites them with each other and separates them from the men. They have formed a powerful normative language that gives them reasons to do something they never could have imagined before they arrived at the Wrights' house. Their interpretations unfold a new, hitherto unthinkable space of action: they choose to hide the bird (conceal evidence), betray their husbands, and break the law.

The reasons of the argument do not appear in terms of the principles, such as justice and equality, that we find in Western theories of practical reason. Certainly such notions inform the background, but they are woven into the textures of their shared imaginaries. Moreover the revisions of their existing understandings occur at the level of the imaginary rather than explicit naming. How does one go from not seeing domination to seeing it? Not through the application of a normative principle but by tacking between accounts of our ontological background and the interpretive normative intervention that we make.[50] In seeking out the background that subtends our first-order speech, we present the presuppositions and horizons of the possible that cradle our sentences. If we enter a debate only with our position and those of others arrayed as individual propositions, as we see in Said, we miss the paths of interrogation that appear when we articulate the background to our positions. Understanding and assessing the effects of globalization on cultures can only come when we open up our collective imaginations rather than hiding from them behind political principles or sociological processes. These collective structures of meaning that constitute us, structures that simultaneously nourish and oppress us, can become a resource and not an obstacle when we understand literature as a normative utterance that speaks to and through these structures.

Notes

1. Max Weber is associated with the first two, Emile Durkheim with the third, and Michael Hardt and Antonio Negri with the fourth. The study of globalization continues this pattern, for as Lynn Hunt says, it concentrates on "macro-historical (worldwide) and especially macroeconomic trends and it ensconces the assumption that economics shapes all other aspects of life. In short, the globalization paradigm reinstates the very suppositions that cultural theories had criticized and thus potentially

threatens to wash away the gains of the last decades of cultural history" (*Writing History in the Global Era* [New York: Norton, 2014], 59).

2. This evaporation of culture is a common assumption of "realism" in political theory and international relations theory, in which the "self-interest" of an atomistic individual is assumed to be the same across cultures: "Realists consider the principal actors in the international arena to be states, which are concerned with their own security, act in pursuit of their own national interests, and struggle for power." W. Julian Korab-Karpowicz, "Realism in International Realism," *Stanford Encyclopedia of Philosophy,* https://plato.stanford.edu/entries/realism-intl-relations. When culture is not evaporated, it is often stigmatized as irrational. In *The Lexus and the Olive Tree* (New York: Farrar, Straus, Giroux, 1999), for instance, Thomas Friedman formulates the political tensions produced by globalization as a struggle between economic growth through modernization (the Lexus) and cultural identity (the olive tree). Olive trees "represent everything that roots us, anchors us, identifies us and locates us in this world—whether it be belonging to a family, a community, a tribe, a nation, a religion or, most of all, a place called home . . . .We fight so intensely over our olive trees" (31). Olive trees (world cultures) are presented as lumps of irrational attachments that compete against the self-evident good of the Lexus.

3. Daniel Little, *Varieties of Social Explanation: An Introduction to the Philosophy of Social Science* (Boulder: Westview, 1990), 85.

4. Carla Bagnoli, "Constructivism in Metaethics," *Stanford Encyclopedia of Philosophy,* http://plato.stanford.edu/entries/constructivism-metaethics/.

5. In Rawls's "original position," the people deliberating about a social contract are deprived of knowledge about their personal and historical circumstances. They do know about certain fundamental interests and the basic facts of the social and physical sciences. See *A Theory of Justice* (Cambridge, Mass.: Harvard University Press, 1971), 17–22, for his first statement on this question. Habermas says, "There is a universal core of moral intuition in all times and all societies and this is because there are unavoidable presuppositions of communicative activity" (*Autonomy and Solidarity: Interviews,* ed. Peter Dews [New York: Verso, 1986], 206).

6. Kant says that the problem of organizing a state can be solved "even for a nation of devils (if only they have understanding)" ("Toward Perpetual Peace," *Practical Philosophy,* translated and edited by Mary Gregor [Cambridge: Cambridge University Press, 1996, 335). People need "universal laws for their preservation," but each is "inclined covertly to exempt himself from them" (335). These private, self-interested struggles "so check one another that in their public conduct the result is the same as if they had no such evil dispositions" (335).

7. Orientalism "is a distribution of geopolitical awareness into aesthetic, scholarly, economic, sociological, historical and philosophical texts." Edward Said, *Orientalism* (New York: Pantheon, 1978, 12.

8. Edward Said, *Culture and Imperialism* (New York: Knopf, 1993), 71.

9. Ibid., 33.

10. Ibid., 41.

11. Ibid., xii–xiii, 4–5, 15–16, 32–33.

12. Said confesses that he is deeply suspicious of the concept: "As for me, though perhaps I am putting it too strongly, culture has been used as essentially not a co-operative and communal term but rather as a term for exclusion" (*Culture and Imperialism,* 15–16). Said is critical of Samuel Huntington's "clash of civilization" thesis because of his use of the words *culture* and *civilization* as "reified objects rather than the dynamic, ceaselessly turbulent things that they in fact are" (*Reflections on Exile* [Cambridge, MA: Harvard University Press, 2000], 381), but he tacitly agrees with Huntington that we cannot reason through culture.

13. Said, *Culture and Imperialism,* 97.

14. Ibid., 279.

15. In postcolonial and cultural studies, "hybridity" is associated with Mikhail Bakhtin and Homi Bhabha. Bakhtin defines it as "a mixture of two social languages within the limits of a single utterance, an encounter, within the arena of an utterance, between two linguistic consciousnesses, separated from one another by an epoch, by social differentiation or by some other factor" (*Dialogic Imagination,* trans. Caryl Emerson and Michael Holquist [Austin: University of Texas Press, 1981], 358). Bhabha gives this linguistic ontology a political animation so that hybridity makes political possibilities available. "If the effect of colonial power is seen to be the production of hybridization . . . [it] enables a form of subversion . . . that turns the discursive conditions of dominance into the grounds of intervention" ("Signs Taken for Wonders: Questions of Ambivalence and Authority under a Tree outside Delhi, May 1817," *Critical Inquiry* 12 (1985): 154). This animation of language and the unqualified valuation of difference and subversion per se leaves out the judgment of the interpreter and the purposes to which these actions are put.

16. "Interview with Edward Said," in *Edward Said: A Critical Reader,* ed. Michael Sprinker (Cambridge: Blackwell, 1987), 134, 137.

17. Said, *Culture and Imperialism,* 314–15.

18. Martin Heidegger, *Being and Time,* trans. Joan Stambaugh (Albany: SUNY Press, 1996), 273. The world does not stand over against a subject; rather "self and world belong together in the single entity of Dasein" (Martin Heidegger, *The Basic Problems of Phenomenology,* trans. Alfred Hofstader [Bloomington: Indiana University Press, 1982], 297. The common link between Taylor and Foucault is Heidegger's ontological turn. At the end of his life, Foucault said that Heidegger was for him "the essential philosopher," the one who determined his entire philosophical development ("The Return of Morality," *Michel Foucault: Politics, Philosophy and Culture, Interviews and Other Writings 1977–1984,* ed. Lawrence D. Kritzman [New York: Routledge, 1988], p. 250.) Heidegger has been an important for theorists of postcolonial and world literature. See in particular Dipesh Chakrabarty's *Provincializing Europe* (Princeton: Princeton University Press, 2000) and Pheng Cheah's *What Is World* (Durham: Duke University Press, 2016). Cheah draws on Heidegger to criticize the cartographical

approach to world literature, which thinks in terms of exchanges in space. "The fundamental shortcoming of this approach is that it assumes that globalization creates a world . . . [and that it] places literature in a reactive position. . . . [The theories] have turned away from questions of literature's worldly causality and avoided examining the normative dimension of worldliness" (5).

19. Charles Taylor, *A Secular Age* (Cambridge, Mass.: Harvard University Press, 2007), 387. Asad, on the other hand, follows Foucault in reading these structures in a way that exposes their surreptitious domination.

20. Taylor has a long-standing objection to reductive, constructivist theories of practical reason because they "cannot articulate" "the background understanding surrounding any conviction that we ought not act in this or that way" (*Sources of the Self* [Cambridge, Mass.: Harvard University Press, 1989], 87). John Rawls himself admits: "Not everything can be constructed. Every construction has a basis, certain materials, as it were from which it begins" (*Collected Papers,* rev. ed. [Cambridge, Mass.: Harvard University Press, 2001], 514. The "ontological turn" has changed the understanding of social sciences, not just philosophy. See, for instance, Tony Lawson's work on economics, "Ontology and the Study of Social Reality: Emergence, Organisation, Community, Power, Social Relations, Corporations, Artefacts and Money," *Cambridge Journal of Economics* 36 (2012): 345–85.

21. Charles Taylor, *Modern Social Imaginaries* (Durham: Duke University Press, 2004), 2, 8–9.

22. Ibid., 3. Taylor clarifies this concept in a subsequent work: "This understanding is both factual and 'normative'; that is, we have sense of how things usually go, but this is interwoven with an idea of how they ought to go, what missteps would invalidate the practice. Take our practice of choosing governments through general elections. Part of the background understanding that makes sense of the act of voting for each one of us is our awareness of the whole action" ("Reply," in *Varieties of Secularism in a Secular Age,* ed. Michael Warner, Jonathan VanAntwerpen, and Craig Calhoun [Cambridge, Mass.: Harvard University Press, 2013], 308).

23. Taylor, *Secular Age,* 3.

24. Charles Taylor, *Philosophy and the Human Sciences* (Cambridge: Cambridge University Press, 1985), 36. I have substituted *secularity* for *negotiation* in this well-known passage from Taylor's work since he is making the same point with secularity. We can contrast this ontological reading with Habermas's account of modernity, in which he signs on to Weber's idea of the instrumental "rationality" "as the process of disenchantment which led in Europe to a disintegration of religious world views that issued in a secular culture" (*Philosophical Discourse of Modernity,* trans. Frederick Lawrence [Cambridge, Mass.: MIT Press, 1987], 1); however, he adds that Weber and the Frankfurt School have missed the possibility of communicative rationality, which is based on Kantian norms.

25. Chantal Mouffe, *On the Political* (New York: Routledge, 2005), 8.

26. Marcel Gauchet, *La Religion dans la démocratie* (Paris: Gallimard, 2001), 12–13.

The current prominence of religion in world affairs is not a return to premodern structuring. Rather religion emerges inside of a modern political ontology as the individual's belief.

27. Taylor, *Secular Age,* chap. 15.

28. Michel Foucault, *Discipline and Punish,* trans. Alan Sheridan (New York: Vintage, 1977), 194. Foucault seeks "to reverse the mode of analysis followed by the entire discourse of right from the time of the Middle Ages. My aim, therefore, was to invest it, to give due weight, that is the fact of domination, to expose both its latent nature and its brutality . . . to show the extent to which, and the forms in which, right (not simply the laws but the whole complex of apparatuses, institutions and regulations responsible to their application) transmits and puts in motion relations that are not relations of sovereignty but of domination" ("Two Lectures," in *Power/Knowledge,* ed. Colin Gordon [New York: Vintage, 1980], 95–96).

29. Foucault does not look for the intellectual manipulation of subjects but for subtle shaping at deeper levels than consciousness: "The control of society over individuals is not conducted only through consciousness or ideology, but also in the body and with the body. For capitalist society biopolitics is what is most important, the biological, the somatic, the corporeal" ("La naissance de la medicine," in *Dits et écrits* [Paris: Gallimard, 1994], 3:210).

30. Talal Asad, *Formations of the Secular: Christianity, Islam, Modernity* (Stanford: Stanford University Press, 2003), 16. Asad insists on large-scale genealogical disclosure: "The important thing in this comparative analysis [of concepts] is not their origin (Western or non-Western), but the forms of life that articulate them, the powers they release or disable. Secularism—like religion—is such a concept" (17). Asad directs his critique at Taylor's "Modes of Secularism" (*Secularism and Its Critics,* ed. Rajeev Bhargava [Oxford: Oxford University Press, 1998] 31–53, which is oriented toward Secularism 1, state policy, in which Taylor advocates a version of Rawls's "overlapping consensus."

31. Ibid., 13; emphasis in original. Asad's project is to examine "changes in the grammar of concepts" (25). Asad, like Taylor, draws on the notion of "habitus" to talk about embodied capacities (95).

32. Ibid., chap. 4. In "The Construction of Religion as an Anthropological Category," *Genealogies of Religion* (Baltimore: Johns Hopkins University Press, 1993), Asad examines how Clifford Geertz's notion of religion as a universal category embeds Christian assumptions within what purports to be a neutral, universal category. Talal Asad, "The Construction of Religion as an Anthropological Category," in *Genealogies of Reason: Discipline and Reasons of Power in Christianity and Islam* (Baltimore: Johns Hopkins University Press, 1993) 27–54.

33. Asad, *Formations of the Secular,* 5.

34. See Saba Mahmood, "Can Secularism Be Otherwise?," in *Varieties of Secularism in a Secular Age,* ed. Michael Warner, Jonathan VanAntwerpen, and Craig Calhoun (Cambridge, Mass.: Harvard University Press, 2010) 282–299, and Peter van der Veer,

"Smash Temples, Burn Books: Comparing Secularist Projects in India and China," in *Rethinking Secularism,* ed. Craig Calhoun et al. (Oxford: Oxford University Press, 2011) 270–281.

35. He introduces the opposition "secular/religious" in the first and last chapters of *The World, the Text, and the Critic* (Cambridge: Harvard University Press, 1983). "Religious criticism," for Said, is not just about religion per se but a kind of discourse that surfaces in many secular forms, such as orientalism, nationalism, and literature. Thus "orientalism" is understood as a secularized Christian story, as "structures inherited from the past, secularized, redisposed, and reformed by such disciplines as philology, which in turn were naturalized, and laicized substitutes for (or versions of) Christian supernaturalism" (*Orientalism,* 122).

36. Edward Said, "Response: A Symposium on Edward Said's *Culture and Imperialism, Social Text* 40 (1994): 24.

37. I will focus on Roy's *Holy Ignorance* (New York: Columbia University Press, 2010).

38. In 1905 the Law on the Separation of the Churches and the State was passed by the Chamber of Deputies.

39. https://www.ac-paris.fr/portail/jcms/p1_1153893/lettre-aux-instituteurs-jules-ferry-17-novembre-1883. Accessed September 23, 2017.

40. Robert Bellah, "Biblical Religion and Civil Religion in America," *Daedalus* 96 (1967): 1–21. Talcott Parsons claims that pluralization in the West was only possible because the Christian ethic had been generalized and institutionalized in the secular world. See "Christianity and Modern Industrial Society," in *Sociological Theory: Values and Sociocultural Change,* ed. E. A. Tiryakian (New York: Harper & Row, 1963), pp. 33–70.

41. Roy, *Holy Ignorance,* 5.

42. "Sécularisme et fondamentalisme: Les deux faces d'un même phénomène," in *Charles Taylor: Religion et sécularisation,* ed. Sylvie Taussig (Paris: CNRS Editions, 2014), 199. Roy notes that mainstream religions have declined and asks rhetorically, "Why have tens of thousands of Muslims in Central Asia become Christians or Jehovah's Witnesses? How can a Protestant evangelical church establish itself in Morocco and Algeria? . . . What is the explanation for the fact that the world's fastest growing religion is Pentecostalism?" (*Holy Ignorance,* 1).

43. Roy, "Sécularisme et fondamentalisme," 212.

44. See Taylor's discussion of the emergence of self, the public sphere, and popular sovereignty through the social imaginary in *Modern Social Imaginaries.* He incorporates large chunks of this work into *A Secular Age* as well.

45. I have developed my theory of the normative utterance at length in "Social Imaginaries and the Theory of the Normative Utterance," *Philosophy and Social Criticism* 43 (2017): 1045–71.

46. Susan Glaspell, "A Jury of Her Peers," in *Best Short Stories of 1917* (Boston: Small, Maynard, 1918), 256–283.

47. Ibid., 272, 277.

48. Habermas brings out the tension between constructivist approaches to normativity and reality: "The tension between normative approaches, which are constantly in danger of losing contact with social reality, and objectivist approaches, which screen out all normative aspects, can be taken as a caveat against fixating on one disciplinary point of view." Jürgen Habermas, *Inclusion of the Other* (Cambridge, Mass.: MIT Press, 1998), 6–7.

49. In "Debating Modernity: Contemporary Chinese Intellectuals and Novelists" (Ph.D. diss., University of South Carolina, 2015), Gengsong Gao shows how Chinese arguments over modernity have ignored literature and how literature can make an indispensable contribution.

50. Constructivists have no place for literature in their conception of practical reason. Habermas says this clearly: "To the degree that the poetic, world-disclosing function of language gains primacy and structuring force, language escapes the structural constraints and communicative functions of everyday life" (*Philosophical Discourse of Modernity*, 204). Rawls claims that the generic model for public debate should be the opinion of the U.S. Supreme Court (*Political Liberalism* [New York: Columbia University Press, 1993], 254).

Altered Realism in Ontological Fiction

Never Let Me Go and *Point Omega*

Chi-she Li

Globalization witnesses the rise of realism. In addition to various literary realisms that narrativize the given social organization of the time,[1] many philosophical realisms that delineate ontologies have also surged.[2] This is not only because globalization intensifies the complex seen and unseen interactions among humans, but also because the coordination of humans enabled by globalization fosters the extensive exploration of the human surroundings, in turn calling "upon us to reorient ourselves profoundly in relation to the world, to one another, and to ourselves" (Coole and Frost 6). The necessity of ontological knowledge is deeply felt. The condition in which ontologies are open to imagination, suspicion, or probing by the global public is prevailing. Think about scientists' dreams of meeting aliens, politicians' controversies over global warming, and comparative-literature experts' debate of planetarity over globalization, for example. Philosophers also resume to probe ontologies, particularly in the last two decades or so. These recent philosophical inquiries, commonly called "new materialism," seriously undermine the Kantian epistemology of human-centered representation, upon which the humanities have been reliant, and these inquiries ask instead the various disciplines of humanities to open up their understanding of meanings not only to humans but also to the "multitude" of nonhumans. In spite of the many shades of new materialism, as Diana Coole and Samantha Frost argue, nonhuman agency, which lends active existence to nonhuman beings, enjoys a consensus: "Matter is no longer imagined here as a massive, opaque plenitude but is recognized instead as indeterminate, constantly forming and reforming in unexpected ways. One could conclude, accordingly, that 'matter becomes' rather than that 'matter is'" (10). A radical assertion of nonhuman agency now reveals in a new light a world in which human dramas are relativized by numerous other "dramas" enacted by nonhumans.

This essay illustrates that contemporary fiction also participates in the global public by probing and articulating ontologies, and that the drastic recasting of humans in these ontologies invokes new hybrid forms. Scholars have already considered the question of what would be the appropriate form of the novel that would express these ontologies. "Terrible Engines" by Brian Kim Stefans asks what writing would be like if it conformed to Quentin Meillassoux's nonhuman, ontology-centered world.[3] The answer is found in the experimental writings he canvases. In "The Realist Novel and 'the Great Outdoors,'" Arne De Boever asks a similar question and points out that the novel *The Map and the Territory* by Michel Houellebecq is paradigmatic of a new form of writing that attends to Meillassoux's radical ontology. These two studies find that texts with highly experimental, quasi-modernist features can eradicate human-centeredness from literary creations. The essay also considers further instances in which realism has been reshaped for the purpose of producing an ontological fiction that maintains a distance from human-centeredness.

Realism, I contend, is renewed in two selected novels in a different way from the classical nineteenth-century human-centeredness. The two novels are Kazuo Ishiguro's *Never Let Me Go* (2005) and Don DeLillo's *Point Omega* (2010). Both writers are quite versed in the accepted forms of either domestic realism (Ishiguro) or postmodernism (DeLillo). Yet in the chosen works, they try out a different style I call "altered realism." They often reuse the conventions of realism to allow concerns of ontology to take center stage, a subject matter not typical in the human-society-oriented nineteenth-century novels. The forms of realism adopted by these writers ultimately threaten to break down the classical conventions on which classical realism is founded, while attempting to ask the question of what reality could be.

The nineteenth-century European realist novel, in recent critical reception, has received a fresh look. Prior to the end of the twentieth century, realism was unfortunately associated with a fixed literary form, in contrast with mid-century modernism's relentless experimentation. In his essay of 1949, George J. Becker offers such a typical definition of realism by delineating three stages. The first is the realism of method, in which the prose description of details is sustained with a belief in objectivity. The second is the realism of subject matter, in which realist writers held the ambition of covering every possible subject matter found in social interaction. The last one is the realism of philosophy, of accepting inevitability. Becker considers what is commonly understood as naturalism to be an offshoot of realism. However, in contrast with the definition of realism as a fixed form, recent studies turn to appreciate the flexibility of its form and its ability to respond to social change. Mihály Szegedy-Maszák argues against an essentialist definition in favor of a historical one, observing how literary conventions dynamically conform to the principle of credibility accepted at a given time. For him the realist novel depicts the historical dialogism of the nineteenth century in the presentation of "a clash between different value systems, conflicting truths, and multiple actual worlds" (51). He considers "chronotopes" (of dialogism) and the phatic use of language (the dialogue between the narrator and the narrate) as terms crucial for a hypothetical definition of realism (54). Simon Dentith, on the other hand, calls our attention to the flexible form of realism by using the term *realist synthesis,* which means that realism is "a whole mode of understanding social and individual life, which combines the widest sweep of history and national geography with the most minutely realized detail of material and affective existence" (48). Similar to the historical emphasis of dialogism, Dentith's synthesis focuses on heterogeneous details of materiality variably gripped by different writers in the same period to achieve a dynamic panorama of diverse subjectivities. These definitional changes chronicle a resurgent interest in realism as historically lived existence rather than an outdated and ossified form and maintain that the realist novel at its best requires vigorous assembling by folding conventions and details into an overarching composite of social subjectivities in clash.

These definitions also entail by implication the prospect that realism can be remade in a different time. Among others, Mikhail Bakhtin theorizes well that the renewing of realism depends on the inventiveness of the composite form in fiction. A well-recognized contribution, relevant to this essay, is the understanding of the novel as polyphony, a wide spectrum of subjects of limited consciousness, each embodying a socially substantial voice, coming into a dialogue. Polyphony describes the ever-renewing form of the novel in its absorption of vocal complexity of the time. This composite nature also implies the openness of the novel to the heteroglot voices in a given social milieu. In addition to this openness to different nonhegemonic social voices, importantly, Bakhtin also seeks the veracity of polyphonic worlds by turning to Albert Einstein's theory of relativity. New scholarship traces the shift in which Bakhtin was gradually disengaged from the epistemology of Kantianism and came to echo Einstein's relativity in his theorization of the chronotope, the figure of time and place, in his revised book on Dostoevsky. Jonathan Stone details Bakhtin's drift from Kantianism to relativity, observing "the transformation of his early implicit and unarticulated interest in an Einsteinian, physically nonobjective universe into an explicit recognition of the Einsteinian nature of his own worldview" (406). In a similar vein, Luis Alberto Brandão maintains the tense inseparability between the metaphor and the concept of relativity in Bakhtinian chronotope: "Time-space and chronotope meet, conceptually and metaphorically, in a common epistemological field that has selected as a basic problem the human determination of knowledge, which includes the debate over the universal and the particular, absolute and relative, fact and discourse, what can be demonstrated and what can be imagined" (134). These two joint qualities, heteroglossia and a transhuman apperception of the space-time continuum, allow us to see Bakhtin as posing the perennial questions of both how we account for the ever-renewing energy of the novel and how the novel's inherently hybrid form functions as way of modeling alternative, and even parallel, realities.

Inspired by Bakhtin's suggestive polyphony, through which the form flexibly articulates what reality could mean in a given sociohistorical milieu, I would like to extend his insights to explicate the two novels under discussion as flexible reuses of realism for dialogism to be opened up to nonhuman participants. Admittedly, in terms of voices, Bakhtin is tied to the kind of polyphony in which only human participants count: "the consciousness of the real people" (Bakhtin 292). Yet if literary realism, in the late-Bakhtinian shape, could be subject to the pull of nonhuman, scientific worldviews, it would be impossible to avoid a likely consequence that humans are embedded in nonhuman contexts to be reassessed accordingly in new realist writings.[4] It would be especially the case in today's hyper-technologized human society when one's experience cannot distinguish what the naked flesh could endow from what nonhuman technology could enable.

To venture a new trajectory of the Bakhtinian polyphony in a highly technologized society, Bruno Latour, who persistently demands one to consider humans and nonhumans on the same plane in terms of actors and agency and asks us to weigh them equally in the public forum in any deliberation, may help. The idea of an actor receives an elaboration in the context of modern epistemology in *We Have Never Been Modern*. Latour complicates the understanding of actors by drawing our attention to the difficulty of identifying them. He critically examines what he calls "purification," an intellectual ossification of knowledge advocated by the Enlightenment, which maintains a black-and-white break between nature and culture, between subject and object. The result of the epistemological purification leaves out many that do not fit squarely into these binaries, and the ill-fit remain unnamed, illegible, invisible, or unthinkable. Against the polarized purification, he foregrounds the nameless multitude jettisoned by the strict structure of the binaries. These nonrecognized, or barely recognizable, Enlightenment jetsams, so to speak, are also actors, equipped with forces of emergence, affordance, and connection. Actors in this context of modernity are interchangeably called other terms. Latour's actor (interchangeable with hybrid, quasi-subject, quasi-object, actant, or agent) appreciates what is usually dismissed in the subject-object divide typical of a Kantian epistemology, existences that are hybrid in form and emerge in complex interaction with nameless others. Latour calls them hybrids, "quasi-objects, quasi-subjects" (*We Have Never Been Modern* 51). These hybrids can be anything the modern epistemology refuses to accept as legitimate: "they compose not only our own collectives but also the others, illegitimately called premodern" (*We Have Never Been Modern* 47).

Later, in his seminal book *Reassembling the Social*, Latour uses the idea of an actor to broaden the scope of society, to contend actor-network theory (ANT) that humans and nonhumans constitute together in changing relationships. To eradicate the assumed distinction between the human and the nonhuman, Latour refers to humans and nonhumans similarly as actors, but an actor as a concept in particular highlights the emergence of nonhuman agency. Lambros Malafouris explains ANT: "Conceptualizing agency as variously distributed and possessed in relational networks of persons and things, ANT proposes that all entities participating in those networks should be treated analytically as of equal importance" (123). What is of interest to literary analysis is that the term *actor* in the case of Latour's oeuvre is inspired by A. J. Greimas's narrative concept of the *actant*," which Latour also uses interchangeably with *actor*. This history of appropriating narrative theory emphasizes the enabling capacity of narrative structure to record and imagine the triggers of sensuous perception and the capacity of linguistic signs that can flexibly cast in imagination the lived experience.

Drawing on the broadened understanding of nonhumans as actors, Latour calls for a comprehensive probing of ontology: "We want the meticulous sorting of quasi-objects to become possible—no longer unofficially and under the table, but officially and in broad daylight. In this desire to bring to light, to incorporate into language, to make public, we continue to identify with the intuition of the Enlightenment" (*We Have Never Been Modern* 142). Such a task—bringing into the global public the nonhuman actors—could substantiate Bakhtin's polyphony with more members and more intense interaction than the human-exclusive dialogism. The following will study how Ishiguro and DeLillo expand the domestic circles to include nonhumans, the "missing masses" (*Reassembling the Social* 241). By so doing they reconfigure realist dialogism to reorient humans in nonhuman ontologies.

▶ *Never Let Me Go*

Ishiguro's novel deploys a sci-fi plot of human clones, but instead of following the convention of the sci-fi future, it places the setting in the near past, narrated in the late 1990s in the first person by Kathy H., aged thirty-one. Written as a bildungsroman of friendship and love among the characters Ruth, Tommy D., and Kathy H., growing up in the Hailsham School in the 1970s, the novel presents seemingly familiar details, such as those typical of British boarding school life, but it turns out that these children are parentless clones programmed to be organ providers when they are adults. The clones only vaguely grasp their objectified status by resorting to the very limited knowledge available. In spite of a keener knowledge of their status as they become adolescents, they still struggle to fit into the human society by seeking their biological origins and imagining a human-like love life.

A prominent category of literary genre available to this novel would be sci-fi fantasy, even though there is criticism that Ishiguro writes nothing of the technological details in *Never Let Me Go.* Margret Atwood, the speculative fiction writer, surmises that Ishiguro does not take fantasy seriously. "All this [cloning and organ transplant technologies] is background. Ishiguro isn't much interested in the practicalities of cloning and organ donation. (Which four organs, you may wonder? A liver, two kidneys, then the heart? . . .)" (Atwood).[5] No doubt *Never Let Me Go* poses a challenge to those who read it in the sci-fi framework. Gabriele Griffin, for instance, who has closely observed the genre confusion of this novel, delineates a gap between biotechnology and the representation of it, because concrete details of the cloning history and its technology are unsatisfactorily missing, at least on the surface of the text (649). Regardless of the difficulty of categorizing this novel squarely as sci-fi, it is often regarded as such.

Such a generic classification, however, elides the fusion of sci-fi and traditional realism, the hybrid that characterizes this novel. The problem of this genre classification, arguably, arises from an assumption of fantasy versus realism regarding characterization. Posthumans (e.g., clones) fit into the sci-fi genre, at least because they are technologically enabled beings, and humans continue to be the taken-for-granted subject matter of realist fiction. However, Ishiguro breaks away from the generic alignment of sci-fi with posthumans by forging a tale of conventional realism in conjunction with otherwise sci-fi clones. To appreciate Ishiguro's hybrid form, one may read this novel as a reversal practice *à la* Donna Haraway's cyborg myth. While her main contention, to break down the imposed boundaries between the sci-fi imagination and the normative discipline, is well known, her cyborg manifesto also conspicuously longs for a new form, not precisely sci-fi but a "cyborg myth," a reversed sci-fi for the real world in the era of modern technology. Significantly this practice would cease being sci-fi per se and mutate into a much more complex fusion of imagination and reality as a form. If Haraway's cyborg rewrites sci-fi for the realism of the contemporary, Ishiguro also endorses a fluid use of genres, only here to rewrite realism into sci-fi for the contemporary, a writing of "clone myth" instead. Specifically, different from the sci-fi reading, in which the reader's disbelief is suspended, this novel establishes a new narrative contract by making the narratee, whom the clone narrator addresses, completely sympathetic with the "artificially" (i.e., "not real" in the traditional realism) created clones, and thus encouraging the reader to adopt a clone's perspective, which is supposed to be real.

The following reading attends to the new realist hybrid of the novel by discussing how three major realist techniques—a limited point of view narration, bildungsroman, and polyphonic dialogism—create a world with the clones' visions detached from typical human-centeredness.

The novel is woven, first of all, by a narrator's limited point of view, which cedes the authority of storytelling to multiple voices (i.e., polyphonies). The three clone characters fall into the snare of a love triangle and fall apart subsequently. In the end Ruth and Tommy die after several surgeries of organ deprivation, and only Kathy lives to tell the tale. She begins the narrative with a self-introduction: "I've been a carer now for over eleven years" (3). She serves as a carer for other clones when they receive organ removal operations. Care, as a supplement to the modern technological production, is symptomatic of the breakdown of social and ontological connections. Intriguingly a real-life equivalent to Kathy's care could be the social work of modern states.[6] Never hesitating to identify herself with her work, she is a bureaucratized being, whose identity is not shaped by kinship or a given cultural status but by a medical profession. Kathy as a carer necessarily contributes to maintaining the organ harvesting system against clones. In this aspect her professionalized voice, which facilitates the exploitative system, is well observed (Whitehead 70).

Nevertheless it is impossible to discredit Kathy's narrative, because the reader has only Kathy's tale even if he or she cannot take her word for it. Kathy relates the tale, one might say, in an ideological slumber. Mechanization of everyday life renders a person, as Walter Benjamin maintains in his essays on modern Paris, into a condition of ideological intoxication, and he identifies those wandering in the city, such as shoppers, men of the leisurely class hidden in the crowd, as flaneurs, urban aimless wanderers, and they indulge themselves in the spectacles of the commercial city while promenading incognito; meanwhile they unconsciously maintain a distance from the same glittering facades in their dreamlike psychological investment in the promises of happiness evoked in the city but unfulfilled (such as love at the last sight). Kathy, a *flâneuse* on the order of Benjamin's daydreaming subjects, steeped in the ideological education for ripping organs from other clones, rides alone on the byroads, dreaming about her clone fellows: "I do like the feeling of getting into my little car, knowing for the next couple of hours I'll have only the roads, the big grey sky and my daydreams for company" (*NLMG* 204). The narrative mirrors Kathy's meandering, slow in pace and unpredictable in plot, and the reader has to be patient to piece together the bits of details. Yet as *flâneuse*, Kath also provides the reader with crucial glimpses of this new biotech world, similar to the Benjaminian dreamers in the urban jungle who reveal the possibility of knowing in their utopian dreaming. Ideologically immersed in the stupor of the super-modern medical system, the narrator in her limited vista also unveils clones' unintentional resistance against the techno regime (even not in a form of revolt).

In addition to the limited point of view, Ishiguro deploys the established bildungsroman convention of children growing up in isolation to give clones voices of their own. If polyphony by definition is a dramatization of a clash of different voices expressing different values, these voices as heteroglossia could facilitate an appreciation of how Ishiguro includes clones to be part of the realist dialogism. Not dissimilar from the Bakhtinian understanding of a given voice as a convergence of different social discourses, the voices of the clones are forged as a result of blending values of the canonical humanities education and the anxious probing of marginalized social positions. The clones are given an education based on literary works, such as Shakespeare and Victorian novels, and drawing. They think, imagine, and write in a manner similar to the characters of nineteenth-century fiction and assume the supreme value of heterosexual love. However, kept in the insular boarding school, they are denied access to who they are, both socially and ontologically, in relation to the wider environments, since they are treated as virtually soulless beings, or at least beings suspected to be soulless. Consequently the clone characters are left to abundant guesswork to compensate for the lack of the social and ontological knowledge, that is, to surmise what is beyond the school and who they are. The voices of the clones spin around their groping for answers: "Take all this curiosity about Madame, for instance. At one level, it was just us kids larking about. But at another, as you'll see, it was the start of a process that kept growing and growing over the years until it came to dominate our lives" (37). The Hailsham students are particularly susceptible to curiosity because they possess an urge to extend their knowledge of their immediate surroundings to a much larger environment, an urge toward ontological knowledge even when there is none available in the education. In lieu of the vacuum of ontological knowledge, the clones unknowingly attempt to transcend the current limitations given to them and conjecture their way out. Even though their guesses always turn out to be wrong, their inferences and conjectures still matter, because they represent the clones' voices in their groping for settlement, their half-formed "cognitive mapping," so to speak.

To avoid an oversimplified binary of clones and humans, rather than lumping the clones into one, it is crucial to acknowledge the different, autonomous voices of the clone trio, Tommy, Ruth, and Kathy, each in his or her own way engaging uncomfortably with the extreme abuse. Tommy expresses the primal noise of resistance. The boarding school is said to be unique among clone-raising institutions, characterized by a "normal" humanities education to provide clones with elementary education. Along with the offer of education, the chief sponsor, Madame, also develops a mechanism of checking to see if a clone could have a soul. Under the pretense of displaying excellent artwork in an art gallery, she collects the clone children's creations for the purpose of examination. In Madame's gallery scheme, Tommy's mediocre paintings seem to prove that he lacks the creative disposition toward arts, and by the evidence of it, he lacks a soul. This ironically places Tommy outside of the ideological indoctrination by the Hailsham system, organized around a romantic philosophy of organic creation and the human soul. As a response to this bad judgment on his talents, he throws tantrums when his peers jeer at him for his poor artwork. Tommy, "the boy with the bad temper," is a stereotype cast in the value system of Hailsham, but, significantly, this anger lets out an instinctive, raw reaction of nonagreement without Tommy's own awareness (*NLMG* 234). Tommy mellows during his adolescent years, partly due to discipline by Kathy, but his violent anger bursts out again after Madame dashes his hope for a hiatus from organ services. After leaving Madame's place, Tommy walks into shrubs at a stop: "The moon wasn't quite full, but it was bright enough, and I could make out in the mid-distance, near where the field began to fall away, Tommy's figure, raging, shouting, flinging his fists and kicking out" (250). Once he returns to the car ride, Kathy ventures a guess: "I was thinking . . . about back then, at Hailsham, when you used to go bonkers like that, and we couldn't understand it. . . . And I was just having this idea, just a thought really. I was thinking maybe the reason you used to get like that was because at some level you always *knew*" (270; emphasis in original). Tommy is surprised at Kathy's inference, but after a few thoughts, he accepts perhaps that is the case. As Bakhtin elucidates polyphony, the meanings of a character's words could not be self-apparent by themselves unless they are understood in a complex weave of discourses from different backgrounds. Similarly these tantrums, expressive of Tommy's frustration, would become meaningful points of critique given the larger context of the dialogism between humans and clones.

In contrast with Tommy's unruly voice, Ruth articulates a suave voice of socialization. Ruth is imaginative and observing. Kathy gets acquainted with her when Ruth shares an imagined tale of a horse squad. The introduction of Ruth reminds one of the classical exposition of the young orphan Jane Eyre, for example, a girl rich in imagination even though in confinement. Indeed Ruth's voice has its origin in the liberal education of Hailsham, as she is the most classically realistic of the three in being intensely sensitive to one's individual position in social hierarchies. For instance she is the first one sensitive to the fact Madame is afraid of clones, and she comes close to the knowledge of the cruelty against clones.

Ruth responds to the human-like education in a voice of an aspiring female who would like to have a strong foothold in the company of humans. Yet in her socializing desire to belong, she also unknowingly falls into the prototype of the creature created by humans who wants to be human. Pricked by a classmate's story that one woman in the modern workplace in the town looks much like Ruth and might be her origin, Ruth goes eagerly to find out. To her great frustration, she later discovers that the woman is far from being like her and thus not a likely candidate for her "possible" (the term denoting the origin of the clone). In her persistent attempt at identifying with humans, Ruth represents the plight of clones, who are not given the knowledge of their ontological status and who consequently think that socialization with humans would be the only important task of being an adult, without knowing the weight of ontology in determining their existence.

In the end Ruth exhibits selfless compassion of which humans in the novel are incapable. Initially her sensitivity and desire to fit in lead her to be manipulative. During the teen years, when she learns of the rumor that Tommy may have a "deferral" in organ donation to enjoy a break with his lover, she feels jealous that her friends Tommy and Kathy might have such a privilege of love and leave her behind, so she mocks Tommy, claiming that it is no more than a rumor of his fancy, and keeps him away from Kathy for fear of being left alone. Years later Ruth confesses to her two childhood friends that her relationship with Tommy is much more of a possessive one than love, and by it she has wrongfully separated Tommy from Kathy. She repents and insists that she has to make it right. In the context of the clone-human polyphony, Ruth's confession and attempted redress set loose the emotional substratum of dejection in clones, implicitly constructed by the unseen obstruction by humans. Upon hearing Ruth, Kathy begins to sob uncontrollably. This is the only moment the repressive Kathy is overrun by what she really feels.

Unlike the voices of Tommy and Ruth, which are understood if directly placed in the conflict with humans, Kathy's voice is marked by the dream of reaching an impossible ontological stability of keeping the clones together permanently, hidden in her intended care of them. Upon hearing of the dismantling of the Hailsham school, she sees a balloon man on the beach. She walks right behind him and sees the human-faced balloons in the man's grip "bumping and grinning down at" her (*NLMG* 209). She likewise would like to clutch clones firmly in her grip if possible. Sharply different from the dispensable use of clones by humans, she becomes a curator of a sort toward these disappeared clones by collecting them in her memory. If Tommy dies with the clear consciousness that clones and humans are separate classes, Kathy still entertains the prospect of nondivision among the Hailsham clones. Before he dies Tommy asks Kathy to let go and demands that she stop being his carer, but the governing strand in Kathy's thought is the opposite, never letting anyone go. After Ruth and Tommy die, Kathy, in her telling of the tale and in her dreaming rides, virtually makes insistent calls to conjure up disappeared clones, never letting any clone go. This melancholic disposition of Kathy could be pathological in terms of human psychology, but in the context of the human-clone dialogism, the reader is forced to reconsider what it means otherwise since Kathy's care of clones is rare elsewhere among humans. In the medical care system as described in the novel, a cruel irony of the absence of care to the clones persists. As Kathy keeps conjuring up the image of disappeared Hailsham, how can clones be ontologically present? This is the main question that effectively resounds in the conflict between humans and clones.

Now we come to the formal structure of the novel, where the third major realist technique is in use: the dual polyphonies that form the plot, one among the clones and the other between clones and humans. In their love triangle, Kathy, Ruth, and Tommy constitute an interaction of voices on their own. In comparison with the clone polyphony, however, the conflict between clones and humans, in which the polyphony of clones is embedded, constitutes the fundamental framework and unsettling dynamism of the novel. The dialogism on this level is complex, since human characters, such as Madame and Marie Claude, embody, via synecdoche, the multiple voices of the debates, controversies, and thought experiments of other humans missing from the novel.

The most acute moment of the human-clone polyphony occurs in Kathy and Tommy's meeting with Madame in her retirement. They meet because the two grown-up Hailsham students assume wrongly that Madame can see the true love between the two by the evidence of Tommy's paintings, and so could grant them a brief reprieve. Noticeably the meeting is depicted in a documentary style. Kathy and Tom cannot outgrow their schoolkids' awe toward the teacherly Madame, and they hold their breath and listen, posing only a few questions. In such a way, Kathy's slumber, "the ideological insensitivity the Hailsham education has inculcated in her, again allows her to record the meeting directly, as if in an interview, to preserve the words of Madame. The meeting is composed of mostly Madame's voice, her long responses to the two young clones. Madame's words require unpacking. She speaks with the voice of authority, in a self-congratulatory tone: "There was only one person in those days who would ask a question like that [the question of mistreating clones], and that was me. . . . And that made it easy for the rest of them, Marie-Claude, all the rest of them, they could all carry on without a care. All you students too. I did all the worrying and questioning for the lot of you" (254–55). Yet her claimed concern for the clones clearly contradicts her fear of them. She has an uncontrollable revulsion against the clones: "We're *all* afraid of you. I myself had to fight back my dread of you all almost every day I was at Hailsham. There were times I'd look down at you all from my study window and I'd feel such revulsion" (264; emphasis in original). Madame refuses to recognize the glaring evil done to the clones even when two of whom stand in front of her, pleading their case. She sends them away: "Poor creatures. I wish I could help you. But now you're by yourselves" (267). In describing this contradiction, Ishiguro plants a crux for the reader to consider. In this crux the critique of Madame is available from the point of view of clones. If a reader sides with the clones against the cruelty of organ harvesting, he or she is given a perspective from which to examine, in a detached manner, some established commonplaces of what humans are.

In unpacking Madame's complex voice, one should discover that she first of all invokes the long-established platitude regarding the ontology of soul. Madame attempts to examine whether a clone possesses a soul like a human being, as previously noted, by collecting the students' artwork. In explaining to Kathy the picture in her mind upon hearing the lyrics to the song "Never Let Me Go" back in the Hailsham days, Madame bares her imaginary of the biotech world: "I saw a new world coming rapidly. More scientific, efficient, yes. More cures for the old sicknesses. Very good. But a harsh, cruel world" (*NLMG* 267). Such an imaginary of a world without ontologies echoes piquantly Matthew Arnold's "Dover Beach":

> . . . for the world, which seems
> To lie before us like a land of dreams,
> So various, so beautiful, so new,
> Hath really neither joy, nor love, nor light,
> Nor certitude, nor peace, nor help for pain. (lines 30–34)

In this passage the negativity, the strong sense stimulation without "light," results from the judgment based on the absence of the ontologies of Christianity and the Greeks. Without the protective enclosure of divine ontologies, Arnold's speaker ends with a vision of ontological ignorance that sends humans into the primordial struggle: "where ignorant armies clash by night" (line 37). Similarly the novel dramatizes this Arnoldian vision, the clash of two "peoples," humans and clones, both ignorant because Madame sees clones in the negativity of ontologies and creates clones in an education that does not allow them to see ontologically, either.

Strikingly this ontological ignorance also serves as an alibi for the crime against the clones on the part of humans. Madame claims that humans are ignorant, confronting a new world in which technological development outruns human knowledge:

> And for a long time, people preferred to believe these organs appeared from nowhere, or at most that they grew in a kind of vacuum. Yes, there *were* arguments. But by the time people became concerned about . . . about *students*, by the time they came to consider just how you were reared, whether you should have been brought into existence at all, well by then it was too late. There was no way to reverse the process. How can you ask a world

> that has come to regard cancer as curable, how can you ask such a world to put away that cure, to go back to the dark days? There was no going back. (240; emphasis in original)

Here the school sponsor, Madame, reveals the common attitude in spite of the debates and controversies about raising clones. No matter how keen the concern for the clones' well-being could be, the selfish need for cures smothers public disagreement and reservations among humans, who then choose to remain ignorant about the source of organs. The Arnoldian ignorance of ontologies here receives an unexpected complication. The ignorance may not be an inevitable condition one has to accept passively; rather a scientific world without ontologies turns into a ground of rationalization to dismiss clones.

This collective ignorance for self-benefitting convenience, from the point of view of the clones, is of note, especially the state of willful ignorance. The humans' selfishness against clones vaguely but decisively draws support from the ontology of soul; the domination structure over the clones depends on their assumed lack of a human soul. However, Madame adopts, it seems, this trope merely to satisfy her conviction of her own progressivism: how she judges if a clone possesses a soul seems irrelevant to other humans and even to herself. In fact, together with her definition of the clone as akin to a human but not quite, Madame, and other humans, also share a perverse self-serving definition of the human; that is, a human is beyond doubt a possessor of a soul and thus deserves to be "complete." A keyword that rings throughout the novel is *complete.* The inevitable death of clones is said to complete after a series of organ snatching. Very ironically, the completion (death) of clones (an event) is to maintain the physiological completeness of the human body, which is vaguely assumed to reflect the presumed completeness of a soul (an ontological condition). However, humans' demand for others' organs exposes the incompleteness of their own bodies. Put simply, the ontology of the soul is mobilized to evade the real problem of exploitation. Madame, the claimed lover of the humanities, turns out to be an accomplice of this exploitation, because she participates in the collective belief in the human soul.

Ishiguro, through a realist point of view of focalizing the clones, produces a narrative that constantly calls into question the arbitrary distinction between humans and clones and therefore the ontology of the soul. This deconstruction of the ontological opposition between the human and the nonhuman is shown to be particularly ironic as the power of the discourse of the humanities is mobilized in service of exploitation and ultimately death. The soul, thus, ironically becomes the predicate of genocide. This is the "banality of evil" Ishiguro writes about. Hannah Arendt coined this phrase to make sense of Adolf Eichmann's willful ignorance of extreme racial exclusion. As a chief Nazi officer that arranged the deporting of to-be-slaughtered Jews, Eichmann, in the tribunal against him, could have claimed he did so simply because he was a good functionary serving the cause of Nazism and denied any monstrous motivation of assisting a horrendous genocide. Likewise Ishiguro sees how Madame serves the biotech regime in the name of the love for creation. Her joint assertion with nameless others that a fundamental ontological distinction exists between humans and clones keeps her callously from facing the moral crime of fatally abusing clones.

In the human-clone dialogism, what is at stake in the recognition of the nonhuman has to be ontological. While trying to place themselves socially in relation to other human characters, the clones are violently denied the ontological recognition. Ishiguro, in depicting the professed liberal Madame, opens up a polemic. Liberal-arts education confusingly endows humans with a self-centered ontological pride that might go seriously wrong. *Never Let Me Go* seems to echo several modern atrocities. Madame's banality of evil reminds one of, for example, Nazis who read Goethe in the shadow of the camps and Japanese fascists who practiced Buddhist nonattachment while ruthlessly exploiting others. However, this novel seeks to consider not just the evil practice of dehumanizing specific downtrodden races but also the dark side of idealizing all humans in terms of the ontology of soul: when humans are ontologized and nonhumans de-ontologized, the former could subject the surroundings to exploitation without critical awareness.[7]

▶ *Point Omega*

In *Never Let Me Go,* the ontological recognition of clones forces the reader to be detached from the human-centered perspective. In Don DeLillo's *Point Omega,* things found to be undetected in routinized urban life loom large to be part of the universe in its long duration. In June 2006 DeLillo went to the Museum of Modern Art (MoMA) in New York City to see *24 Hour Psycho,* an art installation created by Douglas Gordon in 1993. It replays Alfred Hitchcock's *Psycho* (1960) slowed down to approximately two frames per second, thus extending its running time to twenty-four hours. DeLillo was quite taken by this installation and revisited it "two or three times" (McCrum). "The video," he explained, "seemed a kind of meditation on such subjects as time and motion, what we see, how we see, what we miss seeing under normal circumstances" (DePietro interview). This experience was no less than an ontological encounter that seemed to have brought the author to the verge of phenomenological perception. He then determined to write a new novel inspired by this experience.[8]

Arguably *Point Omega* relativizes human loss within the long duration of time of the universe. Critics such as Kate Marshall, Pieter Vermeulen, and Bradley J. Fest have already argued toward this purpose but have not provided an account of how DeLillo experiments with realism to produce this effect.

Point Omega is composed of three parts: a prologue, a long middle section, and an epilogue. The author calls the three-part pattern of the novel a "triptych" (McCrum), but how do the three parts fit together? Interestingly this novel, in its framing and focus, is reminiscent of a French surrealist novel, André Breton's *Nadja* (1928). Their similarities are enlightening. First, as with the MoMA visits of DeLillo, *Nadja* is also derived from Breton's biographical experience. Their personal experiences written into novels challenge the distinction between fiction and reality. Second, they share a similar formal arrangement of three parts. In *Point Omega* the first and final parts are narrated by an anonymous viewer silently absorbing the slow replay of *Psycho.* Similarly *Nadja* is composed of three sections, with two smaller ones sandwiching a major narrative of an encounter with a unique woman, Nadja. Third, the first sections of both novels are set in the public spaces of museums, art galleries, or theaters. The first part of *Point Omega* relates how a viewer is absorbed in experiencing *24 Hour Psycho* and narrates the surrealist perception of discovering previously unobserved movements of things in each scene. Similarly in *Nadja* the first part narrates how Breton the character is immersed in the artwork and performances of fellow surrealist artists and is packed with self-reflexive comments on art and representation. Fourth, in the middle section, both characterize an uncanny woman as their main focus. In *Point Omega* Jessica has difficulty in coordinating her body with changing environments. Self-withdrawn, not responsive, inexplicably she is said to listen to inner voices. In terms of normative social interaction, she may be dysfunctional, but the novel encourages one not to judge but to take her as she is. In this way the acceptance of Jessica is similar to the character Breton's embrace of the insane Nadja. Thus the two novels use a similar tripartite form: the beginning and the ending parts offer personal meditation on artistic and social representation, and the central part invites the reader to look beyond the routine bourgeois horizon via an encounter with an unconventional woman. DeLillo shares with Breton the same desire to remake realism into a new form.

My reading focuses on the middle section to discuss the desert as an overwhelming actor that shares its life with the human characters in the novel. Classical realism evolves around human actors, but human stories in general depend on nonhuman elements, such as stones that make the desert. Jeffery Cohen focuses his attention on stones in the center of narrative in his *Stone: An Ecology of the Inhuman,* in which he enigmatically observes, "Stone opens to challenging story" (38). He continues, "Stony reality is perspectival; a time- and context-bound meshwork that gathers lithic and nonlithic actors without harmonizing; without yielding the unity necessary for secure point of view" (38). Cohen invites one to imagine stones, the backgrounds of human stories, to become the centerpiece. This stone-centerednesss could encourage one, in reading *Point Omega,* to focus on the geological time measured by sand and stones, in addition to the human time of the characters. Then one may read this novel as a forced confrontation of geological time with human time in which characters can make sense of the larger environments, knowingly or not.

The most conventionally realist character in the novel is Jim Finley, an urban middle-class man. He is obsessed with a reductive approach to filmmaking, seeking to produce a long take that eliminates details from within the mise-en-scène, to keep the icon of a face against a wall: "man and wall"; "a face and a voice" (*Point Omega* 99, 36). Conceiving of film as a reproduction of a human idea, Finley says, "film is the barricade" (45). DeLillo emphasizes that "Finley believes, a man's face is his soul" (DePietro interview). The novel pits Finley's impoverished filming against the outward aesthetics of *24 Hour Psycho,* in which the slow replay opens one's eyes to actualities otherwise undetected. For example the anonymous viewer at MoMA counts the shower curtain rings in the murder scene, a detail that could elude the audience's attention in a normal viewing of *Psycho.* This, among other examples, suggests the inclusive capacity of the cinematic eye, which may capture things in scopes, big or small, while presenting any given human drama. In the prologue the anonymous MoMA viewer intuits rightly that Finley is likely to diminish the complex experience of film watching into words. Finley compares his one-face shot to the classical single long take in *Russian Ark* by the Russian filmmaker Aleksandr Sokurov (22). Yet a wide gap exists between Finley's minimalism and Sokurov's incredibly complex operation. In fact Sokurov's take is an omnivorous intake, which includes "a thousand actors and extras, three orchestras, history, fantasy, crowd scenes, ballroom scenes and then an hour into the movie a waiter drops a napkin" (22). In contrast Finley's shot would be a staged one, yielding to a vacuum of the real world. Finley explains his long-shot style to the persons he stays with in the desert, including Richard Elster and Elster's daughter, Jessica. Elster considers this comparison presumptuous. Jessica bluntly returns that it is "so zombielike" (46). This retort succinctly underlines the point that, by taking out things in the mise-en-scène, a given shot misses all that matters.

Finley comes to the desert originally to secure another documentary project but finds himself reoriented by the time and space of his surroundings. He is fascinated with the old scholar Elster's career in the Iraq War. To seek an agreement to make a documentary about Elster, Finley follows him to a desert cottage, whose location is obscure: "somewhere south of nowhere in the Sonoran Desert or maybe it was the Mojave Desert or another desert altogether" (*Point Omega* 20). After his arrival the desert reorients Finley resolutely and unknowingly. Immersed in the slow time and the immense space, he is gradually distracted from his preoccupation with a single-shot documentary, even when his lifestyle does not prepare him to make it known to himself. At first he cannot let go of the interconnectivity of the urbanized life: "I went inside to check my laptop for e-mail, needing outside contact but feeling corrupt, as if I were breaking an unstated pact of creative withdrawal" (25). He has difficulty accepting this lingering in the desert, except in terms of a business term, *retreat.* The slow, indistinguishable time in the desert renders Finley's urban routines meaningless and emerges first in his narrative as disturbing ennui. However, against Finley's ontological unawareness of the desert, this novel points to the jutting appearances of things. For example DeLillo constantly conducts the trick of counting how many "members" are in a given mise-en-scène. In the prologue the anonymous viewer tracks the changing number of people in the exhibit room of MoMA. The number is not simply defined by the incoming guests, since the anonymous viewer's attention reveals other kinds of participants in the room, including the film characters and the museum guards. In the desert section, Finley assumes first that there are only two people in the lodge, but in one scene he counts three, including a trapped mouse, even though Elster is not aware of it (*Point Omega* 31). This counting seems to be a boring mind game, but in each counting the narrative also seems to ask tirelessly an ontological question: how many other different members now unknowingly participate in the human drama of the moment? Thus if one counts in the desert, the number of participants in the drama could vary, not because it really changes but because the desert is a heuristic indicator of infinite things that come to share human life.

Finley has to rely involuntarily on another person to drag him out of his urban lifestyle to appreciate the active, ontological presence of the desert. Such a need necessitates the central dialogism between Finley and Elster. The latter speaks up for the desert, and his voice is complex, ideologically conservative, but imaginatively aggressive. Elster has participated in the Pentagon war council of the Iraq War as a "defense intellectual" by stimulating brainstorming with his unconventional thinking and use of words to package the war, to sell the Iraq War like a neoliberal commercial project (*Point Omega* 28). He stays in the desert for a "spiritual retreat" from his job but does not distance himself from the past involvement. As he says unabashedly, "I still want a war" (30). His pro-war stance and the diatribe against the "old dead despotic traditions" (*Point Omega* 30) of Iraq can be offensive due to his orientalist prejudice. In spite of his conservatism, this novel still gives much room to Elster to ruminate on ontological matters such as human extinction, the death of the universe, and so on. Notably DeLillo does not attempt to create a character of unquestionable credentials to elicit a good reception of the words uttered by the same character. The realist characterization of Elster assumes that the traits of a person can be ideologically disunited and that the imaginative capacity of a person can still probe what is beyond the immediate everyday life. The armchair paleontologist-geologist is real. This characterization of Elster allows ontology to be absorbed by the democracy of realism; everyone, even an ideologically suspicious person, has the right to ontological speculation.

Furthermore, in creating the voice of Elster, DeLillo enriches realism with a poeticization of ontological conjectures, as Elster is a self-assigned poet of the desert. It seems that Elster routinely returns to the remote lodge as a result of bad experiences with timing in the urbanized world:

> It's all embedded, the hours and minutes, words and numbers everywhere, he said, train stations, bus routes, taxi meters, surveillance cameras. It's all about time, dimwit time, inferior time, people checking watches and other devices, other reminders. This is time draining out of our lives. Cities were built to measure time, to remove time from nature. (44–45)

The problem with city time, as Elster sees it, is the exactitude of timing, not allowing one to scale up or down. Elster has the layman's access to ontology. Refusing to see from the human point of view, his perception beyond the human breeds somewhat idiosyncratic visions: "Time slows down when I am here. Time becomes blind" (23). His daughter sees how Elster can comprehend the infinite scale of time in a given period of ten minutes: "He told me it was like watching the universe die over a period of about seven billion years" (47).

The paleontologist-geologist-poet Elster refers to the concept of the Omega Point, a maximum point of destination for the universe to evolve into an entity of complex consciousness, an ontological speculation by the French philosopher Pierre Teilhard de Chardin. Teilhard was an imaginative Jesuit theologian who sought to bring evolution into a system of Christian theology. He speculated about the construction of the "noosphere," said to be the result of the complex thinking of humans, congealing into a kind of collective biological membrane. As a student at Fordham University, a Jesuit institution, DeLillo came to know the theory of the Omega Point and noosphere (McCrum). In a sense the characterization of Elster the desert poet is inspired by Teilhard's evolutionary speculation, but Elster imagines the Omega Point, the end of the world, in an opposite direction (and similarly the title of the novel also reverses Teilhard's term). He says, "Do we have to be human forever? Consciousness is exhausted. Back now to inorganic matter. This is what we want. We want to be stones in a field" (53). Humans originate, Elster seems to assert, from stones and will be stones in the very long stretch of geological time. Here is an ontology-oriented perspective of humans.

While Elster literally lives within the desert, recounting its minimalizing impact on human civilization, Finley at first tends to take his poetic remarks with a grain of salt, as expressions of personal quirkiness. Yet one night, for instance, he discovers the coming of the heavenly bodies: "Behind me, [Elster's] bedroom light went out, brightening the sky, and how queer it seemed, half the heavens coming nearer, all those incandescent masses increasing in number, the stars and constellations" (*Point Omega* 54). He wonders to himself what Elster would say about this.

Soon after Finley is only vaguely enlightened by Elster's poeticization of the desert, the desert reaches him in a raw and direct manner via the disappearance of Jessica Elster. Jessica is sent by her mother in New York to stay away from a potential suitor. Finley's loneliness in the desert (a result of the agency of the desert) welcomes Jessica's presence as she chatters about her city wandering: "I liked these talks, they were quiet, with eerie depth in every stray remark she made" (42). As he listens he grows to be attached to her, but one day Elster and Finley come back to the cottage to discover no sign of Jessica. All of the meager leads as to Jessica's whereabouts come to reveal nothing, and searches by border patrols, helicopters, and volunteers are to no avail.

Significantly the plot twist of Jessica's disappearance is an innovation by DeLillo in rewriting realism, because it allows the nonhuman desert to be a main actor and the center of the story. In his search for Jessica, Finley stumbles on many things in the desert that "occasion" the disappearance of this woman. Two passages in the novel show the staggering company of the elements. Finley follows a lead of the police to a remote site in the desert, to which he tries to find his way after he has to leave his car behind: "The rough path here looked and felt like crumbled granite. Every so often I'd stop and look up and see a sky that seemed confined, compressed. I spent long moments looking. The sky was stretched taut between cliff edges, it was narrowed and lowered, that was the strange thing, the sky right there, scale the rocks and you can touch it" (*Point Omega* 92). This search forces Finley to see the sky with as little assistance as possible, free of human artifacts. The realistic prose of Finley's voice collects things, which are there all the time when he stays in the cottage, but he has to come out in this search to find his emotional loss conjoined with the subdued charisma of various voluminous rocks.

> I looked out into blinding tides of light and sky and down toward the folded copper hills that I took to be the badlands, a series of pristine ridges rising from the desert floor in patterned alignment. Could someone be dead in there? I could not imagine this. It was too vast, it was not real, the symmetry of furrows and juts, it crushed me, the heartbreaking beauty of it, the indifference of it, and the longer I stood and looked the more certain I was that we would never have an answer. (93)

The blinding sunlight in the desert forces the silhouettes, lines, patterns, and alignment of the rock formations into his scan. The beauty of the landscape is not the Kantian sublime, because the "indifference of it" outweighs the significance of a challenged rational mind, and its overpowering (crushing) presence exists regardless of humans' cares. Nor is the immense scale of the landscape a symbol. Its experiential concreteness is kept. The inaccessibility and the immense magnitude of the desert, sky, and rocks ("not real"; "too vast") deeply mark the loss of Jessica to constitute Finley's "point omega," the end of a universe (98). The loss is so final but, paradoxically, so insignificant in the long history of the universe that would return humans to stones. The same nonhuman magnitude also helps Finley to understand the futility of human attempts and to let go. After this futile search, he knows that nothing can be done and then quits waiting and searching. He returns to demand the paralyzed father Elster to leave: "We were leaving her behind" (96).

The desert is *24 Hour Psycho* super-maximized, containing both the immediacy of representation materials perceptible to the phenomenological mind and the immense, incomprehensible nonhuman elements. In *Point Omega* DeLillo reconstructs realism as stark descriptions stripped of communal associations and psychological complications. The narrator, Finley, seeks to put together the scattered, incongruous desert narrative. This narrative of disjointed experiences is not derived from a modernist or postmodernist style but rather from a relinquishing of narrative primacy to stones.

▶ Conclusion

My readings show that Ishiguro and DeLillo take upon themselves to write, in the mode of fiction, about ontology. I highlight their innovations in the altered formalism expressed in clone characterization in *Never Let Me Go* and in the active agency of the desert environment in *Point Omega*. The probing of ontology manifested in the two novels is distinct from the poststructuralist stance. Instead of holding the poststructuralist ambivalence toward ontology,[9] they seek to multiply participants in realist dialogism; at least they are populated with beings (e.g., clones in *Never Let Me Go* and rocks in the desert in *Point Omega*) crucial to, but independent from, humans.

While my intention is not to argue for a totally new realism per se, I still find it necessary to pinpoint what the composite use of realism in these two English novels would suggest. The significance of such a form, which I call altered realism, is to see the viability of novel as ontological knowledge. The normative realism popularized by the form of objective description in nineteenth-century realism, supported by positivism and empiricism, is insufficient and has to be questioned and renewed differently in the time of globalization. These two novels cast ontological knowledge into the clashes of humans versus such nonhumans as the thingness of the nebulous technological environments or the greater geographical environments, and they contribute to the global public by demanding humans to reorient themselves drastically in nonhuman worlds.

Notes

This research is funded by the research grant of the Ministry of Science and Technology: "The Ontological Longing for Form" (MOST 107–2410-H-002–047). I am deeply grateful to Prof. Allen Miller, who closely read the draft of this essay and provided extensive and thoughtful comments. Thanks also go to Bennett Fu for his comprehensive editing suggestions. I am also indebted to Jerry Weng and Mou-Lan Wong. Without the nurture of their intellectual exchanges, this research would not have been possible.

1. One is so-called capitalist realism. Alison Shonkwiler, Leigh Claire La Berge, and others, following Mark Fisher, see it as "that which is measurable within a system of capitalist equivalence," and it institutes itself as the real while not allowing one to accept an alternative real to it (2). Another is instantiated in what Jed Esty calls "realism wars" to suggest media conventions could be mobilized to uphold preferred "national mythologies" (328). Esty ambitiously surveys three historical debates of realism, including Victorian realism, antirealism, and popular realism, in the period of late Victorian years, the first two decades of Cold War, and the post–Cold War present. Realism is heatedly argued for or against during the turnover of dominating "global Anglophone hegemonies" (335), he maintains, because the geopolitical changes that come with the new empires would require cultural forms for manifestation. These realisms assume the antecedent of the literary realism of the nineteenth century and seek to explain how globalization requires cultural forms to validate ideological world-making.

2. The turns to ontology, above all, have strong anchors in sciences, such as Karen Barad's "agential realism," derived from quantum physics, Catherine Malabou's "materialist neuroplasticity" in neurosciences, and Bruno Latour's "realistic realism," derived from the studies of the history of sciences. Some philosophers too attend to the significance of materiality and articulate theories of ontology, such as the speculative realism of Quentin Meillassoux, the object-oriented philosophy of Graham Harman, the vibrant matter of Jane Bennett, the transcendental realism of Ray Brassier, and, last but not least, Michel Serres's "philosophy of the hard and the soft."

3. Meillassoux is an influential French theorist of materialism, who evocatively uses in his book *After Finitude* the terms "the Great Outdoors" and "the ancestrality" to speculate about the existence of the "worlds" human consciousness cannot reach. This radical materialist ontology propelled the formation of what is called object-oriented ontology, which also questions, as Meillassoux vocally does, the ambiguity of Kant's epistemology regarding human knowledge of things themselves. Among proponents of this philosophy, Graham Harman attempts to discuss how literary theory can be understood in a non-human-centered way. Harman in 2012 attempted

in a very succinct fashion to take on the task of theorizing the materiality of literature. On another occasion he remarks, "Any given moment in a literary work (all the way down to specific words and even parts of words, and all the way up to the work as a whole), like any object or thing, is 'fatally torn' between its deeper reality and its accidents, relations, and qualities: a set of tensions that makes everything in the universe possible, including space and time" (*Towards Speculative Realism* 150).

4. In Bakhtin's writings the tension between humans and nonhumans remains.

5. Commenting on Ishiguro's novel *The Buried Giant* in a blog post, Ursula Le Guin expressed resentment, which she retracted later, of how Ishiguro did not play by the rules of fantasy. She blamed Ishiguro for tangentially using fantasy and insisted instead that "the imaginary must *be imagined,* accurately and with scrupulous consistency" (Le Guin). Ishiguro was surprised by this criticism, since he did not assume that the boundary of fantasy should be policed in this strict manner (Gaiman and Ishiguro).

6. Bruce Robbins underlines Ishiguro's experience of being a social worker (295).

7. I thank Prof. Allen Miller for his insightful reading of my manuscript, which helped me to reach this conclusion.

8. In the published novel of 2010, he records the installation exhibit with both a diary-like time marker in the front of the novel and a copyright acknowledgment in the back.

9. Jacques Derrida proclaims "the end of the book" (*Of Grammatology* 6), which refers to the impossibility of '"the idea of a totality . . . of the signifier," "a natural totality" (18). Bronislaw Szerszynsky, among others, takes to heart Derrida's statement if understood in the time of de-anthropocentricism to see how ecologies can be narrated: "So if we are to discern a 'geoethics' or the Anthropocene, it cannot take the form of a good, pure writing, enclosed in and stabilised by the volume of the book of nature, or by the self-present human subject. It will take place in and be conditioned by the much more unstable volume opened up by this multiple dispersal of the human" (181). This interpretation of what deconstruction can mean in the analysis of a new writing is compelling; however, it is still limited by the Derridean operation, which places the making of transparent narratives and the breaking down of them as the twin movement. Consequently ontology is only possible in the breaking down, rendered in the form of the negative, unknown, indescribable. I would say the Derridean breakdown, or "spacing," could be inadequate to designate the positive presence of ontological effects in the two novels in discussion.

Works Cited

Arendt, Hannah. *Eichmann in Jerusalem: A Report on the Banality of Evil.* New York: Penguin, 2006.

Arnold, Matthew. *Selected Poems of Matthew Arnold.* London: Macmillan, 1886.

Atwood, Margaret. "Brave New World." *Slate.* 1 Apr. 2005, http://www.slate.com/articles/arts/books/2005/04/brave_new_world.html. Accessed 21 Feb. 2018.

Bakhtin, Mikhail. "Discourse in the Novel." *The Dialogic Imagination: Four Essays*. Ed. Michael Holquist. Trans. Caryl Emerson and Michael Holquist. Austin: U of Texas P, 1981. 269–422.

Becker, George J. "Realism: An Essay in Definition." *Modern Language Quarterly* 10.2 (1949): 184–97.

Benjamin, Walter. "On Some Motifs in Baudelaire." *Illuminations*. Trans. Harry Zohn. New York: Schocken Books, 1968. 155–200.

Brandão, Luis Alberto. "Chronotope." *Theory, Culture and Society* 23.2–3 (2006): 133–34.

Breton, André. *Nadja*. Trans. Richard Howard. New York: Grove, 1960.

Byron, Glennis, and Linda Ogston. "Educating Kathy: Clones and Other Creatures in Kazuo Ishiguro's *Never Let Me Go*." *21st Century Gothic: Great Gothic Novels since 2000*. Ed. Daniel Olson. Lanham: Scarecrow, 2011. 453–64.

Cohen, Jeffrey Jerome. *Stone: An Ecology of the Inhuman*. Minneapolis: U of Minnesota P, 2015.

Coole, Diana H., and Samantha Frost, eds. *New Materialisms: Ontology, Agency, and Politics*. Durham: Duke UP, 2010. http://dx.doi.org/10.1215/9780822392996. Accessed 21 Feb. 2018.

De Boever, Arne. "The Realist Novel and 'the Great Outdoors': Towards a Literary-Speculative Realism." *Genealogies of Speculation: Materialism and Subjectivity since Structuralism*. Eds. Suhail Malik and Armen Avanessian. London: Bloomsbury Academic, 2016.

DeLillo, Don. Interview by Thomas DePietro. *Barnes and Noble Review*. 1 Feb. 2010, https://www.barnesandnoble.com/review/don-delillo. Accessed 21 Feb. 2018.

——. *Point Omega: A Novel*. New York: Scribner, 2010.

Dentith, Simon. "Realist Synthesis in the Nineteenth-Century Novel: 'That Unity Which Lies in the Selection of our Keenest Consciousness.'" *Adventures in Realism*. Ed. Matthew Beaumont. Malden: Blackwell, 2007. 33–49.

Derrida, Jacques. *Of Grammatology*. Trans. Gayatri Chakravorty Spivak. Baltimore: Johns Hopkins UP, 2013.

Esty, Jed. "Realism Wars." *Novel: A Forum on Fiction* 49.2 (2016): 316–42.

Fest, Bradley J. "Geologies of Finitude: The Deep Time of Twenty-First-Century Catastrophe in Don DeLillo's *Point Omega* and Reza Negarestani's *Cyclonopedia*." *Critique: Studies in Contemporary Fiction* 57.5 (2016): 565–78.

Gaiman, Neil, and Kazuo Ishiguro. "'Let's Talk about Genre': Neil Gaiman and Kazuo Ishiguro in Conversation." *New Statesman*, 4 Jun. 2015, https://www.newstatesman.com/2015/05/neil-gaiman-kazuo-ishiguro-interview-literature-genre-machines-can-toil-they-can-t-imagine. Accessed 21 Feb. 2018.

Griffin, Gabriele. "Science and the Cultural Imaginary: The Case of Kazuo Ishiguro's *Never Let Me Go*." *Textual Practice* 23.4 (2009): 645–63.

Haraway, Donna. "A Cyborg Manifesto." *Manifestly Haraway*. Minneapolis: U of Minnesota P, 2016. 3–90.

Harman, Graham. *Towards Speculative Realism: Essays and Lectures.* Ripley, Hampshire: Zero Books, 2010.

Ishiguro, Kazuo. *Never Let Me Go.* London: Faber, 2005.

Latour, Bruno. *Reassembling the Social: An Introduction to Actor-Network-Theory.* Oxford: Oxford UP, 2005.

——. *We Have Never Been Modern.* Trans. Catherine Porter. Cambridge, Mass.: Harvard UP, 1993.

Le Guin, Ursula K. "'Are They Going to Say This Is Fantasy?'" *Book View Café Blog,* 2 Mar. 2015, http://bookviewcafe.com/blog/2015/03/02/are-they-going-to-say-this-is-fantasy/. Accessed 21 Feb. 2018.

Malafouris, Lambros. *How Things Shape the Mind: A Theory of Material Engagement.* Cambridge, Mass.: MIT P, 2013.

Marshall, Kate. "What Are the Novels of the Anthropocene? American Fiction in Geological Time." *American Literary History* 27.3 (2015): 525–38.

McCrum, Robert. "Don DeLillo: 'I'm Not Trying to Manipulate Reality—This Is What I See and Hear.'" *Guardian,* 8 Aug. 2010. https://www.theguardian.com/books/2010/aug/08/don-delillo-mccrum-interview. Accessed 21 Feb. 2018.

Meillassoux, Quentin. *After Finitude: An Essay on the Necessity of Contingency.* London: Continuum, 2008.

Robbins, Bruce. "Cruelty Is Bad: Banality and Proximity in *Never Let Me Go.*" *Novel: A Forum on Fiction* 40.3 (2007): 289–302.

Shonkwiler, Alison, and Leigh Claire La Berge. "Introduction: A Theory of Capitalist Realism." *Reading Capitalist Realism.* Ed. Alison Shonkwiler and Leigh Claire La Berge. Iowa City: U of Iowa P, 2014. 1–25.

Stefans, Brian Kim. "Terrible Engines: A Speculative Turn in Recent Poetry and Fiction." *Comparative Literature Studies* 51.1 (2014): 159–83.

Stone, Jonathan. "Polyphony and the Atomic Age: Bakhtin's Assimilation of an Einsteinian Universe." *PMLA* 123.2 (2008): 405–21.

Szegedy-Maszák, Mihály. "Notes toward a Historical Definition of Realism." *Neohelicon* 15.2 (1988): 31–54.

Szerszynski, Bronislaw. "The End of the End of Nature: The Anthropocene and the Fate of the Human." *Oxford Literary Review* 34.2 (2012): 165–84.

Vermeulen, Pieter. "Don DeLillo's *Point Omega,* the Anthropocene, and the Scales of Literature." *Studia Neophilologica* 52, supplement 1 (2015): 68–81.

Whitehead, Anne. "Writing with Care: Kazuo Ishiguro's *Never Let Me Go.*" *Contemporary Literature* 52.1 (2011): 54–83.

Ghost in the Machine

Fetishism and the Laboring Body in Marx, Dickens, and Mayhew

Hisup Shin

While many scholars agree that capitalist globalization in the twenty-first century marks the way in which the world is increasingly assimilated beyond national or cultural boundaries, the voice of consent quickly disappears when examining different aspects of assimilation such as patterns of economic networking and social or institutional agents.[1] At the heart of this debate is the difficulty in coming to terms with the paths of globalization that are slipping out of the localized setting of economic and extra-economic situations to ensure the limitless extension of market exchange. The constant need to invent new measures and languages to promote the exchange between different qualities of goods and people entails an act of "redefin[ing] what counts as the given state of society which sets the boundaries of equalization processes" (Hartman 194). No longer bound up in the existing frame of valuation defined by each locality, capitalist globalization prioritizes the means of abstraction by which one's specific situatedness in his or her milieu is compelled to adopt shifting measures of equivalence. While adopting apparently analytical modes of quantification, this task of abstraction is conflict ridden, wrought by the struggles among competing social or ideological forces worldwide. Eva Hartman brings to the fore the concept of "fetishism," a term that she suggests can recall for critical thinking the conflicting realities concealed underneath the quantitative representation of world economy:

> In consequence, the "quantitative" analysis no longer accounts for the context within which the fiction of equality is established, and risks reifying the dissociation. Such a disregard essentially privileges the viewpoint of capital and loses sight of the fetish character of the equalisation process masking the dependence of capital on the always very specific given state of society. (Hartman 190)

The point of interest in this essay has to do in part with the Marxist legacy of the term that has been duly noted in the passage, which goes back to the capitalist economy of Great Britain in the nineteenth century, when the term was first introduced as a sign of violent abstraction obscuring the concrete social realities underneath the functioning of capital. Fetishism, while remaining effective in the critical diagnosis of capitalism in the era of global exchanges and relations, has a very rich interdisciplinary genealogy, whose shifting ideas and images suggest the meaning of the term beyond the Marxist parameter.

My aim in this essay is to explore the theory of fetishism as a site of conflicting discourses traversing a variety of intellectual and social fields from anthropology to economy at a time when England was becoming increasingly materialist in shaping its modern outlook. Originally coined to designate a specific type of material experience that is deemed unscientific and primitive, the term *fetishism* gained further significance when Karl Marx adopted it in order to capture dehumanizing patterns of materialistic life under capitalism. My view is that while Marx's use of the term is primarily critical in diagnosing the way in which individuals (laborers) are compelled to adopt thing-like attributes in their participation in the commodity market, it also offers an alternative insight into the very same features of dehumanization, a fetishist insight extending beyond the Marxist frame of critical thinking. In particular this essay will show how this insight organizes a unique bodily figuration assigned to physical labor—a bodily type whose theoretical and historical significance becomes discernible in its intervention of the way in which the nineteenth-century discourse of political economy reproduces "a recognizably Victorian disgust for the body" (Gallagher, "Body" 104). With this interventionary view in mind, I will later account for, by comparison, a small selection of texts by Marx, Charles Dickens, and Henry Mayhew, all of which deal with the laboring body.

I should also say at the outset that the essay includes different theoretical or textual sites whose involvement with fetishism varies to some extent: while some discussions are directly about fetishism, others are chosen as they fall within its broad theoretical reach covering different variations and implications. As suggested above, the reason for this inclusive scope has to do with the way in which fetishism underwent conceptual or thematic shifts, often crossing disciplinary boundaries. For this reason the essay will account for, first of all, fetishism in its entry to the world of Victorian material culture; at which point it operates not so much as a theoretical or conceptual origin but as an expanding scope of discursivity by negotiating or colliding with different views or claims about material experiences. Particular emphasis will be placed on how this discursive operation is not smoothly carried out, but contains within it a conflicting tension, which will be used as a conceptual backdrop that informs a range of theoretical variations that the essay pursues.

▶ Victorian Material Culture and the Discourse of Fetishism

In *Victorian Things* cultural historian Asa Briggs claims that "it was through nineteenth-century anthropology that the concept of 'material culture' was explicitly introduced to the study of things, from the start bringing into the reckoning materials as well as artifacts, while at the same time relating man-made things to minerals, flora and fauna, which compose the environment in which people live" (30). This remark suggests what can be considered an "anthropomorphic" order of things in Victorian England, an order that in all its biased discourses and implications tends to represent the world of things as a natural habitat for humans. Broadly speaking, the making of Victorian material culture can be seen as a logical response to the way in which England became increasingly "materialized" in its unstoppable drive of industrial-consumerist capitalism. Not only the advent of railways, steamers, and the telegraph but also the broadening market for mass-produced consumer goods were quickly changing the way in which people related to their living environments. In bestowing humanized patterns of thinking and behaviors on the increasing growth and diversity of the material realm, the material culture ensured that things are sufficiently incorporated into the human world, into its existing frames of knowledge and living.

Crucial to this process of cultural signification is how language is used to turn this material world into a domain of human agency in which things serve to reflect its rational, often collective intentions and needs. The problem is that this rationalist view of language can be put in peril by the way in which things, on certain occasions, tend to persist in their own materiality and move beyond the jurisdiction of knowledge, taking on a series of attributes not accessible to human understanding. One such occasion has to do with what recent cultural historian Thomas Richards describes as a kind of linguistic figuration in identifying the common thread of representation in commodity cultures. In a treatment of the commodity culture of Victorian England, he observes how language develops "a maddening way of transforming the means of description into a high drama of human agency, a fantastic realm in which things think, act, speak, rise, fall, fly, evolve" (11). Consisting of "expanded narratives and supplemental metaphors" (11), this "fantastic realm" stands for human ingenuity involved in the task of merchandising products: if things appear animate or even human, it is because manufacturers and advertisers deliberately create this illusion in order to encourage buyers to relate to their products in a personal, subjective manner.

Consider phosphorous matches that were first commercialized in the 1830s and went on quickly to become one of the most common manufactured objects in England. Selling more than 80 million boxes of matches each year by the end of the nineteenth century, several manufacturers were in competition, offering unique kinds with distinct brand names. Bryant and May alone introduced "Brymay matches," "ruby matches" (1862), "tiger matches" (1864), "elephant matches" and "Victoria matches" (1870), "runaway matches" (1864), "Sultan matches" (1871), and, for export, "Cleopatra Flamers" (1878) and "Pillar Box Vestas" (1878).[2] Ranging from jewels and animals to famous rulers and a Roman deity of fire, these names evoke unique qualities of value and power attached to each product. The figural transposition of the things in all their peculiar, fantastic attributes reflects the way in which we understand culture—that is, how culture organizes a distinct, cohesive sense of communal belongingness by sharing codes or symbols of meaning unique to it.

The point of contention is how this symbolic, often malleable sense of cultural cohesiveness formed through acts of signification is counterpoised by a rationalist discourse of things in Victorian England. What is problematic from the latter point of view is how such acts of cultural inscription in bestowing on things humanized attributes potentially undermine what can be considered as the rationalist jurisdiction of human practice in which things emerge only as "tools" subordinate to the rational end of human intentionality. By the rational end, I am broadly referring to the historical or theoretical legacy of the Enlightenment in pursuing the universal moral end of human reason across different levels of experiences, which is what many Victorian intellectuals and critics had in mind when accounting for patterns of human conduct in relating to the material world.

In proportion to the ever-thickening materialist texture of everyday life woven into mass-produced consumer products, critical voices grew louder, warning the public of what they saw as signs of inordinate consumerism. John Ruskin and William Morris, both outspoken critics of culture and technology, wrote disapprovingly about various manufactured objects, whose uniform styles and mechanical features, they feared, would encourage patterns of consumer behaviors adverse to one's organic, moral sense of social belongingness. Underlying their fear is what they saw as an alarming degree to which the world of commodification and consumerism was being incorporated into a new cultural pattern, a pattern in which one's involvement with commodities becomes extremely subjective and arbitrary. In an article titled "The Fashion of Furniture" published in the *Cornhill Magazine* (1865), one of the most famous literary and culture magazines in the latter half of the nineteenth century, an anonymous writer makes such a critical observation: "There is a direct analogy between the spirit which induces a vulgar woman to dress beyond her station in life at a sacrifice of more necessary requirements, and the silly demand of small householders that the fittings of their dwellings should ape those of a much higher rent" (346). In all their different, often whimsical expressions and styles, Victorians were inventing a new culture of tastes and imagination invoked by manufactured objects and technology. Charles Dickens, among others, noted this unique Victorian investment in new objects in *Household Words,* his journal launched in 1850, many of whose articles were devoted to specific things from needles to wine bottles: "The mightier inventions of the age are not to our thinking, all material, but have a kind of soul in their stupendous bodies" (Dickens, "Preliminary" 1). By "the mightier inventions of the age," Dickens of course refers to the likes of railways and steamboats, whose feats of technological revolution are deservingly labeled with terms of "spirituality and soul that transcend commonplace materiality" (Philpotts 209). What is unmistakable, nevertheless, is how such a metaphorical treatment—"a kind of soul in their stupendous bodies"—is typical of the pattern of cultural assimilation traversing all man-made objects high and low or noble and commonplace, in the sense it tends to familiarize and humanize them as part of what I earlier referred to as the anthropomorphic tendency of Victorian material culture.

In trying to counter this cultural influence, the Victorian rationalist discourse of things adopted an anthropological frame of interpretation that delineated not only differences among men and their societies but also how these differences can be diachronically reshuffled as different stages in an evolutionary succession of human development. As many cultural historians argue, anthropology emerged as an eclectic field of investigation combining different disciplines from ethnology to sociology by the second half of the nineteenth century thanks to its effort to explore broadening possibilities and suggestions of Darwinian evolutionary theory. This meant that anthropology operated as a set of assumptions and prejudices, "which saw the development of mankind as a physical being, the growth of human culture, and differentiation of human languages as parts of a single evolutionary process" (Stocking 271). For all its sweeping, often pseudo-scientific narrative of monogenism, it responded most satisfactorily to an ideological as well as rationalist need to underscore the idea of civilization and progress as envisaged by "the 18th-century belief in human rationality"—that is, the way in which Europeans tried to understand and control the world around themselves (Stocking 220).

In particular, relevant to our inquiry is how this Eurocentric frame also tried to tell a story of material progress interweaving all kinds of man-made objects collected from different parts of the world into a coherent evolutionary process. Colonel Augustus Henry Lane-Fox's collection of man-made objects[3] was particularly evolutionary in the sense it tried to embody "the successive ideas by which the minds of men in a primitive condition of culture have progressed in the development of their arts from the simple to the complex, and from the homogeneous to the heterogeneous" (Lane-Fox xi). Unmistakable in his account is the Eurocentric frame of evolutionary progress that marked its heights of achievement by measuring its distance from what was called "primitive condition." In designating the "primitive condition of culture," he assumed a state of cultural stagnation in some parts of the world where "amongst the arts of existing savages we find forms which, being adapted to a low condition of culture, have survived from the earliest times" (Lane-Fox xiv). By eliminating from consideration internal social and historical forces at work, Lane-Fox's theory of cultural anthropology projected the fixed image of savages as a relatively rigid pattern of material practice from fabrication to daily use: "Things themselves are handed down unchanged from father to son and from tribe to tribe, and many of them have continued to our own time faithful records of the conditions of the people by whom they were fabricated" (Lane-Fox xv).

Nowhere is this timeless image of material practice more suggestively deployed than in the discourse of fetishism. In what can be broadly considered as the Eurocentric frame of ethnographic representation, the term *fetishism* was used as early as the mid-eighteenth century in order to designate patterns of material practice among non-European indigenous tribes and groups that were deemed irrational or scientifically backward. Often found in forms of primitive religious worship, the term refers to "the mistake of the pre-enlightened mind [in] superstitiously attributing internal purpose and desire to material entities of the natural world" (Pietz 139). This subjective, often arbitrary attachment to materiality was set in contrast to the secular frame of the Enlightenment rationality, which offered a basically scientific-mechanistic view of the material world—a world of physical nature that could be incorporated into the moral end of human intentionality only through the informed act of production and use. In attributing to the material world various supernatural properties catering to personal whims and desires, fetishism stands for the lowest stage of material experience in which men appear submerged in what William Pietz calls "a sort of libidinal aesthetics," a clear sign of "the perverse submission of intellect and moral will" (140).

▶ Fetishism at Crossroads: Scenes of Exchange between Humans and Things in Marx

What is problematic is that the theory of fetishism and its biased assumptions as a measure of anthropological and cultural distinction was increasingly cast in doubt by the unstoppable momentum of European capitalism, through which the money valuation of material production and wealth fosters what Pietz terms "the fetishistic materializ[ation] of bourgeois production" (147). From labor and other productive resources to commodities and the money-form itself, all forms of value creation and circulation can be seen as a modern fetish in the sense that each of these forms is "magical" in its capacity to designate or even change into something else, abstracted as it is into a measure of value equivalence or commensurability in the capitalist market. This seemingly limitless versatility of the monetarized productive capital—captured by Marx in several memorable terms including "dazzling commodities," "sublime objectivity," and "mysterious equivalent form" (*Capital* 140–49)—is treated as a fetish object of inordinate worship, as it accounts for the drive of human desire at its most arbitrary or volatile degrees. Likewise the world outside the productive capital is no longer an impersonal structure of physical solidity but one that appears directly subject to the arbitrary desire by forming itself into respective relations (exchange relations or values). Seen in this way, the fetishized sensuous perception of materiality in Marx ultimately refers to the troubling fate of modern individuals, whose increasingly obsessive involvement in the capitalist system poses great hindrance to the rationalist need to arrive at the transcendental end of moral pursuits. By obstructing the possibility of moral transcendence, the productive capital, "which had been merely the means to obtain wealth (the power to gratify concrete human desires whose origins and logic are external to its system), becomes identified with wealth" (Pietz 147).

Important to consider here is how the theory of fetishism in Marx can be seen a strategy of defamiliarization with which to unearth a dimension of human experience beyond the conventional frame of thinking about humanity. By adopting "the maximally alien perspective of the primitive fetishist, a cultural other for whom material conditions are themselves spiritual values" (Pietz 143), Marx is able to observe and theorize the "otherness" of European civilization, a world of materialist valuation and obsession that displaces rationalist claims of European cultural or social progress. For all its "primitive" features, this world gains creditability by capturing men in their concrete, fully embodied psychological as well as physical realities, which are brought on by the way their daily lives and pursuits are carried out in the seamless fabric of material relations.

In particular the fetishism discourse is able to focus on the site of materiality at which individuals are formed in different material relations beyond what Jean Baudrillard wryly calls "the splendor of the subject that totalizes the world" (qtd. in Brown 8). For Marx the prospect of this "de-subjectivated" materialist realism culminates in the rise of the modern working class as an otherness to civil society, whose material relations are so extensive and perpetual that they view themselves as a commodity to be exchanged in the market. In all their dehumanizing, often mechanical features of physical activities, their experience brings to light the inextricability of material conditions in the continuum of their lives: "Owing to the extensive use of machinery and to division of labor, the work of the proletarians has lost all individual character, and, consequently, all charm for the workman. He becomes an appendage of the machine and it is only the most simple, most monotonous, and most easily acquired knack, that is required of him" (Marx, "Manifesto" 74). At one level it is clear that the image of miserable working conditions as the dark double of the Enlightenment project emerges only under Marx's fetishist perspective, whose lingering materialist gaze reveals the way in which individuals, far from transcending the material world, remain captive to its inherent law of mechanical motions and applications. It must be said, however, that Marx's fetishism discourse as a defamiliarization strategy is primarily self-cancelling, in the sense that it gives way to a historical struggle for social change in which the shocking features of dehumanization—bodily fragmentation, psychical alienation, and the like—are eventually overcome by a proletarian act of self-realization (Marx, "Manifesto" 78).

At another level the same signs of desubjectification can potentially allude to a field of practice in which the body appears as something quite unfamiliar to itself in its unexpected capacity to mold itself into different adjustments and intensities extending beyond its self-same identity. In my opinion the possibility of such a theoretical reversal is first envisaged by Marx himself, whose account of dehumanization under capitalism gives way to a broad array of figural analogies and fusion intermixing man, animal, and machine. As recounted in the quote shown above, the reduced state of humanity defining the laborers is captured by their physical experience, whose scope of bodily application is such that when caught in the momentum of labor intensity, whatever posits human crosses over into nonhuman, or vice versa: "He becomes an appendage of the machine." Earlier in another writing, he also observes how a similar working condition engenders "the loss of [one's] self" to such an extent that the sense of subjectival coherence is replaced by signs of bodily fragmentation and displacement: "The result is that the worker feels that he is acting freely only in animal functions—eating, drinking, procreating, or at most in his shelter or his finery—while in his human functions he feels himself nothing more than an animal. What is animal becomes human and what is human becomes animal" (Marx, "Manuscripts" 137).

Important to note here is how these features of dehumanization in both passages are occasioned by degrees of abstraction in representing the human body in the capitalist market; the body is thus treated as an object to be measured against or exchanged with other objects. Underlying this abstract thinking is a social as well as epistemological need to forge a sense of similitude with which one can translate the world of difference or multiplicity into an extending network of meaningful relations and sharable properties.[4] What appears dehumanizing is in fact constituted by a rhetorical process of reduction and substitution, by which whatever makes an individual or a thing unique is erased beyond distinction and reconfigured as a measure of abstract value commensurable with each other. It is to this extent that a recent commentator of Marx's value theory argues that "Marx had first seemed to propose that economic exchange was simply a matter of metaphor, of exchange based on resemblance or similitude" (Keenan 166).

I want to argue that such a rhetorical outlook on Marx's fetishism discourse suggests a different line of reading for the negative attributes regarding the laboring body. In my view Marx's emphasis on the sense of physical immediacy or empirical certainty overlaying those features can be conceptually misleading, since the laboring body at its entry to the world of exchange is, he also argues, transformed into an abstract figure—"the human labor in the abstract" (Marx, *Capital* 128)—in order to gain a value of social currency.[5] In other words the very site of physical exploitation and mechanization potentially suggests an individual capacity for abstraction to be socially meaningful, a means by which one considers his labor activities no longer in subjective terms but as a measure of equivalence to be commensurable with any other socially productive activities, human or nonhuman. At the micro-physical level of labor practice, this feat of abstraction spells out a process of bodily objectification and management by which the body becomes depersonalized and emerges as a complex transaction of different functions, impulses, and habits in response to shifting working conditions.

Furthermore this abstract conditioning of the laboring body largely stands in keeping with what Jonathan Crary considers as a major shift in the representation of the human body at the turn of the nineteenth century, which is marked by "an interrogation of the physiological makeup of the human subject" (*Techniques* 70). In a way that overturns the classical model of the mind-body hierarchy, the physiological makeup entails an incessant influx of pulses and impulses, moods and sensations, vibrations as well as motions, which renders the condition of human knowledge and representation highly subjective and unstable. What follows this physiological insight is a language and technology of abstraction devised with a view to treating the body as "forms of investigation, regulation, and discipline throughout the nineteenth century" (Crary, *Techniques* 73). What should not be overlooked here is that this regulatory treatment of the body is not just limited to external forces of ideology or power but also reflects, as suggested above, the way in which each individual goes about in constantly adjusting and recasting one's body in order to relate to the world. What may appear impersonal or mechanical, in other words, reflects in part one's need for a physiological link to the world, without which the body can potentially face the imponderable fate of existential emptiness mired in subjective sensations and impulses. In consideration of this need for "socially articulated physiological functions" (Crary, *Suspensions* 44), Chris Shilling suggests the term *corporeal realism* (12) in order to prioritize all bodily matters as the irreducible condition of possibility for realistic representation. As a result the body is not just an ideological construct but also produces a meaningful pattern of adjustments coordinated by the way in which its irreducible physiological features negotiate with the external environments. It is in this sense that Shilling claims that the body is "an emergent phenomenon that is central to the generation of society," which refers to the way in which the body "intervenes in and molds our natural and social environment in certain ways, and that the physical dispositions and habits we acquire while engaging in such activities are consequential for the viability of existing social structures" (13–14).

To return to my earlier point about the concept of abstraction, then, this bodily negotiation is likened to Marx's account of "human labor in the abstract" in the exchange market, since it too takes on a process of abstraction to establish a range of functional parallels and regulatory analogies between the body and the external environments. As suggested earlier, the physiological abstraction, while taking on the nonhuman attributes of things, machines, animals, and so forth, cannot be said to be totally engulfed by the structural transposition to a level of nondistinction. In a way analogous to what Marx refers to as "phantom-like objectivity," a kind of supersensible leftover from the materiality of human labor remaining after its commodification,[6] this physiological abstraction also leaves behind a shadowy figure of corporeality lingering on those parallels and analogies. Conceptually speaking, this phantom corporeality serves as a point of distinction for selfhood to be made against all its corresponding figures in comparison, without which there will be no exchanging relation between humans and things or humans and animals.[7]

Crucial to note here is how this ghostly corporeality does not just remain as a theoretical necessity but also operates as a kind of slippery momentum lodged in one's sense of physiological beingness, which is marked by its jarring tension with deterministic forces outside—a range of technological rules, institutional disciplines, and the like. It is this residual momentum of the physiological body—lingering pulsations, impulses, and feelings—detected at the site of abstraction and environmental adjustment that often stands as the empirical basis for theoretical challenges and social practices directed at forces of determinism. For instance in what is now called "everyday life studies" among scholars of cultural studies, the ghostly corporeality stands as a micro-physical backdrop of corporeal realism that devises a range of intriguing strategies of bodily adjustment: in a way that complicates the frame of technological or institutional constraints, these strategies often betoken a duplicitous sense of physiological responses or maneuverability, by which one can both obey and challenge technologies and rules of movements prescribed on the body.[8] As a result those parallels and analogies into which the body is abstracted are not exactly in mechanical conformity to the external procedures but are a site of constant negotiations.

▶ Fetishism at Crossroads: Scenes of Exchange between Men and Things in Dickens and Mayhew

Consider, for instance, what Steven Connor calls the "slippery" nature of Dickens's writing, defined by the way in which "it can just as easily be associated with or borrow from the energies of industrial capitalism as it can oppose them" (Connor 9). This paradoxical vitality of Dickens's writing, in my opinion, is most acutely sensed when accounting for his urban characters beset by technologically as well as professionally challenging circumstances. At the heart of comic characterization is the sense of ghostly corporeality lending itself to diverse strategies of physiological adjustment, by means of which his characters challenge as well as conform to the sway of technological and administrative rationalization pervading professions and social relations.

In *Great Expectations,* for example, Wemmick's figure appears, first of all, as an abstract form, merging into the inhuman, mechanical setting of Mr. Jaggers's legal office, where he works as a clerk: "His mouth was such a post-office of a mouth that he had a mechanical appearance of smiling. We had got to the top of Holborn Hill before I knew that it was merely a mechanical appearance, and that he was not smiling at all" (172). However, the physical abstraction and transformation is not of total technological or environmental determinism but unexpectedly discloses what is intrinsically slippery about the character's bodily presence. As a result Wemmick's "mechanical appearance," at the moment it is acted out, becomes complicated by the sense of ghostly corporeality that slips out of the frame of abstraction and serves as a shadowy but palpably unruly physiological backdrop to all his bodily motions and adjustments. It is no coincidence that Wemmick is by far the most persistent itinerant character in the novel—"I have had my legs under the desk all day and shall be glad to stretch them" (204)—whose skillful pedestrian movements and trajectories interweaving different locales and social relations reflect both the almost commodity-like exchangeability of his physical abstraction and a subversive tendency to conceal within it secret signs and meanings. It is thus while engaging in yet another walking tour with Pip along the streets, whose "moves [he] knows" so well (172), that Wemmick slips into their itinerary a casual stop at a church in order to hold his own secret wedding ceremony. Upon leaving the church, he "triumphantly" avows as he quickly resumes his pedestrian mode: "Now, Mr. Pip . . . let me ask you whether anybody would suppose this to be a wedding party!" (454). In the overall frame of Dickens's storytelling primarily geared to the level of bodily figuration and analysis for meaningful characterization and encounters, Wemmick's strategy of dissimulation can only stem from a sense of physical tension within, a ghostly corporeality that jars with the prevailing force of social or technological instrumentality and discipline circumscribing his bodily abstraction. In my opinion this spectral physicality unexpectedly finds a fantasy figuration not referring to itself, which is basically without any stable substance or figuration, but referring to a house where even such a ghostly body is able to rest and leave its more or less visible marks and traces. Wemmick's secret shelter of privacy and family is a diminutive, comical "wooden cottage," which is nevertheless designed to embody, according to his opinion, "the idea of fortification": "It's a principle with me, if you have an idea, carry it out and keep it up" (207). As the source of all the ingenious tactics for deception and secrecy, this "idea of fortification" betokens Wemmick's ghostly body.

Broadly speaking, Dickens's nuanced, interventionary approach to the human body stands in suggestive parallel with the way in which England by the mid-nineteenth century decidedly looked at physical labor as an object of investigation and analysis. In chiming with a growing emphasis on technologies of governmentality with which to treat society as a site of control and discipline, the analytic turn in the representation of physical labor reflects a pattern of Victorian discourse in which the nation's system of social governance as well as economic productivity hinges on the fitness of the laboring body. Consider briefly how Thomas Malthus's influential study of the nation's political economy in *Essay on the Principles of Population* (1798) and Henry Mayhew's much less theoretical but equally influential documentation of urban working classes in *London Labour and the London Poor* (1861) both converge on the "conversion of economic to physiological categories" (Gallagher, "Body" 99) in the representation of the nation's productivity. What appears more empirical and concrete than Marx's value theory in their extensive inclusion of human physiology is, however, complicated by the sense of ambivalence with which bodily matters are related. The sense of ambivalence is derivative of the fundamental ambiguity of the human body caught between two irreconcilable forces: one consisting of socially articulated tasks and technologies designed to represent the laboring body as a coherent, rule-bound frame of physiological functions and the other defined by its very same functions to produce signs of aberration. Thus while recognizing the laboring body's productivity as the basis of their economic discourse dealing with various issues from working conditions to physical welfare, they were doubtful whether the same body would fit into the ever-broadening market of exchange values governed by rules of abstraction and structural adjustment.

Mayhew's following negative depiction of costermongers at the street market, for instance, can be seen as a direct response to this bodily dilemma:

> The pavement and the road are crowded with purchasers and street-sellers. . . . Then the tumult of the thousand different cries of the eager dealers, all shouting at the top of their voices, at once and the same time, is almost bewildering. . . . Such indeed is the riot, the struggle, and the scramble for a living, that the confusion and uproar of the New-cut on Saturday night have a bewildering and saddening effect upon the thoughtful mind. (13–14)

In all their vigorous, often riotous activities of peddling, these street vendors represent the animal nature of human physiology in its direct expression of bodily desires and cravings for food and survival. More troubling is how this image of primitive corporeality is seen as the failure of bodily abstraction, which is a sticking point in the commodity market of exchange turning on the logic of abstraction and value commensurability. In selling goods from various food items to other merchandises, their labor is surely an act of commodification and value creation to be realized by buyers in their corresponding acts of transaction and consumption. And yet the labor of value creation is utterly devoid of physical abstraction, the struggle of peddling and competing for customers a powerful reminder to all that the laboring body as a commodity is potentially conflict-laden, fraught as it is with all the physicality of struggle for living. It is in this sense that Catherine Gallagher calls this site "the theatre of the problematic nature of labor value" ("Body" 102), in which not only those costermongers peddling for penny profit but also poor laborers buying their miserable dinner all embody the sense of labor exploitation and devaluation by which they get far less than what they deserve: "Far from elevating the body to the standard of economic and social value, Mayhew's physicalization of the marketplace creates the fear that society is in danger of reducing human value to its most primitive biological needs" (104).

Standing in contrast to the pattern of bodily figuration in the discourse of political economy marked out by "a recognizably Victorian disgust for the body" (Gallagher, "Body" 104), Dickens's representation suggests a meaningful alternative. If less explicit than the former in expressing the dynamic of the laboring body, Wemmick's body is an enduring presence in the market, which is obtained by the way in which the legal clerk is able to deploy its physiological attributes in negotiation with challenging working conditions. Central to this bodily capacity is, as suggested earlier, the process of abstraction by which the body is able to organize its attributes as a field of shifting socially articulated functions. Far from being merely dehumanizing, the process of abstraction is here self-empowering in the sense that it is incorporated into the laboring body's capacity for social as well as technological involvement. It is this abstract bodily maneuvering that gives a sense of duplicity to Wemmick's physiological beingnesss in the world, one that can deploy degrees of abstraction in his engagement with the world, thus turning his body into an image of "ghostly corporeality." Seen in this sense, Dickens's bodily figuration cannot be simply seen as an upshot of what is often referred to as "Dickensian imagination" in all its idiosyncrasy. Rather it should be addressed as a critical intervention in the Victorian discourse of body economy, informed as it is by a bodily capacity of abstraction in its resistance to the way in which the laboring body is seen as a kind of primitive physiological unruliness.[9]

▸ Conclusion

To return to the earlier point about the discourse of fetishism, then, we should note briefly how Dickens's ghostly corporeality is bound up in the logic of fetishism, as it corresponds to Marx's account of "phantom-like objectivity" detected at the scene of labor commodification. This is, however, where the parallel ends. In departing from Marx's critique of such a physiological reduction remaining at the margin of labor abstraction and interchangeability with nonhuman items, Dickens's figuration turns the same marginalized corporeality into a subversive momentum lurking at the site of labor abstraction—a ghostly corporeality that adds an intriguing sense of secrecy or dissimulation to all the figural equivalents the laboring body assumes in the market.

I am not suggesting that it bodes for some kind of "postmodern euphoria" in which the body is released from any types of social constraints or social identification. What I am suggesting is that the defamiliarization of the body achieved through the fetishism discourse opens up a frame of thinking beyond the Marxist paradigm, a frame that takes into account different bodily adjustments and variations with respect to shifting material contexts. In this sense fetishism can be seen as a potent tool of what Bill Brown calls "a new materialism" (7), as its reference to different material attachments and maneuvers opens up a new arena of conceptualization about subject-object relations. In the new horizon of configuration for material relations, all the symptomatic patterns of subjectivity constructed by the logic of market relations in Marx's fetishism discourse thus anticipate "strategies of deconstruction [that stand] in opposition to totalizing visions of subjectivity" (Amariglio and Callari 191). While fraught with all the biased anthropological assumptions, the theory effectively attends to the condition whose multifaceted link to human lives allows one to discover realities of modern experience beyond all the philosophical or transcendental approaches.

Notes

1. Consider, for example, the debate between William I. Robinson and Leo Panitch and Sam Gindin on the dictates of global capitalism. Robinson argues that Panitch and Gindin neglect to consider social forces within each society in their state-central theory of globalization in which the shape of world economy is primarily governed by "US empire" (Robinson). In defending their view, Panitch and Gindin respond that

the conflict-ridden process of globalization in the final analysis resolves into "a world made in both the American image and its interest" (204).

2. All these and more interesting stories of Victorian common objects are included in Asa Briggs's *Victorian Things.*

3. Lane-Fox's collection is part of the mid-century museum movement that produced many museums, each dealing with different types of material experience from natural history to antiquities (Stocking 263).

4. In a way fundamental to the structure of social interaction beyond any accusations of dehumanization, abstract reasoning, Thomas Keenan argues, is the basis of Enlightenment thinking. For instance in theorizing the notion of human rights, the process of abstraction is crucial in conceptualizing the common denomination of humanity as a point of similitude to be applicable to humans beyond all distinctions. What is apparent here, then, is how this feat of abstraction is basically a linguistic trope obtained by an intellectual effort to "cease to think of properties by which things are distinguished in order to think only of those qualities in which they agree" (Keenan 167).

5. Marx, of course, argues that the process of abstraction is essential in creating values, a process by which all commodities, including human labor, "can be no longer distinguished, but are all together reduced to the same kind of labour, human labour in the abstract" (Marx, *Capital* 128).

6. "There is nothing left of them in each of [the commodities], but the same phantom-like objectivity; they are merely congealed quantities of homogeneous human labour" (Marx, *Capital* 128).

7. Thomas Keenan argues that the logic of exchange hinges on this ghostly objectivity, which "makes possible the relation between things or uses, [and] grants the common axis of similarity hitherto unavailable, precisely because it is a ghost and no longer a thing or a labor" (168). Seen in this sense, the residual materiality of human labor left in the commodity serves as a point of distinction, without which the same commodity, at the very moment of entering the exchange market, will be collapsed into the world of sameness and nondistinction.

8. For instance in Michel de Certeau the challenging practice of everyday life is occasioned by the way in which the social individual is defined not as a stable identity but one that is "far too waywardly and heterogeneous" (Highmore 13). Alluding to, among other things, a medley of impulses, dispositions, and feelings involved at the site of negotiation with various social forces, this sense of heterogeneity hinges on the physiological dimension of one's identity.

9. Dickens's tendency of bodily abstraction is increasingly dominant in his later fiction, where he is particularly concerned with the fate of individuals in a world governed by totalizing frames of representation in dealing with issues from political economy to medicine. In reading his last completed novel, *Our Mutual Friend,* Catherine Gallagher, for instance, draws an engaging parallel between the abstract circulation of money as the bearer of value and the writer's depiction of the suspended

animation of human bodies as potentially life-restoring (Eugene Wrayburn's and Rogue Riderhood's near-death experience). Seen in this way, the positive energy in the novel is mainly marked by the abstract, disembodied mode of potential value outside the domain of physical experience: "The story-telling, value-creating consciousness, like the consciousness of love, like economic value and the vital force itself, are all released from bodies and only exist in their pure form while they remain outside of bodies" (Gallagher, "Bio-Economics" 346).

Works Cited

Amariglio, Jack, and Antonio Callari. "Marxian Value Theory and the Problem of the Subject: The Role of Commodity Fetishism." *Fetishism as a Cultural Discourse.* Ed. Emily Apter and William Pietz. Cornell UP, 1993, pp. 188–216.

Briggs, Asa. *Victorian Things.* Penguin, 1990.

Brown, Bill. "Thing Theory." *Things.* Ed. Bill Brown. U of Chicago P, 2004, pp. 1–23.

Connor, Steven. "Introduction." *Charles Dickens.* Ed. Steven Connor. Longman, 1996, pp. 1–33.

Crary, Jonathan. *Suspensions of Perception: Attention, Spectacle, and Modern Culture.* MIT P, 2000.

——. *Techniques of the Observer: On Vision and Modernity in the Nineteenth Century.* MIT P, 1992.

Dickens, Charles. *Great Expectations.* Penguin, 1996.

——. "A Preliminary Word." *Household Words: A Weekly Journal.* Vol 1. Ward, Lock & Tyler, 1850, pp. 1–2.

"The Fashion of Furniture." *Cornhill Magazine.* Vol. 9. Smith, Elder, Co, 1864, pp. 337–49.

Gallagher, Catherine. "The Bio-Economics of *Our Mutual Friend.*" *Fragments for a History of the Human Body, Part Three.* Ed. Michel Feher, Ramona Naddaff, and Nadia Tazi. Zone, 1989, pp. 344–65.

——. "The Body versus the Social Body in the Works of Thomas Malthus and Henry Mayhew." *The Making of the Modern Body: Sexuality and Society in the Nineteenth Century.* Ed. Catherine Gallagher and Thomas Laqueur. U of California P, 1987, pp. 83–106.

Hartman, Eva. "The Fetish of Global Competition." *Capital and Class,* vol. 38, no. 1, 2014, pp. 184–96.

Highmore, Ben. "Introduction: Questioning Everyday Life." *The Everyday Life Reader.* Ed. Ben Highmore. Routledge, 2002, pp. 1–34.

Keenan, Thomas. "The Point Is to [Ex]change It: Reading *Capital,* Rhetorically." *Fetishism as a Cultural Discourse.* Ed. Emily Apter and William Pietz. Cornell UP, 1993, pp. 152–85.

Lane-Fox, Augustus Henry. *Catalogue of the Anthropological Collection Lent by Colonel Lane Fox for Exhibition in the Bethnal Green Branch of the South Kensington Museum.* George E. Eyre & William Spottiswoode, 1874.

Marx, Karl. *Capital: A Critique of Political Economy,* vol. 1. Trans. Ben Fowkes. Penguin, 1990.

——. "Economico-Philosophical Manuscripts of 1844." *The Portable Karl Marx.* Ed. Eugene Kamenka. Penguin, 1983, pp. 131–46.

——. "Manifesto of the Communist Party." *The Revolutions of 1848.* Ed. David Fernbach. Penguin, 1973, pp. 62–98.

Mayhew, Henry. *London Labour and the London Poor.* Penguin, 1985.

Panitch, Leo, and Sam Gindin. "American Empire or Empire of Global Capitalism?" *Studies in Political Economy,* vol. 93, no. 1, 2014, pp. 193–204.

Philpotts, Trey. "Dickens and Technology." *A Companion to Charles Dickens.* Ed. David Paroissien. Wiley-Blackwell, 2011, pp. 199–214.

Pietz, William. "Fetishism and Materialism: The Limits of Theory in Marx." *Fetishism as a Cultural Discourse.* Ed. Emily Apter and William Pietz. Cornell UP, 1993, pp. 119–51.

Richards, Thomas. *The Commodity Culture of Victorian England: Advertising and Spectacle, 1851–1914.* Verso, 1991.

Robinson, William I. "The Fetishism of Empire: A Critical Review of Panitch and Gindin's *The Making of Global Capitalism.*" *Studies in Political Economy,* vol. 93, no. 1, 2014, pp. 155–73.

Shilling, Chris. *The Body in Culture, Technology, and Society.* Sage, 2005.

Stocking, George W., Jr. *Victorian Anthropology.* Free P, 1987.

Contributors

ALEXANDER BEECROFT is a Jessie Chapman Alcorn Memorial Professor of Foreign Languages, and professor of classics and comparative literature, at the University of South Carolina. He is the author of *Authorship and Cultural Identity in Early Greece and China* (2010) and of *An Ecology of World Literature* (2015), a book that was completed thanks to a Charles A. Ryskamp Research Fellowship in the Humanities from the American Council of Learned Societies.

JULIE CHOI is professor of English language and literature at Ewha Womans University. Her research covers a range of topics in British literature over the long eighteenth century. Her interest in the theme of the city in modern culture stems from research into the work of the German sociologist Georg Simmel, which led to the publication of "The Metropolis and Mental Life in the Novel" in *New Literary History* (2006). Her most recent published work has been on the idea and ideal of the English landscape in the novels of Jane Austen. She is currently working on the rise of evangelical culture and the ramifications for conservative Christian women who sought to improve the plight of nation and world through charity, organized action, and missionary outreach. Ewha was founded by an American Methodist female missionary in 1886 with a single student and is now the largest all-women's university in the world.

BENNETT YU-HSIANG FU is professor in the Department of Foreign Languages and Literatures at National Taiwan University. His research encompasses a variety of areas in Asian North American literature, contemporary Canadian Anglophone and Francophone literatures, and twentieth-century American literature. Over the past decade, he has published extensively in such areas as race/ethnicity/feminism studies, comparative literature, pedagogical innovation, and postcolonial studies. These critical essays have been published in ten countries: the United States, United Kingdom, Canada, Germany, China, Japan, Portugal, Netherlands, Korea, and Taiwan. He is the author of the book *Transgressive Transcripts* (2012). He is currently the series editor of National Taiwan University Press for the book series "East-West Cultural Encounters in Literature and Cultural Studies," copublished with the University of South Carolina Press. He also sits on the editorial boards of several prestigious international academic journals in literary studies.

CHI-SHE LI received his Ph.D. in English (comparative literature) from the State University of New York at Stony Brook and now teaches in the Department of Foreign Languages and Literatures, National Taiwan University. His research interests include literary theory, cultural globalization, and the novel. He has published studies on neoliberalism, Victorian fiction, and East Asian cinema. His publications appear in journals and book chapters published in Korea, the United States, and Taiwan. His current research focuses on the rethinking of aesthetics in the context of new materialisms. He is currently the series coeditor of National Taiwan University Press for the book series "East-West Cultural Encounters in Literature and Cultural Studies," copublished with the University of South Carolina Press.

PAUL ALLEN MILLER is vice provost and Carolina Distinguished Professor at the University of South Carolina. He received his Ph.D. in comparative literature from the University of Texas in 1989. He has held visiting appointments at the University of the Ruhr (Bochum), the University of Paris 13, and Beijing Language and Cultural University. He is the former editor of *Transactions of the American Philological Association* and the author of *Lyric Texts and Lyric Consciousness* (1994), *Latin Erotic Elegy* (2002), *Subjecting Verses* (2004), *Latin Verse Satire* (2005), *Postmodern Spiritual Practices* (2007), *Plato's Apology of Socrates* (2010) with Charles Platter, *A Tibullus Reader* (2013), *Diotima at the Barricades: French Feminists Read Plato* (2015), and *Horace* (2019). He has edited fourteen volumes of essays on literary theory, gender studies, and topics in the classics and published more than seventy-five articles on Latin, Greek, French, and English literature and philosophy. He is currently at work on a book on Foucault's late lectures on antiquity.

HISUP SHIN earned a Ph.D. in literature from the University of Essex (UK) after completing a thesis titled "Experiencing the Unlikely City: The Figuration of Dickens' Street Writing." He was also a 2001/2002 Korea Institute Post-Doctoral Fellow at Harvard, conducting a comparative study of Korean modern urban fiction. His teaching career began at the University of Alabama (2002–4). He currently teaches at Ewha Womans University (South Korea). His research focuses on different areas of literary and cultural studies, ranging from European realist fiction to Korean modern fiction and contemporary popular culture. His numerous peer-reviewed articles deal with various topics of modernity, including city spaces, bodily figuration, and visualities. His recent publications include a book chapter titled "Filth and the Everyday" in *Portable Prose* (2018) and an article titled "Monstrous National Allegory: The Making of Monstrous Otherness in Na Hong-jin's *The Wailing*" in *Journal of Film and Video* (forthcoming).

MEILI STEELE is professor of English and comparative literature at the University of South Carolina and the author of four books: *Hiding from History: Politics and Public Imagination* (2005), *Theorizing Textual Subjects: Agency and Oppression* (1997),

Critical Confrontations: Literary Theories in Dialogue (1997), and *Realism and the Drama of Reference Strategies of Representation in Balzac, Flaubert, and James* (1988). He has also published many articles.

NICHOLAS VAZSONYI (Ph.D. UCLA, 1993) is Jesse Chapman Alcorn Memorial Professor of German and Comparative Literature and chair of the Department of Languages, Literatures and Cultures at the University of South Carolina. His first book, *Lukács Reads Goethe* (1997), was followed by two edited volumes, one on German national identity formation between 1750 and 1871 (2000) and the other titled *Wagner's* Meistersinger: *Performance, History, Representation* (2003). His book *Richard Wagner: Self-Promotion and the Making of a Brand* (2010) was reissued in paperback and appeared in German translation as *Richard Wagner: Entstehung einer Marke* (2012). More recently he completed work as editor of the *Cambridge Wagner Encyclopedia* (2013), became coeditor of the journal *wagnerspectrum*, and is currently coediting the *Cambridge Companion to Wagner's "Der Ring des Nibelungen"* with Mark Berry, set to appear in 2019. His next book project is on Wagner and modernity.

MOU-LAN WONG is associate professor in the Department of Foreign Languages and Literatures at National Taiwan University. He works primarily on Victorian visual culture and nonsense literature and has published chapters in the collections *Alice beyond Wonderland* (2009), *Landscape, Seascape, and the Eco-Spatial Imagination* (2016), and *Humour in the Arts* (2018).

Index